E303 English Grammar in Context
Education and Language Studies
Level 3

D0299770

Book 1

Getting Started

Describing the grammar of speech and writing

Edited by K. A. O'Halloran and C. Coffin

Units 1–7

Series editor: Caroline Coffin

The Open University

This publication forms part of an Open University course E303 *English Grammar in Context*. Details of this and other Open University courses can be obtained from the Student Registration and Enquiry Service, The Open University, PO Box 197, Milton Keynes MK7 6BJ, United Kingdom: tel. +44 (0)870 333 4340, email general-enquiries@open.ac.uk

Alternatively, you may visit the Open University website at http://www.open.ac.uk where you can learn more about the wide range of courses and packs offered at all levels by The Open University.

To purchase a selection of Open University course materials visit http://www.ouw.co.uk, or contact Open University Worldwide, Michael Young Building, Walton Hall, Milton Keynes MK7 6AA, United Kingdom for a brochure. tel. +44 (0)1908 858785; fax +44 (0)1908 858787; email ouwenq@open.ac.uk

The Open University
Walton Hall, Milton Keynes
MK7 6AA

First published 2005. Second edition 2006.

Edited and designed by The Open University.

Typeset by The Open University.

Printed and bound in Malta by Gutenberg Press.

ISBN 978 0 7492 1775 4

2.1

Mixed Sources
Product group from well-managed forests, and other controlled sources
www.fsc.org Cert no. TT-CoC-002424
© 1996 Forest Stewardship Council

The paper used for this book is FSC-certified and totally chlorine-free. FSC (the Forest Stewardship Council) is an international network to promote responsible management of the world's forests.

FSC

Contents

Introduction to Book 1

Read the following two lines.

(a) I hate cockroaches more than rats.

(b) The cockroach is probably the most obnoxious insect known to man.

One of the above pieces of language is written and the other is spoken, both coming from real sources. If you had to say which was which, it probably wouldn't take you very long to decide. You'd probably say that (a) is more likely to be spoken and (b) more likely to be written. But could you say why precisely? Being able to account for this difference actually requires some thought and skills of analysis. For a start, to be able to say quite precisely that (a) is spoken and (b) is written, we need to be able to point to specific features of (a) and (b). And so for me to understand your reasons for choosing (a) as spoken, say, and for you to understand mine, it would help if we had an agreed way of pinpointing the grammatical differences. So if we both understood 'I' as the first person singular pronoun and 'hate' as a verb expressing mental activity, then you would understand me if I said I think (a) is more likely to be spoken since the grammatical pattern – a first person pronoun followed by a verb expressing mental activity – is more common in speech than in writing. But then you might quite rightly say that while you agree with the grammatical description I've made, nevertheless my judgement about the typicality of this pattern is just based on intuition and that I can't know this for sure.

Up until relatively recently, it would be difficult to respond to such an accusation with anything other than saying that I'm a native speaker of English and in my experience this pattern is common in speech. But now we are in a powerful position to be able to answer questions such as these. This is because, in the last few years, technology has been developed for assembling huge databases of English as well as computational methods for searching them quickly. So by consulting a huge database of spoken language, I can find out that my intuition was correct and the pattern of first person singular pronoun and mental verb is much more common in speech than in writing. In Book 1 we shall be making use of such databases of spoken and written English.

Having enormous databases of information can be very useful. But a database in and of itself can only point to how things are; it cannot answer the question why things are the way they are. A census database might tell us that families in the north of a country have on average something close to five children while in the south of a country families on average have something close to one child. So if we came across a family with seven children we might make the reasonable assumption that this family is more likely to be living in the north. But the census information cannot tell us why this is the case. We'd have to consider the differences in context; for example, are salaries bigger in the north than in the south, enabling parents to have more children? We'd have to interpret the data by making meaningful connections with the context. In the same way that the database tells us that 'I hate cockroaches more than rats' is more likely to be spoken than written, it cannot say why this is the case.

To understand this properly, we have to understand the contexts in which we produce speech and writing and why these affect our choice of language. In relating the context to the language and trying to take account of how it affects language, we are making an interpretation of the data. The movement between looking at the general (either a database or the spoken/written context) and a particular example of speech or writing is a rhythm which will inform your study in Book 1. This kind of exploration will give us insight into why we use English in the way we do. So by the end of Book 1, you will understand why English speech and writing differ in terms of grammar, meaning and context. But why would you want to understand this? Why would this be useful to know?

Being able to articulate how English speech and writing work in terms of the relationship between grammar, meaning and context will have benefits for you as a communicator. Not only will your understanding of written and spoken communication in English be improved, but you will be able to comment with some precision on your own written and spoken communication and thus to assess more precisely its effectiveness. An unusual aspect of this course, and in particular of Book 1, is that it will give you a knowledge of English spoken grammar. Comprehensive investigations of English spoken grammar are a fairly recent phenomenon, facilitated by the technological developments I referred to earlier – the capacity to store huge amounts of information on a database and make quick searches through it.

These developments mean that linguists are in a unique position, since the systematic study of language began, to be able to point to regular features of speech which exist because speech is different to writing. This is very significant since, traditionally, assessments of the correctness of spoken English have been made with regard to writing as the 'standard'. Often what was regarded as incorrect in speech was merely because it was incorrect from the point of view of writing. So it was not taken into account that speech had its own grammar which arose through very different contextual conditions. Having a knowledge of the nature of English spoken grammar will enable you to justify your own spoken choices against written choices and thus to assess whether a piece of speech is correct in itself rather than from the perspective of writing.

To enable you to make such justifications, as well as to make links between your use of English, meaning and context more generally, skills of grammatical description are important. All of the units of Book 1 will enable you to learn and to practise these. You will learn how to describe the structure of spoken and written English and also to begin to explore its function in making meaning. But because we also want you to be able to link exploration of grammatical data – both databases and particular examples of English texts – to context and meaning, skills of interpretation will also be practised in Book 1. Throughout Book 1 there are CD-ROM activities and tasks for you to use to practise the skills of description and interpretation of data. There are also exercises for you to practise searching through databases of spoken and written English so as to see how the 'broader' picture can be illuminating about English. We recommend as well that you have a notebook while working through this book; writing down key grammatical concepts and their definitions in your journal and then returning to them from time to time will help them 'sink in'.

There are seven units in Book 1. In Units 1 and 2, you'll be introduced to the idea of a grammatical database and to software for investigating it. You'll also be introduced to the *Longman Student Grammar of Spoken and Written English* (referred to in the units as 'your reference grammar') which accompanies this course. Unit 3 is concerned with how we commonly understand speech and writing in chunks of meaning. Units 4, 5 and 6 examine these common chunks of meaning in greater detail. Finally, it would be odd to have a block on the differences between meaning-making in spoken and written English without some consideration of how meaning can be realised in sound, i.e. in ways which are naturally unavailable to writing. This is what you'll find out about in Unit 7. Now, before starting Unit 1, you might want to pause here and think of your own use of speech and writing in English. How do they differ from one another? Can you account easily for these differences? If you can't, don't worry. The purpose of Book 1 is to put you in a position to do so.

At several points in Book 1, you will be asked to read chapters from the course reader, *Applying English Grammar*, to provide further detail and background on particular topics.

Unit 1
Grammar in context

Prepared for the course team by Ann Hewings

CONTENTS

Materials required

While studying this unit, you will need:

    your reference grammar

    the Activities CD-ROM (in Introduction, at end of unit)

    Guide to the CD-ROMs.

Introduction

I wonder if you understand what Mrs Clark meant, or whether any teacher has ever made a similar remark about your work? Some people think that the difference between speech and writing is that people use longer words in writing. In some writing this is true, but there are also other significant differences, many of which are grammatical. In this introductory unit we look at some of the factors that contribute to differences between speech and writing and at ways of describing them. However, we shall try to avoid just helping you to get descriptive labels right, though that is important. At this early stage in the course we want you to discover that grammar is not a boring system for labelling parts of a sentence, but rather that it can give you an insight into how we present ourselves and our view of the world to other people. Our choices within the grammatical system together with our choices of vocabulary are our most powerful ways of putting together the meanings that we want to communicate. An advanced, sophisticated method of communication is what makes human beings so special, so a study of grammar is a way of exploring how these meanings get made.

Specifically in this unit, you will develop knowledge and understanding of the:

◆ differences between spoken and written English

◆ factors that influence our use of grammar and vocabulary in speech and writing

◆ different ways in which grammar has been described.

In most units we have kept activities requiring you to use your computer until the end of the unit. However, we think it is important for you to decide how much preparatory work you need to do in order to study the rest of this unit and the following units. So we want you to look at the Foundation Grammar on the Activities CD-ROM. Instructions on installing and using the course CD-ROMs are in the *Guide to the CD-ROMs* booklet.

A CTIVITIES CD-ROM

Either look through the Foundation Grammar activities quickly to make sure that you understand how to identify different classes of word such as nouns, verbs, adjectives and adverbs and concepts such as transitivity and subject–verb concord, or work through them thoroughly.

We recommend that you keep notes on the different terms used to help you as you work through the rest of the course.

Explanations and answers are included on the CD-ROM.

1 WHY STUDY GRAMMAR?

Now that you are familiar with the book's structure and some basic grammatical terminology, we want you to start thinking about what exactly we mean by a term like 'grammar' and how and why grammar differs in speech and writing. For some of you this will revise and build on your knowledge of previous study. Activity 1 is a way of raising questions in your mind and you will find some answers or explanations in the rest of the unit. Some activities in this course have specific answers and these can be found near the end of each unit in 'Answers to the activities'.

ACTIVITY 1 (allow about 10 minutes)

Write down a few sentences which explain what you think grammar is about and why it is important. What do you expect to learn by studying English grammar? We shall come back to this activity again at the end of the unit.

COMMENT

In thinking about answers to these questions I have to admit that, in helping to write this course, I have expanded my own knowledge of the variety of interpretations of grammar and the applications of grammatical analysis. I started off many years ago as a teacher of English in various countries around the world, using a form of grammatical description which highlighted 'correct' usage such as knowing when to say *I have gone* and when to say *I went*. More recently, in analysing academic writing, I have applied a different model of grammar, one which foregrounds the idea of grammar as choosing forms to express different types of meaning. Also, in working with my Open University colleagues, I have discovered other grammatical systems and applications. You might be surprised to realise how many different areas of life utilise an understanding of grammar. Computer scientists involved in creating voice-recognition software need to understand grammar and the frequency of the likely patterns of the language; police experts need to trace typical language patterns used by individuals if they are to detect lies and forged documents; doctors and specialists in language disorders in children or in patients with head injuries need to know the typical grammar associated with particular contexts in order to understand where disruption or dysfunction is taking place. Of course, knowing grammar is a basic part of language learning and teaching and is also necessary in professions such as translating and lexicography (compiling dictionaries).

Many of the uses to which a knowledge of grammar is put are also starting to rely on the application of computer technology to language analysis. The new computational tools are changing the way we describe and understand language. Your reference grammar is based on research using these tools. Many of the activities that you will be trying out are similar to those that the grammarians who wrote your reference grammar used and they are also important in writing many dictionaries and textbooks about English. But before we move on to recent approaches to grammar we shall take a short diversion into different types of grammatical description.

2 DEVELOPMENTS IN GRAMMATICAL DESCRIPTION

ACTIVITY 2 (allow about 10 minutes)

As a way of helping you to consider what we mean by 'grammar' look at the following sentences and see how many meanings of the word 'grammar' you can identify.

1   It's a really complicated area of grammar.
2   Why don't you look it up in a grammar?
3   Her spelling is good, but her grammar is almost non-existent.
4   Children don't do enough grammar at school.
5   We had to do generative grammar on the course.
6   He needs to work on his grammar and punctuation.
7   Systemic functional grammar is generally associated with the work of Michael Halliday.
8   I've always had problems with German grammar.
9   It's a grammar for learners of English as a foreign language.
10   Oh no! We're doing grammar again today!

(Based on Hewings and Hewings, 2004)

COMMENT

There is clearly overlap in these uses, but I have grouped them into five meanings.

(1) In 1 and 8, it refers to the way in which words are organised in a language in order to make correct sentences; here 'grammar' is the description of the way in which words combine into larger units, the largest being the sentence.

(2) In 2 and 9, it refers to a book in which these organising principles are laid out. Sometimes these are given as a set of rules.

(3) In 4 and 10, it refers to the study of these rules.

(4) In 3 and 6, it refers to whether a person follows the 'rules of grammar'.

(5) In 5 and 7, it refers to a particular theory of language description.

Different theories of language result in different types of grammatical description based on different premises and with different purposes. In this course, you will be using two complementary grammatical descriptions. The first is what is sometimes referred to as traditional or structural grammar, a grammar that divides language on the basis of **parts of speech**, units such as nouns, verbs, and adjectives. This is the type of labelling that you will have seen in the Foundation Grammar on the Activities CD-ROM and it is used in your reference grammar.

In looking at parts of speech, or **word classes** as they are also called, grammarians divide up sentences or smaller units into their constituent parts; for example:

David	played	his	guitar	in	the	concert
noun	verb	possessive determiner	noun	preposition	determiner	noun

See Foundation Grammar or your reference grammar for 'word classes' ('parts of speech') and the terms used here.

Don't worry if you do not know terms such as 'possessive determiner'; when you need to know these terms they will be introduced. In addition to this type of description, grammarians and others can also concentrate on how words combine to make meanings and this gives rise to a **functional grammar** which uses a different descriptive vocabulary. Functional grammar is the other main approach to describing language that we take in this course. In a functional grammar the emphasis is on describing words or groups of words according to the function they are fulfilling in a sentence. You will start to find out more about functional grammar in Unit 3.

The particular type of functional grammar that we shall use in this course is *systemic functional grammar* (SFG), associated with Michael Halliday. If you are interested in reading more about this approach, see the functional grammar references section at the end of the book.

Both traditional grammars and functional grammars are largely **descriptive grammars**, that is, they set out to account for the language we use without necessarily making judgements about its correctness. However, the word 'grammar', as we have seen, can be used to indicate what rules exist for combining units together and whether these have been followed correctly. For example, the variety of English I speak has a rule that if you use a number greater than one with a noun, the noun has to be plural (I say 'three cats', not 'three cat'). Books which set out this view of language are **prescriptive grammars** which aim to tell people *how they should speak* rather than to describe *how they do speak*. Prescriptive grammars contain the notion of the 'correct' use of language. For example, many people were taught that an English verb in the infinitive form (underlined in the example below) should not be separated from its preceding *to*.

So the introduction to the TV series *Star Trek*

...to boldly <u>go</u> where no man has gone before

is criticised on the grounds that *to* and *go* should not be separated by the adverb *boldly*. In this course we shall not be arguing that one form is better than another. Rather, you will be analysing examples of English as it has been used and looking at the different choices that have been made and the factors that might influence those choices.

The final type of grammar is a **pedagogic grammar**. These grammars are generally based on descriptions of 'standard' English and are designed to help people learn English if they are not native speakers of the language. Pedagogic grammars often give some of the 'rules' of English and lots of examples and practice material. They thus combine elements from descriptive and prescriptive grammars. Your reference grammar is a pedagogic grammar, but it relies on description rather than prescription to explain how English works.

Of these three approaches, prescriptive grammars are probably the best known. Originally associated with describing ancient Greek, a system of labelling parts of speech developed into a way of laying down rules on the socially correct usage of language. Because of their origin in the ancient languages, prescriptive grammars introduced rules into English which arguably imposed labels and expectations that had not evolved from within the living language.

Descriptive grammars in the USA and Europe have a more recent history. Linguists, and particularly grammarians, take examples of language that they have read, heard or invented to work out the rules underpinning our language use. The rules underlying actual practice are the structure or grammar of the language. The most notable attempts to make thorough descriptions of language occurred in the USA at the beginning of the twentieth century when anthropologists sought to describe North American Indian languages which were disappearing as English became more powerful. There was no written record relating to these languages so careful description of speech patterns was necessary.

At approximately the same time, a European anthropologist, Bronislaw Malinowski, was working among islanders in the Pacific. The importance of his work lies in his understanding that it is not enough to translate words into their rough equivalents in English or another language. In order to understand a language it is necessary to understand the contexts in which language is used and the cultural significance of different choices of words and grammar. Words and their meanings are not independent of their culture or of the situation in which they are being used.

This anthropological work illustrates a more dynamic approach to the study of language which is still influential today, particularly in functional approaches to grammar. Many linguists are exploring ways of grounding their description of language in the cultural, geographical, social and economic conditions stressed by Malinowski. These factors are seen as influencing how language is used in **context**; that is, how variations in what we are doing, who we are communicating with, whether we are face to face or separated in time and space from our listener/reader and so on affect the grammatical and other language choices we make. This is a wide definition of context, and is sometimes called **sociocultural context**. This term is to distinguish it from a narrower meaning of context which refers to the words in the immediate textual environment of the word or grammatical feature that you are looking at. So in the following sentence we might be looking at how, for example, the word *wide* is used.

This is a wide definition of context.

All the words that surround it form its immediate context, as does the whole paragraph. The notion of context and its influence on grammatical choice are central to this course. You will constantly be reflecting on how the local textual context affects grammar and how the wider context of the local culture and the particular situation of people communicating influence the variations that you will observe in grammatical choices.

A CTIVITY 3 (allow about 10 minutes)

Before you continue reading, think about what the contextual factors are that might be influencing me as I sit here typing this unit. What would be affecting me in the wider sociocultural context and in the immediate textual context surrounding each word I write?

C OMMENT

If we are using context in its broader sense then wider influences on my selection of grammar than simply textual context can be considered. My choices of language would reflect my evaluation of the social relations between myself as writer and you as student reader. We are strangers, but I wish to create a feeling of friendliness and dialogue within the text. I am conscious that I am trying to achieve a purpose through writing – helping you to understand more about grammar. I therefore select words and put them together in sentences which I hope will convey the point I am trying to make. I can't refer to things in my immediate environment because you do not share it – we are not communicating face-to-face or even simultaneously. I must make myself clear just by the ordering of the words on the page. Such contextual factors can be described and accounted for in a comprehensive description of grammar and such a grammar can also help me to think about how I can make my meanings more clearly.

❸ GRAMMAR AND CONTEXTUAL VARIATION

3.1 Spoken and written modes

Variations in context that can affect grammatical choice may relate to different **modes** of communication, such as whether it is speech or writing, telephone or email, and so on. I am communicating with you now through the written mode. I have no idea where you are or what motivates you to study this course. I don't know if you are alone, inside, outside, whether it is morning, afternoon or evening. To make my meanings clear to you, I type words into a computer that fit together in strings of phrases and clauses with boundaries marked by full stops and initial capital letters. I try to make what I write as clear as possible because you do not have the chance to ask me for clarification. If you were sitting with me here in my study and we were discussing grammar, most of the communication would be oral, though we might also make use of various reference books that I have on my shelves. There would be no full stops or capital letters in my speech. Instead there would be a stream of sounds, some of which would receive greater emphasis than others. The sounds would be broken up with pauses and often I would stop part way through and start to rephrase my thoughts. While we are talking I would be looking at you to make sure that you have understood what I have to say. I would be automatically monitoring your gestures, such as a nodding of the head to indicate understanding or a furrowing of the brow to indicate non-comprehension. You might interrupt and ask me to say something again or retell something in your own words to check your understanding.

In this way, the inherent difference of face-to-face communication and written communication creates different contexts which tend to lead people to communicate meanings differently through making different grammatical choices. The way I speak and write is different from the way you speak and write. However, the way I speak is probably closer to the way you speak (if you are a native speaker of English) than to the way either you or I write. Let me put that in a different way. Language varies for each individual, but it varies in systematic ways in different situations. So the language choices we make when we write will show similarities because the mode is writing and not speech.

To start you thinking about what the study of grammar can tell us about these systematic variations, let us consider the following two bits of language which come from some longer texts which you will read shortly.

1   So she piles her in the car and they go off.

2   Since 1840, maximum life expectancies have increased at a rate of about three months per year.

Like the examples in the introduction to Book 1, one of these is spoken and the other is written. You can probably guess that (1) is spoken and (2) is from a written text. What clues are you using to make this judgement? What choices have the speaker in (1) and the writer in (2) made that enable you to identify one as speech and the other as writing? You might say that (2) is more formal and (1) less formal. If you know some grammatical terminology, you might relate this to the long noun phrases like *maximum life expectancy* in (2) and the less formal 'phrasal verbs' such as *pile in* and *go off* in (1). In writing we often consider more carefully the words we use. We have time to plan and revise what we have to say to fit in with the meanings we want to convey and the person or people we are addressing. In speech we often do not consider our words so carefully, particularly in casual conversation. However, we are still making choices about how to express ourselves – just so quickly that we rarely have time to reflect on it. The speaker in (1) probably based her selection of informal-sounding phrasal verbs on the basis that she knew the friend she was talking to well. Or perhaps she thought that those choices would add to the contrast between the everydayness of the activities she was describing and what she was about to say next. Most of our language choices are subconscious choices, but they are nevertheless motivated. There must be a reason why you chose one word or expression and not another. One of the factors influencing this choice is whether or not we are in face-to-face contact with the person we are communicating with. While this is a major influence on variation in grammatical choices it is not the only one. There are many factors which influence our choices and this course will help you to see what some of these are.

As we have said, one of the most significant factors affecting our grammatical choices is whether we are speaking or writing. We can see these differences if we compare a spoken text and a written text. **Text** here is not being used in its usual sense to mean a piece of writing. 'Text' in language analysis can refer both to speech which has been prepared in a written form that can be analysed and to writing.

A CTIVITY 4 (allow about 30 minutes)

Read Texts 1 and 2 below. Which do you think is spoken language and which written? Make a list of the differences between them that indicate to you that one is a written text and one is a spoken text. Don't worry about using grammatical terminology to describe things – just make notes that mean something to you.

Text 1

A friend of mine told me this amazing story the other day she a ... she'd been shopping and she came back to this multi-storey car park that she's been in and it was kind of deserted ... erm ... and as she was walking towards her car she saw this figure sitting in the passenger seat ... and she thought what's that I've been burgled and as she walked towards the car feeling a bit scared this person got out of the car and it was a little old lady ... so she thought oh well probably it's not a burglar and ... er ... anyway she asked her and the woman said ... er ... apparently she'd been sitting there waiting for her daughter to arrive and the daughter hadn't turned up and she was feeling a bit giddy and faint and so she went and sat in the car ... it seems a very strange thing to do ... I mean ... apparently she'd been trying all the door handles one was open so she sat in it ... so anyway ... this friend of mine ... erm ... said ... you know ... what are you going to do now ... when are you meant to be meeting your daughter and the woman said half an hour ago so she said well ... what are you going do now and anyway ... finally this woman asked her if ... er ... she could possibly giver her a lift home because it was freezing and this old lady looked really ill and my friend thought oh ... I'd better be nice and it was a bit out of her way but she thought she'd better do the ... do the ... do the right thing ... so she piles her in the car and they go off ... and as they're driving along she just happens to look across and sees her hands ... and they weren't woman's hands at all ... they were man's hands ... it's got hairy big hairy hands...

(Brazil, 1995, pp. 24–5)

Text 2

Industrialized societies throughout the world are greying. Since 1840, maximum life expectancies have increased at a rate of about three months per year and this trend shows no sign of slowing down. The good news is that people are getting healthier. But one downside is the net impact on healthcare. The overall improvement in health is more than countered by the much greater number of individuals reaching ages at which age-related health problems occur. An obvious example is Alzheimer's disease, which was almost unknown a century ago. The same is true of age-related macular degeneration, now the leading cause of blindness. Ageing is bad for us and yet it happens to everyone. So why does it occur at all?

(Partridge and Gems, 2002, p. 921)

COMMENT

There are many differences between these two texts that you might have noted and many of these will be dealt with during the course. Let us look at just a few of them. To start with, Text 1 looks very different from language that you normally see written down and this is the first clue to the fact that it was originally spoken not written. It is a **transcript**, a written version of something that someone has said. This is a very simple transcript, partly because there is only one speaker and partly because of the way it has been transcribed. As you go through the course you will read lots of transcripts and will see that there are many different ways of representing spoken language on a page.

In this transcription many of the features that we associate with written language are missing. There are no sentences or paragraphs, for instance. Three full stops (an ellipsis) are used to indicate gaps or pauses, not sentence endings. It is consequently difficult at first to make sense of what is said and to guess how it sounded. The speaker repeats parts of **utterances**, e.g. *she'd better do the ... do the ... do the right thing* and hesitates, e.g. *er, erm* and pauses. (The word 'utterance' is used in preference to 'sentence' because, as we shall see, the notion of a sentence does not fit neatly with describing spoken language.) The utterances often seem incomplete or to change direction as they proceed, e.g. *anyway she asked her and the woman said ... er ... apparently she'd been sitting there waiting for her daughter to arrive*, and there are changes in verb tenses, e.g. *but she thought she'd better do the ... do the ... do the right thing ... so she piles her in the car and they go off*. The string of events in the story are linked predominately by *and*, e.g. *...apparently she'd been sitting there waiting for her daughter to arrive <u>and</u> the daughter hadn't turned up <u>and</u> she was feeling a bit giddy and faint <u>and</u> so she went and sat in the car*.

Many of the features of Text 1 are in direct contrast to Text 2 where the meanings are divided into sentences. Sentences and parts of sentences are linked together not predominately by *and*, but by other linking words such as *but, yet* and *so* which not only link bits of text but give us an idea of the logical unfolding of a text. One of the most significant differences between speech and writing is the amount of information that is packed into written texts in relation to the number of words used.

We can demonstrate this through looking at the following sentence from Text 2.

1   The overall improvement in health is more than countered by the much greater number of individuals reaching ages at which age-related health problems occur.

Imagine how you might convey all that information in speech. If I were in a seminar discussing this I think I might say something like:

2   There's been an improvement in health generally but at the same time this has led to problems ... more people are living into old age and this is when they start to have illness and diseases that are only associated with being old.

But if I were talking to friends it might be more like:

3   Health's getting better yeah overall ... more people are living longer ... but but the problem is the problem is they're not as well ... they've got lots of diseases and stuff ... things that you get when you're old.

In (2) I have used 42 words (I am counting contracted forms such as *they're* as one word) and in (3) 36 words to say what took 24 words in the written text. How we convey all this information in relatively few words is one of the main grammatical differences between speech and writing, especially between informal conversation and formal writing. Both formality and whether something is spoken or written can affect the choice of grammatical structures and also the choice of vocabulary. For example, the noun *improvement* in (1) is replaced by a verb and an adverb in (3): *'s getting better*. Vocabulary differences can also be seen: for example, the word *individuals* in (1) is replaced by *people* in (2) and (3).

The technical word for vocabulary is **lexis**, and this is combined with the word grammar in the term **lexicogrammar**. In this course our primary focus is on grammar, but it is important to realise that it is often the choices of both lexis and grammar, i.e. lexicogrammar, that convey the meanings we make with language. For this reason, we shall also at times highlight lexical choices alongside those that are more formally considered under the heading of grammar.

3.2 Features of speech

Texts 1 and 2 were both **monologues**, that is, one person speaking or writing. Speech is more often a **dialogue**, a communication between two or more speakers and this influences the grammar choices made. We can see this in the dialogue transcribed below.

A: Oh well she wouldn't be there after the bingo then would she? Probably went to I know that she does go. She there most of the evening and she goes to bingo and

B: Yeah

A: Cos they live down round near Tina's but not like Tina's house before that off Allard Avenue round the back of Allard Sherwood is it?

B: Sherwood, yeah Sherwood Avenue

A: Yeah

B: Yeah they live up yeah.

(BNC-OU spoken corpus)

This transcript looks different from Text 1 (p. 18) and is even more difficult to make sense of. In natural speech, people often speak at the same time as each other, or complete each other's remarks. There are therefore many utterances that seem incomplete when read on the page. Although transcripts of conversation may seem 'ungrammatical' in comparison to text specifically composed to be read, the participants in them have no problem understanding and responding. This indicates that the grammatical choices made in speech are often just different from those we make in writing. The use of the context surrounding the participants means that they do not need to make everything explicit. In fact, they need to do different things in conversation and therefore need different grammatical resources. For example, in the context of a face-to-face conversation we see grammatical features such as **question tags** (*would she? is it?*) which invite a response, either verbally or through gestures such as nodding the head, from the other member of the dialogue. This helps to keep all participants in the conversation involved. Missing out words such as personal pronouns is common, e.g. *Probably went to*, where the pronoun *she* is omitted. This is allowable in conversation because such words can be inferred from the surrounding text. It also helps to create a feeling of closeness between the participants. They can leave out words because they can rely on their shared understanding to fill in the meanings.

Once we start to consider the ongoing interactive nature of speech, many of the differences between speech and writing become explicable.

ACTIVITY 5 (allow about 15 minutes)

Read the extract below from a conversation among three people. Using your own words, underline and describe things that indicate that this is spontaneous conversation. To get you started, here is an example from the first two lines.

A: I've got [informal everyday expression with contraction] something [general noun rather than specific] new on the computer [specific reference to a particular computer shows shared context] here [reference to specific place that is clear to those in the conversation].

B: What do you got? [questions reflect interactive style: *do* and *got* show a lack of concord (agreement) as perhaps the speaker changed his/her mind halfway through the utterance.]

A conversation

A1: I've got something new on the computer here.

B1: What do you got?

A2: If you turn it on, it turns on here and that turns on the monitor, the speakers and the uh, printer so now <unclear> shut off my printer. I just put a, a plug strip in here.

B2: oh okay.

A3: And there there's another switch inside here that allows me to turn everything off, the computer, so like when I go away I can hit that and then everything is down.

C1: The one I like is the uh, little console.

B3: Yeah.

C2: You can, well you know <unclear>

A4: Well you know the other thing is though, see I can shut this off.

COMMENT

Some of the points that you might have noticed were:

◆ Avoiding elaborations or specification of meaning, and the use of general nouns and of pronouns e.g. *something new*; *the other thing*.

◆ Interactiveness with questions: *What do you got?* (note the dysfluency – a term we introduce more fully on p. 23).

◆ Real-time production by add-on strategy: *If you turn it on, it turns on here and that turns on the monitor, the speakers and the uh, printer so now* <unclear> *shut off my printer.*

◆ Vernacular range of expressions such as contractions (*I've*), and informal and non-standard usage e.g. *so like when I go away*; *What do you got?*

◆ Repetition and hesitation: *I just put a, a plug strip in here.*

(Based on Biber, 2002b, pp. 100–101)

Many of these features can be put down to the pressures of thinking and translating our thoughts into comprehensible language in the milliseconds available during face-to-face conversation. They also rely on the sharing of immediate physical contexts and often much sociocultural context knowledge as well. They result in the range of features noted above. Easily observable in most conversations is the increased use of pronouns to refer to people and things in the vicinity or recoverable in the wider context of the conversation. Writing, in contrast, usually uses fuller combinations of nouns and adjectives to specify who or what is being referred to.

Another feature of relying on the shared linguistic or sociocultural context is **ellipsis**. This occurs when some elements of a phrase or other unit of language are not specified because they can be inferred from the context. Ellipsis occurs in both speech and writing, but is more common in speech. The following two-part exchange between myself and my daughter is an illustration. We have a cordless phone which can be used anywhere in the house and my daughter, like many teenagers, is constantly phoning and being phoned by her friends.

> MOTHER Suzanne, have you got the phone up there?
>
> SUZANNE No. Dad's using it.

The ellipsis occurs in the first part of Suzanne's response. *No* could be expanded to 'No, I haven't got the phone up here', but this is unnecessary because we both know what she is saying 'no' to.

ACTIVITY 6 (allow about 10 minutes)

In the examples below there is ellipsis. Try to work out what words have been omitted. The place where they could go has been indicated with the symbol ^. Write a version of each of these sentences with the ellipsed material included.

1   He and his mate both jumped out, he ^ to go to the women, his mate ^ to stop other traffic on the bridge.
2   Perhaps, as the review gathers steam, this can now change. It needs to ^.
3   A: Have you got an exam on Monday?
    B: ^ Two exams ^.

(Biber et al., 1999, pp. 156–7)

See 'Answers to the activities' for feedback.

Another of the differences between conversation and writing is sometimes referred to as **dysfluency**. This is the use of **hesitators** (sounds such as *erm, um*), pauses and repetitions which reflect the difficulty of mental planning at speed. We can see all three of these dysfluencies in the next example.

> That's a very good – er very good precaution to take, yes.
>
> (Biber et al., 1999, p. 1053)

There is a pause after *good*, a hesitator *er* and repetition of *very good*. While such dysfluencies might be considered as random occurrences during unplanned speech, analysis of large amounts of conversational data shows that there are systematic patterns in how they are used. Before you read on, consider when you might use a pause as opposed to a hesitator in conversation.

Hesitators are devices for indicating that a speaker has not yet finished their turn, and thus does not want to be interrupted. Hesitators are commonly used at a point when a speaker has not yet finished all they want to say, but they need to give themselves time for forward planning. In contrast, a pause occurs more often at places where a speaker is about to start on a new part of their utterance. They are often followed by words such as *okay* which signal this new section, as in this example:

> Mmm I just thought you know I okay it's only a cheque I know
>
> (BNC-OU)

This transcript does not have pauses marked. However, when I say it in my head I certainly feel that there would be a pause before *okay*.

ACTIVITY 7 (allow about five minutes)

Read the examples below which show uses of repetition. Do you think repetitions function more like hesitators or pauses?

1   I hope that, uh, Audrey sent in that article to the News Press to, to get back with them

2   Hopefully he'll, er, he'll see the error of his ways.

(Biber et al., 1999, p. 1055)

COMMENT

The repetition of *to* and *he'll* are not at major points in the utterance, rather they are like hesitators, they allow forward planning time and indicate that the speaker has not finished. They can also be used to indicate emphasis.

In our discussion of dysfluency above, we specifically avoided the use of the word 'error'. In the past, because written grammar was used to judge speech, common features of speech were judged as errors because they do not occur in the more planned environment of written text.

Thus what type of data is analysed is crucial to what the grammatical findings are. We said earlier that grammar descriptions were increasingly being developed on the basis of examining how language is really used. This is in contrast to methods which rely on introspection; that is, grammarians consider examples of the language that they use or that is published and devise ways of accounting for the word combinations they find. This method has two consequences. The first is that it is associated with a particular variety of the language, usually that used by those with higher levels of education. The second is that written rather than spoken language often forms the basis of the description. Nowadays, many authors writing grammar books or books to help learners of English are using large databases of natural language to give them insights into how language is used in real life, not just how we think it is used. This will be part of the approach adopted here and you will learn more about it in Unit 2. For now, we just want to show you an example of a grammatical feature which would not have been evident to grammarians using just introspective methods or even those describing actual uses of language based on limited examples.

The example comes from a project investigating grammatical patterns in speech. One of the discoveries made by the project team is referred to as 'heads and tails'. These are items that are placed at the beginning or the end of the main utterance. Example (1) illustrates 'heads' (in bold) and (2) exemplifies 'tails' (in bold).

1 **Paul** in this job that he's got now when he goes into the office he's never quite sure where he's going to be sent.
2 A: I'm going to have Mississippi Mud Pie **I am**.
   B: I'm going to have profiteroles. I can't resist them **I can't** ... just too moreish.

(McCarthy, 1998, p. 78)

I think you will agree that it is highly unlikely that such utterances would occur in writing, with the exception perhaps of dialogue in novels. However, they have been found to occur frequently in speech. They must therefore serve a communicative purpose in speech that would not be necessary in writing. It has been suggested that heads play an important role in helping the listener to prepare for what is coming next. In (1), the word *Paul* is used as a signal by the speaker to the listener that a new topic of conversation is being introduced. It reflects the importance of helping the listener to process incoming information in the short time span typical of face-to-face interaction. In contrast, tails are often used in evaluative contexts where they reinforce a particular point, as in B's remarks which contrast with A's. These are examples of features that are only now being discovered through analysis of authentic, naturally occurring language, particularly in association with computational analysis.

To illustrate what I mean about not basing our study on how we think we use language, look at the transcripts below from a television news programme. Earlier, in Activity 4, we contrasted speech and writing, now you are looking at two different types of speech.

A CTIVITY 8 (allow about 30 minutes)

The video is accessed from the Unit 1 page on the Activities CD-ROM.

Below are two transcripts from a BBC news programme. In Text 3 you will read a short part of what the newsreader said when introducing a news item on rioting in Genoa during a summit conference of world leaders. In Text 4 you will read what a demonstrator at the conference had to say to a reporter. Read the texts and try to put in punctuation for both of them. Make a note of any differences in how the newsreader organises his speech and how the demonstrator organises his. Before you read the comment you may want to watch the video clip 'Rioting in Genoa' on the Activities CD-ROM and see if you want to change your mind about the punctuation.

> Text 3
>
> Newsreader: Good evening dozens of people have been hurt in fighting between police and protesters outside the G8 summit of world leaders in Genoa Italian riot police fired tear gas at demonstrators after an anti-globalisation rally erupted into violence
>
> Text 4
>
> Man: A peaceful demonstration broke up round here you know with them mindless thugs that set fire to that bank for a start it's it's just devastating

See 'Answers to the activities' for my versions.

COMMENT

Here we can observe yet more variation in how language is structured. The newsreader is reading from a script, so his words have been carefully worked out for him; his speech has a lot in common with written language and is therefore much easier to punctuate with conventional punctuation. The demonstrator, however, is thinking and formulating his thoughts into words almost simultaneously. We can see the result of this in the pauses, repetition, fillers such as *you know* and the lack of clear sentence boundaries – features you observed earlier in Activity 4 and other subsequent examples. What is interesting is that before the invention of the tape recorder, people were not consciously aware of many of these features of spoken language. In the same way, having access to lots of language data is also revealing new features of how we actually use language.

ACTIVITIES CD-ROM (allow about 40 minutes)

(1) Work through the activities for Unit 1.

(2) Watch the video clip 'Face to Face' (a split screen of a man and woman talking). This is an unscripted conversation, though obviously the participants knew they were being filmed.

Try to write a transcript of the conversation. Look out for the features of spoken language that we have discussed in this unit.

See 'Answers to the activities' for my transcription of the video clip.

The video is accessed from the Unit 1 page on the Activities CD-ROM.

Conclusion

Once we start to look at naturally occurring language we see that there is systematic variation in the choices people make. These choices relate to both the meaning and the context of the communication. Specifically we have started to look at differences in mode between grammar in speech, especially conversation, and in writing.

You may already be familiar with the idea of variation within a language. For example, there are different varieties of English used in different parts of the world. India, the USA and Australia, for example, all have different varieties of the language we refer to as English. But variety also occurs within countries where different lexical and grammatical choices may be associated with regional dialects. Often people have a choice over whether to use their dialect or to communicate using what has come to be called standard English. In exploring the grammar of English on this course you will be looking at a level of variation which is much more subtle. So far we have used a very crude distinction between written and spoken modes. As the course progresses you will have opportunities to explore for yourself how grammar is a tool for adapting our communications in ways which present us and our message in different lights and how it is dependent on many contextual factors.

Earlier in the unit you were asked to note down what you thought grammar was about. Look back at what you wrote down. Have your views changed at all? We hope that in this course you will see that grammar is not just about labelling parts of speech or judging whether something is right or wrong. Studying grammar opens doors into how we organise our world. Exploring grammar will allow you to see how language is intertwined with both describing a view of the world and interacting with others in it.

Learning outcomes

After completing this unit, you should have developed a knowledge and understanding of the:

◆ importance of context in the grammatical choices we make

◆ reasons for differences between spoken and written English

◆ historical impact of written grammatical descriptions on our view of spoken language.

In the light of your increased understanding, you should be able to:

◆ identify and describe key features of spoken grammar (e.g. ellipsis, heads and tails)

◆ identify and describe some of the key differences between speech and writing.

Key terms introduced

context	monologue
descriptive, prescriptive and pedagogic grammars	question tag
dialogue	sociocultural context
dysfluency	structural grammar
ellipsis	systemic functional grammar
functional grammar	tail [tag]
head [preface]	text
hesitator	traditional grammar
lexicogrammar	transcript
lexis	utterance
mode	word class [part of speech, grammatical class]

Near equivalents are given in [ ].

Answers to the activities

ACTIVITY 6

Ellipted material is enclosed in < >.

1 He and his mate both jumped out, he <jumped out> to go to the women, his mate <jumped out> to stop other traffic on the bridge.

2 Perhaps, as the review gathers steam, this can now change. It needs to <change>.

3 A: Have you got an exam on Monday?

   B: <I've got> two exams <on Monday>.

ACTIVITY 8

Text 3

Newsreader: Good evening. Dozens of people have been hurt in fighting between police and protesters, outside the G8 summit of world leaders in Genoa. Italian riot police fired tear gas at demonstrators after an anti-globalisation rally erupted into violence.

Text 4

Man: A peaceful demonstration broke up round here you know with them mindless thugs that set fire to that bank for a start. It's, it's just devastating.

VIDEO CLIP ('FACE TO FACE') TRANSCRIPT

I have not included punctuation in this transcript. However, there are many different ways of transcribing speech, as you will see throughout the course. If you have included punctuation that is acceptable.

MAN but the second thing is I wondered about the characterisation of the lads whether the fact that men playing the girls was actually sharper because it was men or whether it actually missed a lot

WOMAN I'm at a disadvantage here because you know I've observed this these kids at a very much younger age I used to be a teacher and it was exactly the kind of thing that they would've done you know the girls oh the the scene in the hairdressing salon was absolutely beautiful they were all, they were all getting themselves prettified

MAN now there's the caricature with that hairdresser and the hair going 6 feet above the girls' head

WOMAN yeah yes

MAN you know

WOMAN yes but its its not an anachronism is it I mean it wasn't a bee hive hair do it was a it was a

MAN no no

WOMAN but was it a punk either I I thought

MAN no no

WOMAN that was a little bit over the top

MAN it wasn't punk

WOMAN because he was he was doing all this kind of thing wasn't he behind her head

MAN yes but that's right there were several occasions on that when there were quite clearly where that they took something and just played it well beyond reality

Unit 2
Corpus and grammatical description

Prepared for the course team by Ann Hewings

CONTENTS

Materials required

While studying this unit, you will need:

    your reference grammar

    the course reader (Activity 3)

    the course CD-ROMs (at end of unit)

    Corpus Tasks

    Guide to the CD-ROMs.

Knowledge assumed

From Foundation Grammar:

    word classes (parts of speech).

From Unit 1:

    mode of communication

    descriptive, prescriptive and pedagogic grammars.

Introduction

This cartoon reflects what we learned in Unit 1 about the ways in which language, and grammar in particular, has been researched and described. We discussed traditional methods of writing grammar books based on introspection, describing the sort of language you think you use. We hinted at the more recent methods based on describing large amounts of naturally occurring data, both speech and writing. This is represented in the second picture by the researcher sitting in front of her computer which can store masses of texts for analysis.

Of course, in reality, the grammarian with his/her computer will probably not ignore all the work that has gone before, but will test it to see whether it is an accurate description of how the language actually works.

In this unit, you will be introduced to methods for investigating grammar based on using large amounts of data stored on computer and analysed using special software tools. You will have the opportunity to use these tools yourself and to begin exploring grammar in speech and writing. You will also look at some of the findings presented in your reference grammar and relate those to how the authors explored large quantities of data using computers.

By the end of this unit you will:

◆ be familiar with new computerised methods of exploring English grammar

◆ be able to use a corpus and a concordancing program to explore a limited number of grammatical features

◆ understand how the authors of your reference grammar have used similar techniques and what their findings are in relation to grammar in conversation.

❶ INTRODUCING CORPUS ANALYSIS

What is this large amount of data stored on a computer and what use is it in exploring grammar? To answer these questions we first look at what has become known as 'corpus linguistics' and then at how the techniques of corpus linguistics have been used in your reference grammar. At the end of this unit you will start to practise your own corpus analysis skills and to consolidate some of the grammatical points that have been introduced.

1.1 Terminology of corpus linguistics

We start by defining some of the important terms in corpus linguistics. There are many different definitions of a **corpus** and many different types of **corpora** (the plural of corpus). For our purposes, a corpus refers to a collection of naturally occurring language data (usually many millions of words). The data are in the form of texts, which can be written ones, e.g. books, letters and newspaper articles, or spoken ones, e.g. transcribed speech from radio and TV programmes and from spontaneous conversation. Usually this large collection of texts is stored on a computer and analysed using special software. The software allows language analysts such as grammarians and dictionary writers to find out how frequently different words are used and to display on their computer screens hundreds of examples for analysis in detail. Figure 1 shows you an example of the type of computer view a corpus linguist might study.

The purpose of a corpus is not to access texts in order to read them, but to allow the texts, as data, to be studied in new ways.

> Concordance lines bring together many instances of use of a word or phrase, allowing the user to observe regularities in use that tend to remain unobserved when the same words or phrases are met in their normal contexts.
>
> (Hunston, 2002, p. 9)

The most common way of accessing corpus data is by using a **concordancing program** also known as a **concordancer**. This displays the texts in the form of **concordance lines** as shown in Figure 1. You can see that a concordancer presents a particular word at the centre of the page, or screen on the computer. The word or phrase that is searched for is called the **node** or **key word** and it is displayed with the other words that occur to the left and right of it. These other words are referred to as context or **co-text**, here meaning only those words found immediately to the left or right and not anything further away. This type of display is known as **key word in context (KWIC)**.

```
MonoConc Pro - [Concordance - [because]]                                          _ □ ☒
File  Concordance  Frequency  Display  Sort  Window  Info                        _ ᵬ ×

... Nelson called this the 'I-Scream' bar. This was  because a slogan " which he himself coined " had been  ..
no room for blackboards or instructional pitches  because every inch is covered with pin-ups picked for prot
e.      The British had been taken to the cleaners  because foolish politicians in post-war Britain had elected ·
om the first agents but they refused, arguing that  because he had given them his credit card number he had
used entry clearance to come to England, mainly  because he could not say what were his long term intentioi
final opponent couldn't have had it much easier,  because Hill booked his place courtesy of a remarkable 21·
... thing he's got. Try to get it before Christmas,  because I've got a bit of time off then, and  ...
oak round his shoulders. 'Sometimes I am proud  because I have the King's ear, but our royal master ...
... job for you.' I almost ignored his last words  because I was still thinking about Billingsley's dishonesty,
was scared. But not just by Quigley. I was scared  because if what Quigley had said to Pikey was true and ...
isees to join us in encouraging sensible drinking  because it in their own interests.'      Rather than cutting ti
... a match that has put the Cypriot police on alert  because Juventus, the other Heysel disaster club, are also
.. after pledge was given. Each year it was put off  because of the impossibility of devising an acceptable sch
hen justify the exclusion of some students purely  because of the severity of their disability.      However, t
not widely used for research outside the military  because of the cost of high fidelity simulator time. A compl·
She was admitted to hospital in September, 1991,  because of fever, productive cough, and weakness. She ha
n world, yet he also thinks that he understands it  because of his own (despite the tennis lessons and joggin:
se Adam was broke and Mary was close to broke  because that first time it had been so beautiful and peacefu
ganisms were present in the Cambrian, however,  because the colonization of the land did not take place for
branches and less attack than those without but,  because the few larger workers have a ferocious sting and
ourse is that you haven't got any choice anyway,  because the yen to have children is about as basic as ...
because of the tragedy that befell a little boy but  because they have made people realise how much their ov
s unlawful means when he withdraws his labour  because this situation does not appear to fall within sectioi
young person, probably male. Able to dissemble,  because those lads had not expected to be killed. Or so ...
e of the speed of internal storage operations, and  because use of such a calculation allows the unbroken key

27 matches              1st right          Strings matching: because
152 files in current corpus                                              119.48 mbytes, 152 files
```

Figure 1 A corpus search for the word 'because'

The words to the right and left of the key words can also be sorted, that is ordered on the basis of their initial letter of the alphabet. In Figure 1 the lines have been sorted alphabetically 'to the right'. This results in examples of the key word followed by words beginning with the letter 'a' coming at the top of the list. The concordance lines could be resorted alphabetically 'to the left' to see if there are any patterns to the words that occur before the key word. When we talk about concordance lines we often use the word 'pattern'. This is because, when you sort the lines, you often notice that certain words or classes of words occur to the left and right in blocks and these can be noticed visually as patterns.

Because is a simple word to search on as it does not change its form. However, if you wanted to search for *house* you are also likely to be interested in the plural form *houses*. A concordancer can help you do a search for both forms. In Figure 2 we have chosen to look at all the forms associated with the **string** of letters F A S T. You will notice that there are concordance lines for *fast, faster, fastest*, etc. This is because I searched for the key word *fast**. The symbol * is called a **wildcard** and it means that the concordance program will find any words that begin with the letters *fast*. This shows another useful feature of the concordancer: it can search for and display the different forms of a particular word. Usually we are interested in all the forms of a verb. So for the verb *walk* we would need to look at the forms *walk, walks, walking, walked*. Collectively these forms are known as a **lemma**.

The word 'string' refers to a sequence of letters used in conducting a computer search.

The concordancer does not recognise lemmas in the way that you and I do. It does not know that *walks* and *walking* are part of the same lemma. It finds them using wildcards which just match the first string of letters such as W A L K and then accepts anything which follows them. That is why in Figure 2 we have examples such as *fasten* and *fast-growing*.

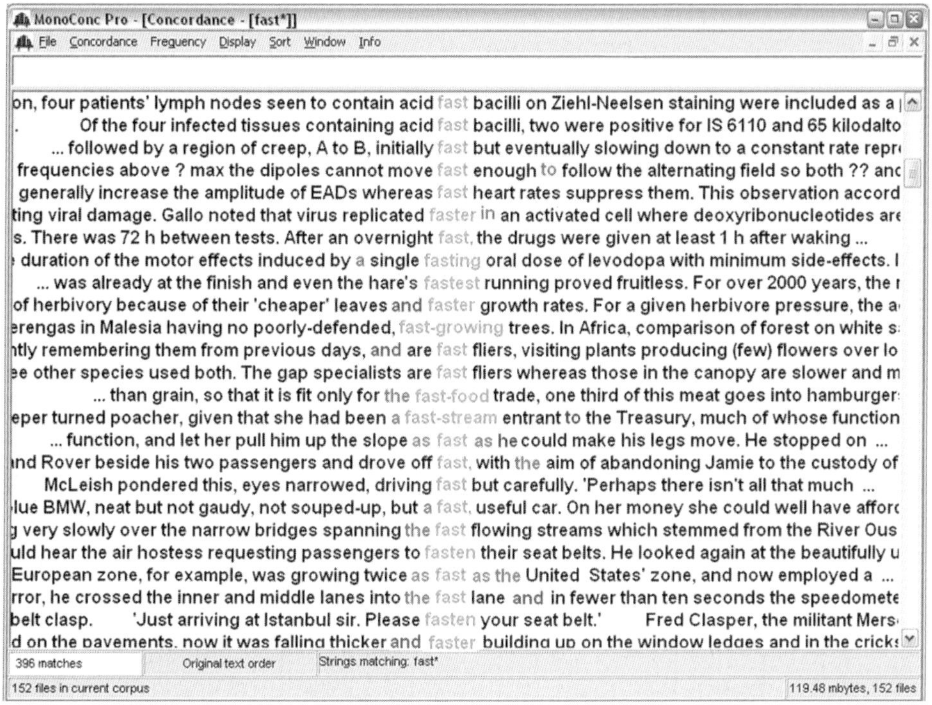

Figure 2 Concordance lines for *fast**

Because a concordance program can sort words only on the basis of their form, it will include words that are of different grammatical classes but have the same form. It is an important point to remember that even though words can have the same or similar forms, they may belong to different grammatical classes or have different meanings.

ACTIVITY 1 (allow about five minutes)

Consider the difference in both grammatical class (noun, verb, adjective, etc.) and meaning of *fast* in the following examples from a corpus of English spoken and written texts.

1 I go fast because I want to get back quick.
2 By early September it seemed that the fast might go on indefinitely.
3 I'm normally a fast learner.

See 'Answers to the activities' for feedback.

This activity illustrates the point about concordance data – they need to be skilfully interpreted. A computer is very good at pattern recognition, sorting and counting, but human beings need to interpret the findings.

In addition to concordance data, most corpus-analysis software can also create lists of word frequencies in a text and analyse the words that frequently co-occur. The tendency for two or more words to co-occur within a short distance of each other is called **collocation** and the co-occurring words themselves are called **collocates**. Figure 3 shows unsorted concordance lines for *flower*. The concordancing program highlights the main collocates, for example, *kinds of, beds, garden, the* and *a* in a different colour on the computer screen. These are only visible as a lighter grey colour in the figure.

```
MonoConc Pro - [Concordance - [flower]]
File   Concordance   Frequency   Display   Sort   Window   Info

ping, it brushes against the pollinia and in the next flower these are lodged in the stigmatic cavity. Eulaema ic
er the anther grooves on the central column of the flower, the pollen being precisely positioned on the thora:
hich opportunistically visit many different kinds of flower, generally small ones, and specialized nectar eater:
nectar eaters, which concentrate on a few kinds of flower, mainly larger ones. Nectar never provides a compl
destructive: mechanisms reducing damage to the flower include the development in many groups of the info
ianensis (Marcgraviaceae) in Brazil, the rest of the flower being inconspicuous. The unspecialized humming
nators between plants. Bird nectar thieves like the flower piercers are found in many species, but the bromel
cies decreases through the day during which any flower is presented. Although the inflorescences last just
.. S. macroptera, which is the first of the section to flower, when the pollinator numbers have not yet built up
empts at photography, proudly framed, a pressed flower that reminded her of her first proper date. Small thi
nage changing, he had seen her as a bright exotic flower. He could remember every detail of that first meetin
d the freshly-turned earth and looked around for a flower she could place on the grave, but it was the ...
    She cherished those walks. Every tuft of grass, flower, bird, was precious to her and she wanted to store
Would her bonnet take more ribbon, or perhaps a flower or two, to give her height?      'And now I ...
ow agapanthus africanus , the blue lily, was in full flower, Hilbert and Lewis and Beryl sat in old-fashioned d
been looking after the garden, you could see that. Flower beds,had been weeded, dead heads removed, the
ight to the stone doorstep and was bordered by a flower garden at one side and a summer house at the ...
was but merely a streak of sunshine bordering the flower garden now. He reached out for his tie that was ...
    ... did them up top have to go and stop the flower trains coming from Cornwall? There was nothing li
s coming from Cornwall? There was nothing like a flower to cheer you up on a dark day. It was ...
Miranda sniffed the heavy scent of the lilies; in the flower room beyond the bar, she could hear Elinor and Bu
erconnecting rooms faced the sea over lawns and flower beds, though they were bleak at this time of the ...
ng. Vaulted ceilings, everything white, one perfect flower spotlit in the centre of each table, impeccable fettuc
metals.        The third is the tobacco plant: a ., the flower: b ., the leaves plucked and drying. I know you kno
unning out. eyes left and right. watching out. a red flower in her teeth. and she makes passes over the dead
69 matches              Original text order      Strings matching: flower
                                                                              119.48 mbytes, 152 files
```

Figure 3 Concordance lines for *flower* showing the collocates

◆ **A**CTIVITY **2**   (allow about five minutes)

This activity is to help you remember some of the important terms in corpus linguistics and to make sure you understand what you are seeing when you look at a screen of concordance lines.

Using Figure 3, complete the following paragraph.

Figure 3 shows _____ _____ for the _____ _____ or node *flower*. We cannot see lines for *flowers*, *flowering*, etc. because the _____ character * was not used for this search. The lines have not been alphabetically _____ to the left or to the right. However, we can see that the main _____ to the immediate right are _____ and _____ and the main collocates to the immediate left are _____ and _____.

See 'Answers to the activities' for feedback.

1.2 Data-driven language analysis

A CTIVITY 3 (allow about 1 hour 30 minutes)

Now that you have had an introduction to what a corpus can show you, it is time to read about corpus linguistics in more detail. Chapter 1 in the course reader *Applying English Grammar*, entitled 'Working with Corpora: Issues and Insights', by Elena Tognini-Bonelli, takes you through considerations such as definitions of different types of corpora and different ways of using corpora. Before you read the chapter, look at the subheadings, the text in boxes and the figures. The quotations on the subject of 'What is a corpus?' are particularly significant. Your view of what a corpus is and what it can be used for will influence how you think it can be used. We shall return to issues such as designing a corpus later in the course and you will be asked to read parts of this chapter again.

A CTIVITY 4 (allow about five minutes)

Before we complete this section introducing corpus analysis, let us check your intuitions about a common word against corpus findings. Jot down two sentences with the word *post* in them to illustrate the common meaning of *post*.

See 'Answers to the activities' to check if the meaning or meanings you think are most common are borne out by looking at large amounts of data.

Letting us view the unexpected facets of language and grammar is one of the joys of working with corpus data and concordancing software. Intuitions about how we use language can be tested against the evidence of a corpus and new hypotheses or descriptions generated. You will be using the corpus and software supplied with this course to help you explore English grammar as you work through the units. You will find that different types of corpus show you different things about English. This highlights the relationship between corpus design and the types of result obtained. In the next section we look specifically at your reference grammar and how the authors have used a variety of subcorpora to inform their analysis of English.

2 INTRODUCING THE *LONGMAN STUDENT GRAMMAR OF SPOKEN AND WRITTEN ENGLISH*

You read in the introduction to this book that the *Longman Student Grammar of Spoken and Written English* is your reference grammar. It is there for you to refer to whenever you want additional information on points of grammar. Sometimes we ask you to read particular sections or we discuss specific points made in the reference grammar. You will notice that in this unit we introduce quite a lot of the technical language that is used in describing grammar. We recommend that you make notes on new terms as you go along. You will find many of them defined in the course units and in the reference grammar.

One of the important reasons for choosing this particular grammar book is that it is based on analysing grammar using the methods of corpus linguistics. It is a smaller version of a much larger reference grammar, the *Longman Grammar of Spoken and Written English* (Biber et al., 1999). This original grammar book was based on an analysis of a corpus of 40 million words of text. By using such a corpus, the analysts were able to analyse more language than any one person will hear or read over many years. In this section you will be thinking about how this type of analysis has changed the way we look at language and the different understandings it facilitates. You will be able to see how your reference grammar fits into the developments that have been taking place and how the tools that you will be using allow you to start researching language in a similar way.

Your reference grammar and the original work done by Biber and his fellow analysts follows a relatively recent tradition of reporting on findings from the analysis of large quantities of naturally occurring data. Pioneering work was done in this field by the Cobuild project based at the University of Birmingham UK. Originally set up to provide data for the compilation of dictionaries, the Cobuild project also gave rise to grammar and other reference books. The editor of the *Collins Cobuild English Grammar* wrote in the introduction:

> We have tried to produce a grammar of real English – the English that people speak and write. It contains detailed information about English, collected from the large corpus we have built up, and it is new both in what it says and in the relationship between statements and the evidence on which they are based.

(Sinclair, 1990, p. x)

ACTIVITY 5 (allow about 15 minutes)

As an introduction to your reference grammar, you should now read sections 1.1, 1.2 and 1.3. Some of the information covered in these pages revisits our earlier discussions in this unit and in Unit 1 of types of grammar, including lexicogrammar, and the importance of corpus, so it should help you to revise these concepts. It also introduces the important new concept of 'register' which we shall return to later.

The reading introduces the terms: **corpus-based grammar, lexicogrammatical patterns, register, subregister, dialect, 'standard' English.**

Now that you have finished reading, you are ready to do the quiz in Activity 6. The quiz is from a workbook (Biber et al., 2002b) written to accompany your reference grammar. If you have this workbook you may find it useful to look at the exercises on topics that interest you or that you are finding difficult.

ACTIVITY 6 (allow about 15 minutes)

Part A

Identify each of the following statements as either true or false. If it is false, revise it so that it is true. The first one is done for you.

1   A descriptive grammar presents rules about correct and incorrect stylistic choices.

False: a *prescriptive* grammar presents rules about correct and incorrect stylistic choices.

2   A prescriptive grammar describes the grammatical patterns that speakers and writers follow when they use the language, regardless of whether the patterns conform to standard English that is presented in usage handbooks.

3   A corpus is a collection of written texts that is stored on a computer.

4   The *Longman Student Grammar of Spoken and Written English* describes the grammatical preferences of speakers and writers, so it includes information about the frequency of grammatical choices.

5   One of the advantages of a corpus-based grammar, such as the *Longman Student Grammar of Spoken and Written English*, is that it can describe how speakers and writers vary their grammatical choices for different communicative situations.

6   Another advantage of a corpus-based grammar is that it can reveal associations between grammatical structures and vocabulary (i.e. lexicogrammatical patterns).

7   A register is a variety of language that is associated with speakers who share certain characteristics, such as gender, socio-economic class, or geographic region.

8   A **dialect** is a variety of language that is associated with certain characteristics of a communicative setting, such as the purpose of the communication, the amount of time for planning and the mode (i.e. spoken versus written).

9   Different registers often have different frequencies for the use of certain grammatical structures.

10   'Standard' English is one unvarying form of English that is always easy to identify.

11   There is a group of experts that officially decides whether or not a grammatical form is 'standard' English.

Part B

Give an example for each of the following (try to think of your own original examples, but if you can't, you can find examples in Chapter 1 of your reference grammar):

(1)   a very specific subregister and a more general register

(2)   a geographic dialect

(3)   a social dialect

(4)   a lexical item from the semantic domain *furniture*.

(Based on Biber et al., 2002b, pp. 7–8)

2.1 Longman registers

In looking at your reference grammar you will have noticed that it is not a prescriptive grammar. Rather it is descriptive, using a corpus-based approach to look at the grammatical and lexical choices that we make in using English in different registers, namely news, fiction, academic prose and conversation. The authors define **registers** as 'varieties of language that are associated with different circumstances and purposes' (p. 4). This includes factors such as mode (speech or writing), interactivity (monologue or dialogue) and communicative purpose (telling, requesting, ordering, etc.). As we have noticed already, the typical grammatical choices that people make vary in different circumstances. In your reference grammar certain of these circumstances have been grouped together under the broad headings of the registers of conversation, fiction, news and academic prose. In using this grammar you will find out about the typical grammatical choices in English used in these specific registers. Frequency information is given so that you can see which grammatical features are more common in particular modes and registers.

Before we look at the significance of frequency, we need to be clear about what we are comparing. In compiling their corpus, the authors selected texts which broadly represented four registers. They are careful to note that these are not the only registers of English but that they are important because they are frequently encountered by a student of language. Also they show sufficient variation to illustrate the principle of differences and similarities in the frequency of grammatical features in different registers. Each collection of texts which represents a register can be analysed separately and can therefore be considered as a **subcorpus** of the total Longman spoken and written English (LSWE) corpus. The first subcorpus is for the register of conversation which differs from the other registers most markedly as it uses the spoken mode. Speakers were selected to be representative of a variety of age groups, genders, social classes and geographical regions. Their conversations were compiled and treated as a cross-section of the general population of the United Kingdom. The conversations were recorded and transcribed to form the spoken register subcorpus. This is supplemented by a further subcorpus of spoken American English. The other three registers all use the written mode. The fiction subcorpus is composed mostly of British English texts, supplemented with a large number of American English and a few other varieties such as Caribbean, Australian, and Irish English. A British English news subcorpus contains texts from national broadsheet and tabloid papers as well as regional newspapers. In addition, there is a further subcorpus of American newspaper texts which the authors have used for comparative purposes. The final subcorpus is composed of academic prose such as extracts from books and research articles in disciplines within the sciences, social sciences and humanities.

ACTIVITY 7   (allow about 15 minutes)

How a corpus is compiled is very significant in terms of the types
of analysis that can be undertaken using it. This is a subject we shall
return to a number of times during this course. To make sure you
understand what is included in the LSWE corpus, you should
now read pages 7–9, Section 1.4, of your reference grammar. The tables
in it will give you detailed information about the number of words in
different types of text and in the different subcorpora.

COMMENT

An important point to notice is the variety in the number of words
analysed for each subcorpus. To illustrate the significance of this we
can consider an extract from Table 1.2 on p. 8 of your reference
grammar on the overall composition of the LSWE corpus.

Table 1 Overall composition of the LSWE corpus (Biber et al., 2002a)

Core register	Words
Conversation (BRE)	3,929,500
Fiction (AME and BRE)	4,980,000
News (BRE)	5,432,800
Academic prose (AME and BRE)	5,331,800

If you look at the figures for each register you will see that the number
of words in each subcorpus is not identical. However, to make
comparisons of frequency it is important to compare like numbers. In
your reference grammar, comparisons are made per one million words.
In studies where there are far fewer words analysed, frequency figures
are often quoted as the number of occurrences per 500 words or even
per 100 words. Once the figures are standardised it makes comparisons
between registers meaningful and allows easier visual representation
of findings. If you look at the left-hand side of Figure 4 in Activity 8 you
can see that frequency is given per million words and that the graph is
calibrated in units of 5,000. Thus the total frequency of *and, but* and *or*
in the conversation subcorpus is 29,000 occurrences per million, as
compared to 37,000 occurrences per million in the fiction subcorpus.

ACTIVITY 8 (allow about 15 minutes)

Figure 4 presents information about the frequency of the **coordinators** *or, but* and *and* across the four registers. You will learn more about coordinators and other conjunctions in a later unit. This activity is to help you further in interpreting the frequency graphs and information given in your reference grammar. You will also get the opportunity to think about the implications of the quantitative findings you are seeing.

Part A

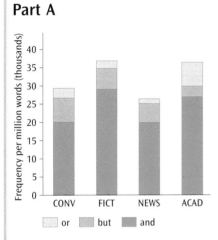

Figure 4 Distribution of co-ordinators across registers (Biber et al., 2002, p. 228)

Use Figure 4 to answer the following questions.

(1) What are the four registers included in the figure? (Do not write abbreviations, write out the full names.)

(2) Which two registers have the highest frequency of all three coordinators combined? Which has the lowest frequency?

(3) Which coordinator is the most common for all registers? Which two registers have the highest frequency of this coordinator?

(4) Which register has the highest frequency of *but*?

(5) Which register has the highest frequency of *or*?

Part B

Now connect this frequency information to the actual use of the common coordinators in texts. Look at the samples of conversation and academic prose below and answer the following questions.

What is the function of *but* in these samples of conversation? Why is it useful for this register?

What is the function of *or* in the samples of academic prose? Why is it useful for this register?

You do not need to give technical explanations in your answers. Use everyday language to describe the meanings and uses of these coordinators. The instances of each coordinator are numbered so that you can refer to them easily. For each question, consider whether the register uses the coordinator just to add one idea to another, to show contrasts, or to cover alternatives. Think about why the register needs to use the coordinator more often than other registers.

Conversation examples

The symbol <...> indicates that a section of the text has been omitted.

1   A: So do you guys feel like – do you feel like she is an acquaintance that you feel inclined to keep in touch with or do you feel like this is my mother.

    B: Well I feel that way **but**[1] I don't think Willy and Sarah really do.

    A: **But**[2] you feel like she's your mother.

    B: Oh yeah.

2   A: Then we change trails and we go into a primitive trail kind of <...> and it's steep at times, and there's poison oak along the way, **but**[3] it's, you know, you can walk around in it, you don't have to worry about it <...>

3   A: Our dog gets cranky if he doesn't get his sleep and he's too big to be cranky.

    B: Oh great.

    A: **But**[4] he's new so don't worry.

Academic prose examples

1   In a text we can study style in more detail, and with more systematic attention to what words **or**[1] structures are chosen in preference to others.

2   These areas may have either high **or**[2] low sulphur content.

3   Plants of several natural orders were grown in surrounds free from ammonia **or**[3] any other nitrogen compound.

(Based on Biber et al., 2002b, pp. 9–10)

See 'Answers to the activities' for feedback.

2.2 Importance of 'words'

Looking at the three words *or, but* and *and* brings us to the importance of the basic concept of a **word**. The authors of your reference grammar note that the definition of a word is not straightforward and this is particularly the case for texts analysed by computer software. If we take

> don't do not

we recognise that the meanings are the same, but in one we have a single written (**orthographic**) **word** bounded by spaces and in the other we have two words, each bounded by spaces. In normal speech it is more difficult because we don't have orthographic clues. For the sake of convenience in computerised counts of words, the spaces on either side of a letter or group of letters are used to define an orthographic word. Thus most computer software would recognise *don't* as one orthographic word and *do not* as two.

Definitions of words become significant when we want to compare the frequencies of words in different text types. Word frequencies are an important feature of different registers, but it is not enough just to count the number of words. The number of *different* words is also highly significant. Let us use the beginning of Text 1 that we looked at in Unit 1. You may recall that this is a spoken monologue that has been transcribed into a written form. (Pauses are indicated by ...)

Corpora can contain plain text and 'tagged' text. These corpora are analysed by concordance software. How a 'word' is defined and counted depends on whether it is tagged and on the programming of the concordancer.

Text 1

A friend of mine told me this amazing story the other day she a ... she'd been shopping and she came back to this multi-storey car park that she's been in and it was kind of deserted ... erm ... and as she was walking towards her car she saw this figure sitting in the passenger seat ... and she thought what's that I've been burgled and as she walked towards the car feeling a bit scared this person got out of the car and it was a little old lady.

If we count the words, that is forms separated by spaces, we get a total of 87 (hyphenated words and contractions such as *she's* count here as one word). This is referred to as the number of **tokens** in the text. If we look again, we see that a number of the tokens are identical to each other: for instance, there are three tokens with the form *of*. The number of *different* tokens in a text is referred to as the number of **types**. Below is a list of the types that are represented by more than one token in the text.

Table 2 Word types in Text 1 (extract)

Type	Tokens	Type	Tokens
of	3	car	4
this	4	that	2
the	4	in	2
she	6	it	2
a	3	was	3
been	2	as	2
and	6		

So these 13 types occur more than once, and 44 types (not listed above, for instance *friend*) occur only once, making a total of 57 types used in this piece of speech. So the text has 87 tokens, but only 57 types. The relationship between types and token is called the **type-token ratio**. The more types you have in comparison to tokens, the more varied is the vocabulary. Another way of saying this is that the text will show greater lexical variety. The formula for calculating the type-token ratio is the number of types divided by the number of tokens, and the result is multiplied by 100 in order to make a percentage score:

$$\text{type-token ratio} = \frac{\text{number of types}}{\text{number of tokens}} \times 100$$

For our example, the calculation is:

(57/87) × 100 = 66%.

ACTIVITY 9 (allow about five minutes)

Calculate the type-token ratio for the text below.

Text 2

Industrialized societies throughout the world are greying. Since 1840, maximum life expectancies have increased at a rate of about three months per year and this trend shows no sign of slowing down. The good news is that people are getting healthier. But one downside is the net impact on healthcare. The overall improvement in health is more than countered by the much greater number of individuals reaching ages at which age-related health problems occur.

(Partridge and Gems, 2002)

See 'Answers to the activities' for feedback.

The value of calculating type-token ratios lies in what it tells us about different texts and registers of English. When we investigate speech and particularly conversation, we find that the type-token ratio is usually low. This may be because conversation is produced spontaneously, with little time for planning and therefore contains many repetitions of the same word tokens. For example, eight words were repeated more than twice in the spoken text (Text 1) and only three were repeated more than twice in the written text (Text 2). There is more practice in calculating type-token rations on the Concordancer and Corpus CD-ROM.

A CTIVITY 10   (allow about 15 minutes)

Your reference grammar discusses words and their categorisations on pp. 13–15. Read sections 2.1 and 2.2 to the end of 2.2.1 and make notes on the meaning of the terms *morpheme, syntax, orthographic word,* **lexeme** (another word for 'lemma'), *token* and *type*.

2.3 Categorising words by grammatical function

In addition to counting types and tokens, we also need to categorise words on the basis of meaning and grammatical function. Your reference grammar classifies words according to their main function and their grammatical behaviour into three categories: those that carry the most meaning in text, **lexical words**; those that bind the text together, **function words**; and **inserts**. These are explained and illustrated in your reference grammar.

A CTIVITY 11   (allow about 10 minutes)

Read section 2.2.2 of your reference grammar. Pay particular attention to lexical words and function words.

The reading introduces the terms: 'lexical word', 'function word', 'insert', 'open class'.

The term open class applies to lexical words. It signifies that it is not possible to list all the members of the class and that new members can be added.

Lexical words carry the main information content of a text and belong to four grammatical classes: nouns (e.g. *Peter, Moscow, table, dictionary*); lexical verbs (e.g. *walk, think, pray, cook*); adjectives (e.g. *hot, thirsty, angry, early*); adverbs (e.g. *slowly, recently, interestingly, carefully*). In carrying out analyses of the different registers of English it has been noted that there are different frequencies of different types of word. This is shown in Figure 5 in the next activity.

ACTIVITY 12 (allow about 10 minutes)

Look at Figure 5. Which register uses the most lexical words? What are the most common two groups of lexical words? Which register uses least lexical words – can you think of why this is the case?

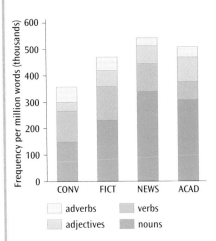

Figure 5 Distribution of different lexical word classes in the registers specified within the LSWE corpus (Biber et al., 2002a, p. 23)

COMMENT

The graph shows that the news register uses the most lexical words and that for the corpus as a whole nouns are the most frequent lexical words, followed by verbs. It also shows that overall there are fewest lexical words in conversation. This might be because in conversation we substitute pronouns (*I, he, you,* etc.) for nouns, and pronouns are function words not lexical words. However, the number of nouns and verbs used in conversation is roughly equal. This is in contrast to the written registers where nouns are much more frequent. Information like this starts to show us the value of looking at language with the benefits of computer technology. Knowledge of such statistically significant differences between registers would be practically impossible to ascertain without computer-aided classifying and counting mechanisms.

Computer **tagging** of word classes is helpful for structural approaches to grammar (see p.13), but automated identification of functional elements of a text (to be outlined in Unit 3) is not yet generally possible.

The same technology allows us to find out about function words. This is a large category of words which provide information on the relationships between the lexical words or larger units of a text such as phrases, clauses and sentences (e.g. in *fast and furious* the word *and* signals a function of addition) or indicates the way in which a lexical word or larger unit should be interpreted. For example, in the following sentence *unless* functions to show that the first half of the sentence will occur if the condition stated in the second half is not met.

He later went on national television to state that he would stand-down <u>unless</u> his new government gained public backing.

(Biber et al., 1999, p. 61)

Function words are generally **closed classes** of words; that is, there are a finite numbers of words in each category such as pronouns (*I*, *she*, *they*, etc.) and prepositions (*on*, *in*, *by*, *through*, etc.). The authors of your reference grammar demonstrate the significant differences in distribution of different types of function word by comparing conversation and academic prose. For example, in conversation the frequency of pronouns is about 165,000 per million words. In academic prose, however, the frequency is about 39,000 per million words; that is, pronouns occur four times as frequently in conversation as in academic prose. Prepositions show the opposite tendency, being about three times more frequent in academic prose.

ACTIVITY 13 (allow about 30 minutes)

Distinguishing between lexical and function words can be tricky. For that reason we want you to at least skim through sections 2.2.6–2.6 in your reference grammar. You are not expected to understand or remember everything in these sections. It is a long passage and some of it covers aspects (such as how to recognise a noun or verb) that you may already know, while other parts contain detailed and complex information on **morphological**, **syntactic** and **semantic** tests to help you classify words. However, it is a useful reference section and you may wish to return to it again during your work on this course. Notice in particular section 2.6 on word-class ambiguities. It is important to remember that any classification system will have grey areas because some items are difficult to assign to one class rather than another. This is particularly true of language which is constantly changing and used in so many creative ways.

One of the advantages of being able to distinguish between lexical and function words is that it allows us to calculate a measure of difference between texts called **lexical density**. Let us use Text 2 again. This time we shall count the number of words that are lexical and the number of words that are functional. I have underlined the words which we are classing as functional in this text. The rest are lexical.

Text 2

Industrialized societies <u>throughout</u> <u>the</u> world <u>are</u> greying. <u>Since</u> 1840, maximum life expectancies <u>have</u> increased <u>at</u> <u>a</u> rate <u>of</u> <u>about</u> <u>three</u> months <u>per</u> year <u>and</u> <u>this</u> trend shows <u>no</u> sign <u>of</u> slowing <u>down</u>. <u>The</u> good news is <u>that</u> people <u>are</u> getting healthier. <u>But</u> <u>one</u> downside is the net impact on healthcare. The overall improvement in health is more than countered by the much greater number of individuals reaching ages at which age-related health problems occur.

(Partridge and Gems, 2002)

I have classified 34 words as functional and 40 as lexical, making a total number of 74 words. To calculate the lexical density, divide the number of lexical words by the total number of words and multiply the result by 100 to make a percentrage score:

$$\text{lexical density} = \frac{\text{number of lexical words}}{\text{total number of words}} \times 100$$

i.e. $(40/74) \times 100 = 54\%$

ACTIVITY 14   (allow about 15 minutes)

The function words have been underlined in Text 1 below. Calculate the lexical density of this text. Can you think of any reason why it is different from the lexical density for Text 2?

Text 1

A friend of mine told me this amazing story the other day she a ... she'd been shopping and she came back to this multi-storey car park that she's been in and it was kind of deserted ... erm ... and as she was walking towards her car she saw this figure sitting in the passenger seat ... and she thought what's that I've been burgled and as she walked towards the car feeling a bit scared this person got out of the car and it was a little old lady.

See 'Answers to the activities' for feedback.

Lexical density is practised again on the Activities CD-ROM.

The final category of words identified in your reference grammar are inserts, words such as *erm, like* and *yeh* which occur in speech and fictional speech. (For simplicity, we have treated inserts as function words in the calculations of lexical density above.) Inserts are often marked off in speech by intonation and pauses, or by punctuation marks in writing. They generally carry emotional meanings or contribute to the ability of speakers in a conversation to manage taking turns such as preventing themselves from being interrupted. Many of these words can also be classified as **discourse markers**; that is, they separate off different sections of what people have to say. Next time you are in a conversation, try and notice, for example, how often people use the word *okay* to indicate a change of topic.

ACTIVITY 15 (allow about five minutes)

You should be aware that some words can be lexical, functional or inserts depending on their particular use. In Figure 6 you can see a screenshot of lines showing different uses of *like*. Try to identify examples of *like* as a lexical word, a function word and an insert.

MonoConc Pro - [Concordance - [like]]

File Concordance Frequency Display Sort Window Info

Like if you look like er Woking, you're W he's Woking and you're Enfield.

ote.	People who are denied political privileges	like	this on the ground that they are not standard items
inisations, and to a financially hard pressed charity	like	HealthWatch, which has to step in where the profes
constable appeared in the doorway, they stood out	like	sore thumbs, causing more than a ripple of interest
ren then, that this self-administered absolution was	like	a drug in the bloodstream. It was comforting and ea
... But don't forget you're welcome any time you	like	to come.' He half turned from her looking towa
for herself might temper any onslaught. He did not	like	Daniel, or her marriage, and made that clear. Sh
... he put the paper back in his pocket. 'You	like	being famous, Mr Adam Nicholson? Your photograp
idoned. He saw himself then, and now, and did not	like	what he saw. Act One concluded. The curtain c
... 'The babby likes to stroke the fur, they're	like	cuddly toys'; and I says, 'Jesus, woman, you ...
ered over the edge. His flames whipped in the wind	like	a tattered kite. The fireball became tiny and winked (
. three weeks. It was lovely. Just heaven. I wouldn't	like	to tell you how often I've thought back on ...
... Pike isn't a big guy, but he did this	like	he had been in secret weight-training. As the table fo
... a distraction.' 'Is it just that he is	like	you?' Zeinab asked Owen. 'Or are all men ...
At sunset the slabbish, orange peaks had appeared	like	ghosts out of the clouds and then, in less time ...
... years to the 1940s. Here and there it felt more	like	the Middle Ages. What brought all this on was d
... Mm. it's not as if you're	like	selling them at cost and making a few pence becaus
... got fifty four. Oh well he's just pulling away.	Like	if you look like er Woking, you're W he ...
... I've got a sweet tooth when it comes to	like	chocolates and things like them Mm but ...
. n't even make the semi finals and erm they reckon	like	that, that channel nine that's supposed to be backin
... she goes I'll do porno's look's	like	you went and like all the clothes and I suppose ...
... minute, like, turned all the lights off hoping he'll	like	pass out you could just hear him like laughing to ...
n you move them fingers there? Go	like	that, like that. Shut up. What's up

| 22 matches | Original text order | Strings matching: like |

C:\Documents and Settings\Guy\My Documents\EZD303\BNC Corpus\speech\KD0.xml   168.69 mbytes, 183 files

Figure 6 Concordance lines showing the variety of word classes that *like* can belong to

COMMENT

You should be able to see examples of *like* used as a lexical word (in this case a lexical verb), e.g. *He did not like Daniel*, as a function word (preposition), e.g. *People who are denied political privileges like this* and as an insert, e.g. *I've got a sweet tooth when it comes to like chocolate and things*.

Like used as an insert is now very common, particularly in the speech of young people. However, if you look back at grammars and dictionaries from say the early 1980s, you probably won't find it mentioned.

Grammar books, even those using the latest technology, can only show us a snapshot of how language is organised at a particular time. Human beings are constantly inventive, and playing with language is common. So a grammar book may give you a rule or description of, for example, when to use the function word *not* to make something negative. It may tell you that *not* must come before the main verb, e.g.

He did**n't** remember.

However, it is less easy to account for the uses my teenage children come up with:

He's really attractive. NOT

where the *not* is emphasised. Or,

She is so NOT cool.

In a prescriptive grammar both these utterances would be deemed incorrect, but in fact they are acceptable uses among a particular group of the population. Much of the humour or effect of these types of expression relies on our intuitive knowledge or expectation of the typical grammatical patterns of the language and the contexts in which they would be appropriate. When these are not followed we have new patterns emerging which may persist and change the language for ever, or may be current for a while and then fade.

⬦ CORPUS AND CONCORDANCING
ON CD-ROM

You will now start to use corpus approaches to study grammar yourself. You will be using a four-million word corpus which has four subcorpora of conversation, news, fiction and academic prose similar to the much larger corpus used by the authors of your reference grammar. The corpus is a small part of the British National Corpus (BNC) which was also used by the team writing the grammar books. In addition, you will be using a software program called MonoConc which allows you to look at concordance lines and find out frequency information about the corpus. MonoConc can also be used to examine texts from other corpora, including ones you compile yourself. You could therefore explore some of the lexicogrammatical features of your own writing, or of news articles or fiction that you have collected, using the corpus and concordancing skills introduced in the *Corpus Tasks* booklet.

CD-ROMS (allow about seven hours)

1   Work through the tasks for this unit on the Concordancer and Corpus CD-ROM using the *Corpus Tasks* booklet (allow about five hours).

2   Work through the activities for this unit on the Activities CD-ROM (allow about two hours).

Conclusion

This unit has introduced you to ways of researching language using computer software and large collections of texts stored electronically. This method of analysis has been used by the authors of your reference grammar. In particular, by dividing the corpus into separate registers they are able to make grammatical descriptions which relate more closely to the contexts of those registers. This type of grammatical analysis will be supplemented in later units by techniques which build on and extend methods for relating the language choices we make even more closely to the particular contexts in which communication takes place.

Learning outcomes

After completing this unit, you should have developed a knowledge and understanding of:

◆   lexical words and functional words

◆   new methods of analysis using computational techniques that can be used to explore grammar

◆   how corpus analysis can help to highlight differences in the frequency of grammatical features in different registers, including speech and academic writing.

In the light of your increased understanding, you should be able to:

◆   load a corpus and concordancer and search for particular words or groups of words

◆   compile your own corpus of text files, load them into the concordancer and carry out simple searches

◆   interpret the frequency graphs and information given in your reference grammar

◆   calculate the type-token ratio for a test

◆   calculate lexical density.

Key terms introduced and revisited

closed class	lexicogrammatical pattern
collocate	morphology
collocation	node/key word
concordance line	open class
concordancing program [concordancer]	orthographic word
coordinator	prescriptive grammar
co-text	register/subregister
corpus/corpora	'standard' English
corpus-based grammar	string
descriptive grammar	subcorpus
dialect	tagging
discourse marker	token
function word	type
insert	type-token ratio
key word in context (KWIC)	wildcard
lemma [lexeme]	word
lexical density	word classes [parts of speech]
lexical word	

Near equivalents are given in [ ].

Answers to the activities

ACTIVITY 1

In (1), *fast* is an adverb showing that something happens at speed. In (2), *fast* is a noun meaning to go without food or drink, usually for religious reasons, and in (3), *fast* is an adjective denoting that something takes place quickly over a short period of time.

ACTIVITY 2

Figure 3 shows **concordance lines** for the **key word** or node *flower*. We cannot see lines for *flowers, flowering,* etc. because the **wildcard** character * was not used for this search. The lines have been not been alphabetically **sorted** to the left or to the right. However, we can see that the main **collocates** to the immediate right are *garden* and *beds* and the main collocates to the immediate left are *the* and *a*.

ACTIVITY 4

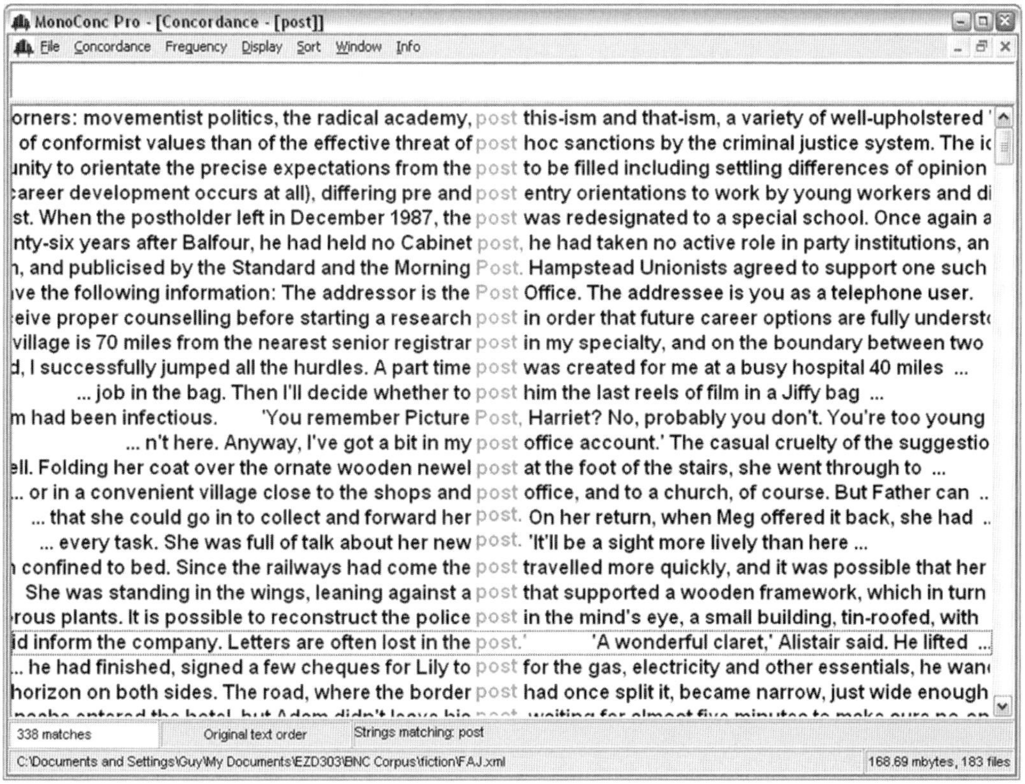

Figure 7 Unsorted concordance lines for *post*

Before looking at the lines, I wrote the following two sentences.

I'm going to the post office.

The post usually arrives at about 9 o'clock.

I didn't think of meanings such as a newspaper (*the Morning Post*), a job or position (*she was full of talk about her new post*), or an upright piece of wood (*the ornate wooden newel post at the foot of the stairs*).

ACTIVITY 6

Part A

1   False: a *prescriptive* grammar presents rules about correct and incorrect stylistic choices.

2   False: a *descriptive* grammar describes the grammatical patterns that speakers and writers follow.

3   False: a corpus can include both written texts and transcribed spoken texts on computer.

4   True.

5   True.

6   True

7   False: a *dialect* is a variety of language that is associated with speakers.

8   False: a *register* is a variety of language that is associated with certain characteristics of a communicative setting.

9   True.

10   False: there is considerable grammatical variability within 'standard' English.

11   False: there is no official group that designates 'standard' English.

Part B

There are many possible answers. Some examples follow.

(1)   A specific subregister: methodology sections of medical research articles; a more general register: research papers or academic writing.

(2)   A geographic dialect: the variety of English spoken in Yorkshire.

(3)   A social dialect: the language of middle-income Hispanic women in the USA.

(4)   Chair, table, bed, etc.

ACTIVITY 8

Part A

(1) Conversation, fiction, news and academic prose.

(2) Academic prose and fiction have the highest frequencies; news has the lowest frequency.

(3) *and* is most common across all registers; fiction and academic prose have the highest frequency.

(4) *but* is most frequent in conversation.

(5) *or* is most frequent in academic prose.

Part B

There are many ways to describe the use of the coordinators. An example follows.

But is used to show contrast in the conversation samples. It appears to have several specific uses in these samples. Sometimes *but* marks contrasts within a speaker's own ideas (1, 3, 4). These contrasts can be used to reassure the other participants in the conversation (3, 4) or they can be used when a speaker wants to clarify the last speaker's utterance (2). These functions are useful in conversation since the interactions among people are an important concern of that register.

In the academic prose, on the other hand, *or* is used in giving specific and thorough descriptions and explanations which are important for conveying precise, accurate information. For example, *or* can present alternative conditions or choices (2), specific and general terms (3) and collections of items covered in a study (1).

ACTIVITY 9

type-token ratio = (63/74) × 100 = 85%.

ACTIVITY 14

lexical density = (no. of lexical words/total no. of words) × 100 = (34/87) × 100 = 39%.

Unit 3

The units of grammar: function and form in spoken and written English

Prepared for the course team by Clare Painter

CONTENTS

Materials required

While studying this unit, you will need:

your reference grammar
the course reader (at end of unit)
the course CD-ROMs (at end of unit).

Knowledge assumed

You should be familiar with the following before starting this unit.

From Foundation Grammar:

types of phrase
subject of a clause
active and passive voice.

From Unit 1:

heads and tails
influence of context on grammatical choice
hesitators, pauses, repetitions and question tags.

From Unit 2:

coordinator
use of a corpus for data analysis
discourse marker
lexical density
register.

Introduction

Because communication is so central to human life, an understanding of how a language works can illuminate many interesting and important issues in a variety of different domains. But before we can seriously address such questions – for example, about how English is used differently in different contexts to create effective texts, or how English is best learned or taught, or what is special about our most-valued English literary texts, or how power, attitudinal stance or ideology operate in particular English texts – we need gradually to build up the terminology and concepts that will allow us to talk about spoken and written English in precise and useful ways. In other words, we need to further our understanding of the nature of English grammar (or, more precisely, lexicogrammar).

In this unit we begin our description of English grammar by exploring the very basic building blocks of the language – the chunks that we need to be able to recognise and identify both in order to describe the way English is organised and to discuss the choices that are taken up in different contexts. This will involve identifying and classifying some of the *forms*, or 'formal' units, of the grammar and seeing what jobs they do in communication, i.e. the *functions* of grammatical units. For some of you, some of the terminology we introduce at this point may be familiar from your previous studies of English or another language, while other terms may be quite new to you. But whatever your previous knowledge of grammar, this unit will give you an opportunity to reflect on some of the principles underlying traditional terminology and to think further about grammatical categories in relation to the two basic modes of communication (speech and writing).

◆ CONSTITUENTS OF THE SENTENCE

Let us begin by looking at a brief passage of written English from which the punctuation has been removed. As you make sense of the text, put in full stops where you think they would be appropriate.

> rabbit is a great favourite in Tuscany we had a fantastic rabbit dish at a restaurant on our way back to our villa from the market one day the saddle of the rabbit had been boned and stuffed with various tasty ingredients and then was roasted it came with a sauce made with grapes from the restaurant's vineyard the chef had preceded this dish with a tiny sage and lemon sorbet and cleverly used the ingredients in season

What grammatical units can we identify in this passage? In the first place, we can all agree that it consists of 78 words, since these are signalled to us by the spaces on the page. Of course these words are not separated out when we speak them, and this is one of the difficulties we face when learning to converse in a new language. Interestingly, some of the earliest written manuscripts were closer to the spoken mode in that they did not separate words with spaces.

ThisstyleofwritingwasknowninLatinasscriptiocontinua. (This style of writing was known in Latin as *scriptio continua*.) The reason that spaces soon began to be used between words in written text is that they provide a visual signal of this key grammatical unit and thus aid our comprehension. But even with the word boundaries made clear as they are in the text about rabbit, you may have found this excerpt rather difficult to digest at first because of the lack of punctuation, which provides another visual signal to the grammar.

Here is the text with the original punctuation included:

> Rabbit is a great favourite in Tuscany. We had a fantastic rabbit dish at the restaurant on our way back to our villa from the market one day. The saddle of the rabbit had been boned and stuffed with various tasty ingredients, and then was roasted. It came with a sauce made with grapes from the restaurant's vineyard. The chef had preceded this dish with a tiny sage and lemon sorbet and cleverly used the ingredients in season.
>
> (Adapted from Alexander and Beer, 1998, p. 146)

If you were able to punctuate the passage correctly, then you were able instinctively to identify at least one further grammatical unit – the written sentence. And even if you could not explain exactly why full stops go where they do, you probably feel that everything within a sentence seems to 'belong together' as a unit of meaning more closely than it does to the rest of the passage. So far, then, because of our familiarity with written text we have been able to identify two grammatical units – that of the word and the sentence.

Now compare the first and last sentences from the passage (ellipted elements are in angle brackets):

1   Rabbit is a great favourite in Tuscany.

2   The chef had preceded this dish with a tiny sage and lemon sorbet
and
<he> cleverly used the ingredients in season.

To explain the differences between the two sentences we need to recognise that in the first case we have a simple sentence consisting of one single **clause**, but in the second case there are two clauses linked together by *and* to make a longer sentence. In Unit 6 you will explore the ways clauses join together to form sentences, but here we shall be most concerned with individual clauses. By the end of the unit you will have a clearer idea of how to recognise a clause, but, for the moment, you can think of a clause as the simplest kind of sentence.

Recognising the units of word, clause and sentence, however, will not be enough to allow us to explain how the passage makes sense, because if we rearrange the words within the individual clauses we come up with nonsense, such as:

great in favourite rabbit is Tuscany a

The problem is not that the words are difficult or unfamiliar but that we cannot discern any meaningful *patterns* among them. Yet some rearrangements of wordings within a clause certainly are possible.

◆ **ACTIVITY 1**   (allow about 10 minutes)

Before reading on, take the following clause and see how many ways you can rearrange the wording without changing the sense:

We had a fantastic rabbit dish at the restaurant on our way back to our villa from the market one day.

COMMENT

Here are just some of the possible variations:

At the restaurant we had a fantastic rabbit dish on our way back to our villa from the market one day.

At the restaurant one day we had a fantastic rabbit dish on our way back to our villa from the market.

On our way back to our villa from the market one day, we had a fantastic rabbit dish at the restaurant.

On our way back to our villa from the market, we had a fantastic rabbit dish at the restaurant one day.

One day, we had a fantastic rabbit dish at the restaurant on our way back to our villa from the market.

One day on our way back to our villa from the market we had a fantastic rabbit dish at the restaurant.

One day at the restaurant on our way back to our villa from the market, we had a fantastic rabbit dish.

We had a fantastic rabbit dish one day at the restaurant on our way back to our villa from the market.

We had a fantastic rabbit dish at the restaurant one day on our way back to our villa from the market.

We had a fantastic rabbit dish at the restaurant on our way back to our villa from the market one day.

While some of these variations are more likely than others, all are quite acceptable English clauses, so clearly it *is* possible to rearrange certain chunks of a clause and still end up with something meaningful. But as we've already seen, we cannot rearrange just any individual words. Some words 'stay together' as larger groupings in all our rearrangements.

What has become evident from this activity is that we need to recognise some intermediate-sized units between those of word and clause. These intermediate units are made up of groups of words that seem to belong together more closely than they do to other words inside a clause. For this reason they are referred to by grammarians as 'groups' and/or 'phrases'. In this course we shall follow your reference grammar (Chapter 3) and refer to these groupings of words as **phrases**. To sum up, then, we have established a basic hierarchy of the building blocks, or **constituents**, of grammar. We have found that words combine in particular ways to form phrases, which in turn combine to form clauses, as shown in Figure 1.

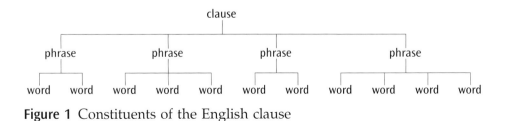

Figure 1 Constituents of the English clause

We can extend this by recognising that words too may be broken down into meaningful parts. Think of a word like *kicked*: it has two parts, *kick* providing the core meaning and *-ed* signalling past tense. The meaningful constituents of a word are called **morphemes** and the study of word structure is **morphology**. A morpheme is a unit of the grammar not the sound system; it is not the same as a syllable. A word may have several syllables but be a single morpheme (e.g. *catastrophe*), or be a single syllable and contain two morphemes (e.g. *cat-s*). Many words in English, such as *on, yes, lady, scratch,* consist of only one morpheme.

If we include morphemes as the very smallest building blocks of the language, then we arrive at a hierarchy of parts and wholes with four levels, or **ranks**, as shown in Table 1.

Table 1 Hierarchy of ranks in English

Rank	Example
Clause	⏐ Several children are playing near the river ⏐
Phrase	⏐ Several children ⏐ are playing ⏐ near the river ⏐
Word	⏐ Several ⏐ children ⏐ are ⏐ playing ⏐ near ⏐ the ⏐ river ⏐
Morpheme	Several - child - ren - are - play - ing - near - the - river

Both one-morpheme and multi-morpheme units are called words. On a similar principle, at the next rank up, both one-word and multi-word units are called phrases and at the next rank, both one-phrase and multi-phrase clauses are called clauses. (And we are used to referring to both one-clause and multi-clause units as sentences.) Here are some examples of simple English clauses to illustrate this point:

In the hall / the girl / was play-ing / the piano / very soft-ly

(One clause consisting of five phrases, 11 words, 13 morphemes)

Now / they / play / it / fast

(One clause consisting of five phrases, 5 words, 5 morphemes)

Stop!

(One clause consisting of one phrase, 1 word, 1 morpheme)

Biber et al. (1999, p. 50) sum up the **rank system** (or rank scale) of English grammatical units in the following way:

Most typically a unit consists of one or more elements on the level below, i.e. a clause consists of one or more phrases, a phrase consists of one or more words, a word of one or more morphemes, etc.

ACTIVITY 2 (allow about five minutes)

Identify the phrases, then the words and then the morphemes in the
given clause. (When marking off the phrases, you may want to change
the position of *soon*.)

Rank	Example
Clause	The discomfort of internal gastrointestinal examination may soon be a thing of the past
Phrase	The discomfort of internal gastrointestinal examination may soon be a thing of the past
Word	The discomfort of internal gastrointestinal examination may soon be a thing of the past
Morpheme	The discomfort of internal gastrointestinal examination may soon be a thing of the past

See 'Answers to the activities' for feedback.

In the rest of this unit we shall begin to look at the units of clause and
phrase in particular, and to discuss some aspects of how they vary in
spoken and written modes of communication.

❷ IDENTIFYING CLAUSES I

In the first of three sections on identifying clauses, we look at the clause
as a representation of experience.

2.1 Functional parts of a clause

To get a better understanding of what we respond to when we identify
a stretch of text as a clause, we need to think about what function such
a unit of language performs. To begin to explore this, look at the picture
below and write a few statements about what you can see in this scene.
I have begun with two examples of my own below.

Example statements:

    A bird is pecking some bread.

    Several people are having their lunch on the grass.

By constructing your statements you have been finding ways to turn
some non-linguistic experience into language. And this is one of the
prime jobs of the grammar of any language: we put words together in

particular ways to give meaning to what we experience. Our experience of our world in terms of happenings, states and relationships between different phenomena must be shaped into grammatical structures if we want to share it with other people. But what is the nature of these grammatical structures? Let us look at four of the statements made by someone who was given this task:

A toddler is laughing happily.

A family is eating a picnic under a tree.

A dog is playing with a ball.

A young woman is photographing her brother.

Each of these is a single simple clause and each performs the same job: it provides a representation of something going on. Most of the specific words in each example are different, but the examples are similar in that they contain similar groupings of words – that is, similar in that they do the same job. The key grouping is perhaps the one that lets us know that some **process** is going on. In the first example it is the constituent *is laughing*; in the others: *is eating, is playing, is photographing*. So all these examples are similar in having some words that 'go together' as a grammatical unit by functioning to represent some process that is happening.

In these examples, each process involves at least one entity that is participating in the process in some way, typically by doing it or being affected by it. In the first example, this is *a toddler*. We can see that, despite their different specific wordings, our examples contain similar chunks of wording functioning as the **participants** in the process. In Table 2, the participants are identified for each example.

Table 2 Constituents functioning as process and participant

Participant	Process	Participant
A toddler	is laughing	
A family	is eating	a picnic
A dog	is playing	
A young woman	is photographing	her brother

You will notice that a participant is not necessarily a person: it can be something inanimate like *a picnic*. And it need not be a single entity: it can be *a family* or *several people* or *parents and children*.

Now let us turn our attention to the remaining words in our example clauses – what is their function? In every case the remaining words are playing a generally similar role. They do the job of describing something of the setting or **circumstance** accompanying the process. In the first example, *happily* explains how the toddler is smiling, while in the next, *under a tree* describes where the process takes place. Circumstances add information concerning the process as to how, where, when, by what means, who with, for how long, etc. Table 3 shows the complete structure of all our examples.

Table 3 Constituents functioning as processes, participants and circumstances

Participant	Process	Participant	Circumstance
A toddler	is laughing		happily
A family	is eating	a picnic	under a tree
A dog	is playing		with a ball
A young woman	is photographing	her brother	

We can now begin to explain a little better what we mean by a simple clause in English. A key function of clauses is to represent the phenomena of our experience in terms of processes, participants and circumstances. This means that a basic clause (where there is no ellipsis) will always have a process element and (unless it is a **command** like *Stop!*) at least one participant. Circumstances are less central, functioning rather to add extra detail and so may or may not be present. If present, there may be only one (as in these examples) or there may be more than one, as in *At the moment the toddler is laughing happily in the park.*

Before we elaborate on this idea of the clause as a representation of experience, try the following activity to check your understanding so far.

ACTIVITY 3 (allow about 10 minutes)

Match up the following example clauses with the correct structural description. In the descriptions, the symbol ^ means 'is followed by'.

Clauses

1   The old woman was scrubbing the table with vigour.
2   Before breakfast, Peter unenthusiastically swept the footpath.
3   In the heat the flowers were drooping.
4   My cousin smashed the car.
5   John went to the cashier.
6   Explain this problem.

Descriptions

(a) participant^process^participant
(b) participant^process^participant^circumstance
(c) circumstance^participant^circumstance^process^participant
(d) process^participant
(e) participant^process^circumstance
(f) circumstance^participant^process

See 'Answers to the activities' for feedback.

Once you become familiar with seeing a clause in terms of a process with participant(s) and circumstance(s), you will be able to reflect more easily on how experience has been represented in particular texts of interest to you. An important point here is that different people will represent the 'same' experience differently, not only by choosing a different lexis, but by representing it with a different grammatical pattern. For example, I included the following statement in my own list describing the picture on page 70: *A young man is posing for a photograph.* This statement has the following structure.

A young man	is posing	for a photograph
participant	process	circumstance

Let us compare this with the final example from Table 2 (p. 71): *A young woman is photographing her brother.*

A young woman	is photographing	her brother
participant	process	participant

Here we can see a difference in lexical choices (*brother* as against *young man* for example) and also a difference in the way the grammatical structure represents the experience. In the first clause (*A young woman is photographing her brother*) we have a process in which two participants are involved: one that does the action (the '**agent**') and one that is affected by the action. In the other clause (*is posing*) we have a different process involving only one participant: the agent (*a young man*). In the first example the man in the picture is represented as the participant who is 'acted on' and in the second, as the agent. Another contrast between the two representations concerns the action itself. In the first example, *is photographing* has the central place grammatically as the process in the clause. In the second example, this action is merely implied in the circumstance that provides the extra detail (*for a photograph*). The point is not that one version is better or truer than another, but that the two versions create slightly different meanings; they make subtly different interpretations of the same reality. Every time we create a clause we are transforming experience into a structure, and every time we do this we are making meaning – but not the only possible meaning. Just as our choice of words contributes to meaning, so does our choice of how we pattern those words into configurations of process, participant(s) and circumstance(s).

You may have noticed as you did Activity 3 that the units we are identifying as participants, processes and circumstances involve similar groupings of words. Every participant, for example, is expressed either by a noun or a group of words that centres on a noun. Such groups of words are therefore known as **noun phrases**.

Here are some examples of noun phrases with the central or **head** element in bold:

> **Mary**; the little **boy**; this spritely **fellow**; **you**; **they**; the two old **men** with long beards; **him**; sixteen **bananas**.

As you can see, noun phrases include personal pronouns such as *you, they, him* as well as single nouns like *Mary*. All the examples given are of single noun phrases, but sometimes two or more linked noun phrases function as a single participant. For example in the clause *We met Mary and her friend*, the second participant is *Mary and her friend*.

Turning our attention to the process in our examples, we can see that this is expressed, or **realised by** (made real by, made actual by), a verb or a group of verbs. Such a verb or group of verbs is known variously as a **verb group**, a **verbal group** or, as we shall refer to it, a **verb phrase**.

Here are some examples of verb phrases:

> Went; might take; has drunk; will be going to eat; is; has been expecting; said; had become; could have been going to ask; having spoken; whistling.

As you can see, the verb phrase may vary considerably in size. As long as there is no ellipsis, there will always be a lexical verb; that is, a verb that is a lexical or 'content' word (see Unit 2), but this may be preceded by a number of function words of the type known as auxiliary verbs. You will find out more about these verb phrases in a later unit; at this point, it is important to understand that the process in a clause may be realised by a single lexical verb or by a phrase made up of two or even several verbs (such as *could have been going to ask*).

See Foundation Grammar for 'lexical verb' and 'auxiliary verb'.

Finally, looking at circumstances we can find two different structural patterns. Sometimes a circumstance is realised as an **adverb phrase** like *(very) happily*. In other cases, circumstances are realised by longer units where a noun phrase is linked into the clause by a preposition. These longer units are known as **prepositional phrases**. Here are some examples of both structures.

Table 4 Examples of adverb phrases and prepositional phrases

Adverb phrases	Prepositional phrases (prepositions in bold)
happily	**under** the umbrella
very loudly	**on** the ground
as soon as possible	**for** a long time
enthusiastically	**to** London
over there	**during** the summer
more loudly than ever	**for** Mary
quite effectively	**before** lunch

If we now return to our original text, we can see more clearly how each clause divides into meaningful units consisting of groupings of one or more words. Here is the passage from page 65 displaying how the clauses are made up of participants, processes and circumstances realised by phrases of different kinds. (The conjunctions linking clauses together have been placed in brackets to indicate that they are not themselves part of the structure of the phrases.) A clause boundary is indicated by ‖, a group/phrase boundary by | and an embedded element (to be explained in a later unit) enclosed in [ ]. Processes are in bold and participants are underlined.

> <u>Rabbit</u> | **is** | <u>a great favourite</u> | in Tuscany. ‖ <u>We</u> | **had** | <u>a fantastic rabbit dish</u> | at a restaurant | on our way [back to our villa | from the market] | one day. ‖ <u>The saddle [of the rabbit]</u> | **had**

been boned ‖ (and) **stuffed** | with various tasty ingredients ‖ (and then) **was roasted**. ‖ It | **came** | with a sauce [made with grapes [from the restaurant's vineyard]]. ‖ The chef | **had preceded** | this dish | with a tiny sage and lemon sorbet, ‖ (and) cleverly | **used** | the ingredients in season. ‖

ACTIVITY 4 (allow about 20 minutes)

Try to analyse the following text yourself into processes, participants and circumstances. (The excerpt comes from a letter written by a Year 6 schoolchild telling his parents about a school excursion). Each clause has been numbered and displayed on a separate line with the conjunctions in parentheses.

1   We sat on a hill

2   (and) observed the plants.

3   We saw bushes and grass

4   (but) we didn't see many plants because of the pollution.

5   We climbed on the bus again

6   (and) went to Mt. Kiera rainforest.

7   We got off the bus

8   (and) ate our little lunch in the clearing area.

9   We saw many different types of plants and trees.

10   We saw wattle trees, tall trees, thin trees and rock plants.

11   We returned to school at 12 o'clock.

12   (Then) we went into school

13   (and) talked about our excursion.

(Adapted from Derewianka, 1990)

See 'Answers to the activities' for feedback.

2.2 Form and function

We have now identified the English clause as consisting of a component that represents a process, together with one or more components representing participants and (optionally) one or more components representing circumstances. We have also seen that the intermediate grammatical units of noun phrase, verb phrase, adverb phrase and prepositional phrase are the groupings of words that realise these roles. It seems then that we have two ways to describe a clause structure: one that focuses on the meaning, i.e. the function, of each unit in the clause (as process, participant or circumstance) and one that focuses on the classification of that unit in terms of its own structure (its form or formal category). The following example gives the function that is realised by each form.

	the old woman	was scrubbing	the table	with vigour
Function realised by	participant	process	participant	circumstance
Form	noun phrase	verb phrase	noun phrase	prepositional phrase

Putting these descriptions together we can say that in this particular clause there is a participant realised by a noun phrase, followed by a process realised by a verb phrase, followed by another participant realised by a second noun phrase, followed by a circumstance expressed by a prepositional phrase.

At first it may seem redundant to have these two ways of describing the parts of the clause, but there are distinct advantages in distinguishing function and form in this way. In the first place, you have already seen from these examples that a particular function is not always realised by the same formal category. Consider the following structures:

The old woman swept the floor **very vigorously**.
The old woman swept the floor **with great vigour**.

In terms of their function, *very vigorously* and *with great vigour* play the same role in the clause – that of circumstance. But in terms of their own structural form they are different units, one is an adverb phrase and the other is a prepositional phrase. If we wish to focus on the jobs they are doing in a particular text, we need a function term, but if we wish to focus on their classification as units of a particular shape, then we need structural form terms. (Class, form, formal unit and structural form are all terms used for a grammatical term that focuses on form rather than function.) And it is not only circumstances that may be realised by different classes of unit. This is also true of participants – for example, in the case of a passive voice clause with two participants. This can be shown if we change the previous example from active to passive:

See Foundation Grammar for an introduction to passive voice and active voice.

The old woman swept the floor with great vigour (active)
The floor was swept with great vigour by the old woman (passive)

When the order of the participants is changed in this way, the agent of the process is realised by a prepositional phrase (*by the old woman*) rather than a simple noun phrase.

Just as a single function may be expressed by different forms, so a single form like a noun phrase or a prepositional phrase may serve different functions on different occasions. For example, while the noun phrase *the floor* is a participant in the clause above, the noun phrase *great vigour* is part of a circumstance and, in our opening text, the noun phrase *one day* is a circumstance.

To illustrate this further here are two apparently identical formal patterns to consider:

He groomed the horse with a stiff brush.

He groomed the horse with a white tail.

Do these clauses divide up in the same way? The answer is no. Each clause ends with a similar prepositional phrase but the phrases are not doing the same kind of job. *With a stiff brush* is a circumstance giving us extra detail about the process. It tells us how the process was done. *With a white tail* almost certainly does not describe the process but refers to the horse and is part of the noun phrase *the horse with a white tail*. This is readily shown when we break the clauses into their functional units.

He	groomed	the horse	with a stiff brush
participant	process	participant	circumstance

He	groomed	the horse with a white tail
participant	process	participant

A functional category like circumstance is not then simply 'the same thing' as a prepositional phrase. A prepositional phrase has the potential to be used as a circumstance but might also serve a different function.

ACTIVITY 5 (allow about 10 minutes)

Look at the following examples and decide which of the prepositional phrases (in bold) are functioning as a circumstance.

1   'I expect you saw us **from the window**', she said.
2   At first they were too busy to notice the little cat **with matted fur**.
3   The young man dived **into the pool** and made a huge splash.
4   We left the car **for twenty minutes**.
5   A girl **in a raincoat** was stroking and patting her pet dog.
6   Peter bought a small brown suitcase **with a strong leather handle**.
7   Peter bought a small brown suitcase **with his last bit of money**.
8   The students discovered the answer **by chance**.
9   Unfortunately the school cancelled the special class **for advanced students**.
10   **At five o'clock** we had coffee and cake **by the pool**.

See 'Answers to the activities' for feedback.

ACTIVITY **6** (allow about 15 minutes)

To check that you have understood the points I have been making in this section, look at the following descriptions of grammatical units and decide for each whether it characterises a structural form (i.e. a class) or a grammatical function. For each class and function, give an example term. I have done the first ones for you to provide a guide.

(1) What the unit acts as (in a particular instance).

A function, e.g. a participant.

(2) What the unit is (by virtue of its form).

A structural form, e.g. a noun phrase.

(3) Can only be determined from text.

(4) Can be cited (e.g. in dictionary) regardless of context.

(5) Gives the actual role in an utterance.

(6) Has the potential for certain role(s).

See 'Answers to the activities' for feedback.

2.3 Processes and participants

In this section we look at processes and participants in spoken and written English.

Whether using speech or writing, English sentences will be made up of clauses structured in terms of participants, processes and circumstances. But there are considerable differences in how information is distributed among these components in spoken and written modes and in the forms that realise them.

ACTIVITY **7** (allow about 20 minutes)

Below are two texts of the same length that exemplify some of these contrasts. Processes have been printed in bold and participants are underlined. Read the texts and answer the following questions.

(1) How do the texts compare in terms of the number of processes found in the 103 words?

(2) How do the texts compare in terms of the number of pronouns functioning as participants?

(3) What other contrasts are there in terms of the participants in the two texts?

A written text

The steady increase in life expectancy in human populations **shows** that longevity **is** plastic. Although lifespans **are** species-specific, they **can be modified** greatly by the environment as well as by genes. For many human populations, the fixed three score years and ten allotted for human longevity **are** already but a distant memory. Much of this increase in lifespan **has been achieved** by improvements in public health, medical care and domestic circumstances. We **are beginning to view** ageing-related damage as a side-effect of other adaptive processes. This **may allow** us **to reduce** the impact of ageing-related diseases as the limits on human lifespan **recede**.

(Partridge and Gems, 2002, p. 921)

A spoken text

(The speaker, W., is describing a friend's first skiing holiday.)

W: He **was coming** down this- this track ‖ and he**'s been** a few times ‖ so he**'s got** some idea of it ‖ um so he **said** ‖ that he **saw** this slight rise ‖ so he **said** ‖ he **headed** up the rise ‖ and he **found out** ‖ it **was** a ski jump! ‖ he- he**'d lost** one ski at the top ‖ and eh apparently he **was flying** through the air ǀ with one leg up in the air with a ski on it ‖ and he **landed** head first in the snow ‖ but he **caught** his head ‖ his mate with him, he **hit** a tree on the way down ‖ **came back** all bruised and scraped … ‖

(Eggins and Slade, 1997, p. 250)

COMMENT

- There are more processes (and therefore more clauses and more conjunctions) used in the spoken version than the written.
- Participants in the spoken version are more often realised by pronouns than in the written.

Here are some other points of difference you may have noticed.

- The participants in the written text tend to be very long and often include several nouns or other lexical words; in the spoken they are realised by shorter noun phrases. (This relates to the phenomenon of lexical density discussed in Unit 2.)
- In the written text more than one participant is realised by a prepositional phrase (such as *by the environment, by improvements in public health*…) because of the use of passives (*can be modified, has been achieved*).
- The participants in the written text are often 'abstractions' like *increase, lifespan, memory, limits* while in the spoken text there is more reference to 'concrete' entities including people (*he, one ski, a tree*).

We can in part explain the differences between the written and spoken texts above by recognising the contextual constraints on the written and spoken modes. A passive structure can be used for information flow (see the final section of this unit) and to place stress on the appropriate participant. It is less needed in spoken language because these can be achieved through the use of intonation, a resource not available to the writer. On the other hand, a long tightly structured unit at the start of the clause is not easily achieved in the dynamic context of speech, which allows no time for preparation, so an elaborate noun phrase for an initial participant is not typical in this mode. A writer, however, has the opportunity to create such structures in a more considered way, away from the pressures of 'online' production. Moreover, units in written text can be rapidly scanned by eye and so 'lexically dense' structures are more accessible in this mode. The greater abstraction of participants in writing is in turn related to lexical density and is a result of a phenomenon known as 'nominalisation' that you will learn about in later units of the course.

 IDENTIFYING CLAUSES II

In the second of three section on identifying clauses, we look at the clause as an interpersonal move.

3.1 Classes of clause

So far we have been concerned with the way every clause is some kind of representation of experience and has a constituent structure that creates this. Now let us adopt a different perspective and think about the clause as a way of interacting with another person. This will allow us to see that there are different classes of clause as well as different classes of phrase.

We can best begin an exploration of what basic kinds of simple independent clause there are in English by turning our attention to the spoken mode of language. This of course precedes written language, not only in the history of the language, but in the history of the individual native speaker's life. For this reason, many information books written for English-speaking children attempt to adopt a conversational tone so as to be more accessible to the beginning reader. As an example, consider the following excerpt of text which is the opening to a child's picture book on the topic of sound. (The words are accompanied by illustrations, which are not shown here.)

Talk about sound

Do you enjoy making sounds? What sounds do these things make if you bang them? What different sounds can you make with your body and your voice? Put your fingers on your throat as you talk or sing. What can you feel? Hold a ruler on the edge of a table. Press down the end and let go. Can you hear a sound? What do you see? Whenever you hear a sound, there is something moving. This movement is called a vibration...

(Webb, 1987)

The author's strategy in this text is to try to make learning enjoyable and interesting by getting the child to carry out simple activities and to observe the results before giving the child any factual information. Consequently the text uses a range of different wordings associated with different conversational moves or **speech acts**. For example, the reader is directed at various points to carry out activities, using structures of the kind: *Put your fingers on your throat...*, *Hold a ruler on the edge of a table...* . Then the writer elicits information from the child, asking: *What can you feel?*, *Can you hear a sound?*, and so on. Only then is the child given information such as: *This movement is called a vibration.*

We can identify three different speech-act functions here, each realised by a different type of clause. This is summarised in Table 5.

Table 5 Three major types of English clause

Function	Class of clause	Example
Command	imperative	Hold a ruler on the edge of a table.
Question	interrogative (yes/no)	Do you enjoy making sounds?
	interrogative (wh)	What can you feel?
Statement	declarative	This movement is called a vibration.

(Adapted from Biber et al., 1999, p. 202)

The terms **imperative**, **interrogative** and **declarative** are labels for different classes of clause, each identifiable in terms of its own distinctive grammatical structure. We can make this clearer by manipulating a single example – noun phrases are underlined and auxiliary verbs are in bold:

<u>You</u> **can** hear a sound   (declarative)
Can <u>you</u> hear a sound? (interrogative)
What **can** <u>you</u> hear?   (interrogative)

When we do this, we can see that the sequence of units creates the different forms with their different meanings. In the declarative we have a noun phrase before the (auxiliary) verb. In the interrogative, the auxiliary verb comes before the noun phrase. You may already be familiar with the grammatical term '**subject**', which is used to refer to the noun phrase whose position is important here. In our examples, this noun phrase is a simple pronoun, but it could be a much longer phrase, such as:

> Her expensive new vase **has** been broken.

> **Has** her expensive new vase been broken?

You will already realise that the subject is also the noun phrase that 'agrees with' or has **concord** with the auxiliary verb in English: for example, we say *I have* but *he has*. This holds true also for the repetition of subject and auxiliary that takes place when a question tag is added to a clause, as in the following examples where the tags are in bold.

> You can hear a sound, **can't you?**

> Her expensive new vase has been broken, **hasn't it?**

The imperative clause is distinct from the other two types because it usually has no subject and (unless negative) no auxiliary verb as in *Put your fingers on your throat.* (There is an implied or 'understood' subject, which is always *you*.)

ACTIVITY 8 (allow about 10 minutes)

Check your understanding of the three basic structural types of clause (declarative, interrogative and imperative) by finding examples of each in the next part of the text *Talk About Sound*.

Talk about sound (continued)

Strike a triangle with a beater. Touch the triangle while it is ringing. What can you feel? When something stops vibrating, the sound stops. How does someone's voice reach you? The sound travels through the air as sound waves. Throw a stone in a pool of water. Watch the waves spreading out. Sound waves move through the air in a similar way.

(Webb, 1987)

See 'Answers to the activities' for feedback.

3.2 Form and function revisited

You may wonder why we should need two sets of terms to discuss clause types. Why do we need both *declarative* and *statement*, both *interrogative* and *question*, both *imperative* and *command*? The reason we need two terms, one focusing on the structural form and one focusing on the function in the text, is that – as we have found before – there is not always a one-to-one relationship between the two. For example, a mother might say to her son *The television is very loud* and expect him to respond by turning the volume down, rather than replying *Yes, it is.* In other words, the mother is giving the child a command but is using a declarative clause to do so. Or, to take another example, that mother might say to her son *You've done your homework*, but use rising intonation as she does so: *You've done your homework?* The structural form of the clause is again declarative, but the intonation signals that the speech function is a **question** rather than a **statement**. As you can see, structural form and speech-act function do not always match up in a one-to-one relation. (When and why this is the case is a fascinating question to follow up when you come to examine authentic English spoken texts in different contexts! Meanwhile, in a later unit you will be learning something more about English intonation and how it relates to speech function.)

3.3 Distribution of clause types

In this section we look at the distribution of clause types in spoken and written English.

Your reference grammar provides you with some information about how the various classes of clause and their speech-act functions are used in communication. It will come as no surprise to find that interrogatives and imperatives are many many times more frequent overall in the spoken language corpus than in the written one. It is in the give and take of dialogic interaction that we most naturally use language to elicit information or action from the addressee, while writing serves more readily to give information using declaratives, since the reader is not actually present to respond. (We have already seen that a writer *can* choose to adopt a dialogic tone that requires a variety of clause types in order to set up a (simulated) personal relationship with the reader.)

What is not so obvious is how frequent the different types of clause are within conversation and the extent to which conversation favours one particular form of clause for one particular speech function.

ACTIVITY 9   (allow about 10 minutes)

To see whether your intuitions are supported by corpus data, look at the following questions and note down your guess as to the answers. Then examine the table in 'Answers to the activities', which provides data drawn from the LSWE corpus of conversation.

(1)   Which is more frequent in conversation: yes/no-interrogatives or wh-interrogatives?

(2)   What proportion of questions in conversation are expressed as an independent clause: 90%, 70%, 55% or 35%?

(3)   What proportion of questions in conversation are realised by declaratives: 50%, 25%, 10% or 5%?

COMMENT

How accurate were your intuitions? You may have been surprised by the fact that only a little more than half the questions in the corpus are realised by full clauses, and also by the fact that as many as 10 per cent of questions are realised by declaratives, not interrogatives. This use of declaratives shows the importance of intonation in signalling speech-act function. Not surprisingly, declaratives rarely function as questions in writing.

The frequency of questions outside the structure of an independent clause points, on the one hand, to the frequency of question tags added to declaratives. These function as a way of handing a turn of talk over to the hearer by eliciting a response from them. The question tag is a structure almost absent from the written corpus, reflecting the essentially monologic nature of writing. On the other hand, the use of clause fragments is partly due to the phenomenon of ellipsis, where wordings can be 'understood' from the preceding speaker's clause:

A: Have you got an exam on Monday?

B: <I've got> Two exams.

A: What exams <have you got>?

B: <I've got> German reading and French oral; French oral's a doddle.

A: Is it <a doddle>?

(Biber et al., 1999, p. 157)

In the activity you looked at information from a corpus of conversation without distinguishing between the speakers. It is possible to set up a corpus so that the distribution of clause types among different groups of people can be explored. For example, evidence from small corpora of tape-recorded conversations shows that female speakers of English seem to ask more questions, especially through tags, than male speakers (Coates, 1993). Some analysts have claimed that this demonstrates that females lack confidence and certainty, while others argue that it is because females take more responsibility for bringing other speakers into the conversation and for keeping the talk going smoothly. Males on the other hand seem to be more concerned to make statements and display knowledge. Both the corpus findings and the debates they have generated have played an important part in public discussions about the roles of men and women in English-speaking societies in recent decades.

Another early corpus study examined recordings made in English classrooms and found that, although the educational theory of the day stressed the importance of a critical, questioning and hypothesising attitude by students, school pupils rarely asked any questions in the classroom. Instead it was the teachers (who already knew the answers!) who were using interrogative clauses; talk by pupils was very much restricted to short elliptical responses (Coulthard and Sinclair, 1975). These facts raise for educators important questions about translating educational theory into practice and, more generally, show how speech is constrained by social context. In the school classroom, the teacher has authority over the pupil because of their superior expertise and because society gives the teacher responsibility for the care and control of the pupil. Thus the social context of the school classroom accords a superior role to the teacher and a subordinate one to the pupil. This is manifested in the language choices taken up in classroom discourse, where students do not generally initiate or prolong topics, or control the direction of the talk by using questions. As you can see, investigating a language corpus, even with some very basic grammatical concepts, can provide some illuminating findings about the social roles and relationships of speakers in a society.

❹ IDENTIFYING CLAUSES III

In the third of three sections on identifying clauses, we look at the clause as a package of information in spoken and written English.

When we focus our attention on differences between spoken and written English, we are reminded that the structure of a clause not only signals the speech function and constructs a representation of experience, but is also a form for packaging information in ways that make it accessible to the hearer/reader. Lexical density is one means that has already been discussed. In this section we look at some other aspects of how we organise information within and around clauses.

The comment on Activity 1 gave the following versions of a declarative clause from the text on page 65.

> At a restaurant we had a fantastic rabbit dish on our way back to our villa from the market one day.

> On our way back to our villa from the market one day, we had a fantastic rabbit dish at a restaurant.

> One day, we had a fantastic rabbit dish at a restaurant on our way back to our villa from the market.

> One day at a restaurant on our way back to our villa from the market, we had a fantastic rabbit dish.

> We had a fantastic rabbit dish one day at a restaurant on our way back to our villa from the market.

You may agree that they do not differ as representations of a process with its participants and circumstances, but they do differ in subtle ways as packages of information. In English, what we put at the beginning and end of a clause in particular can be important for making the meaning clear. Looking at the clause beginnings in the above examples, you can see that there is a reasonable amount of choice concerning which element we begin the clause with, but it isn't the case that the variations made are simply random.

Let us first think about written English. When you are writing, you have no phonological resources to help you structure the information – there is no opportunity for the addressees to interrupt and ask for clarification if they find it difficult to understand you and there is no contextual information available to help 'fill out' the meaning. The writer has to take all the responsibility for making the meaning clear. The consequence is that writers have to structure their information carefully both within and between clauses. They have to be careful to make their wordings 'flow' well and to signal when they are shifting to a new point or angle. Because of this, written English is more likely to exploit two particular patterns that provide flexibility in the organisation of information.

One of these is the use of a circumstance rather than a participant to begin the clause with. Generally speaking, when an English clause begins with a circumstance there is more likely to be some small change in the organisation of information than when it begins with a participant in the subject role. In other words, the initial circumstance plays a role in structuring the information in the text as a whole. We can illustrate this with the following fragment of written text for children on the topic of locusts. (Circumstances at the beginning of the clauses are given in bold type, ellipted elements have been included in angled brackets, sentences are numbered.)

[1] The young locusts have no wings and <they> are known as 'hoppers.' [2] They live mainly in sandy desert areas. [3] **In dry years**, when vegetation is sparse, locusts resemble green grasshoppers. [4] They prefer to hunt about by themselves for food and <they prefer> to stay away from each other. [5] Their desire for solitude disperses them over wide areas, thus helping the species to survive. [6] But **during the rare intervals of heavy rains in the desert**, they begin to breed in enormous numbers.

(Extract from an information text for children)

As you can see, the use of the circumstance at the beginning of the third sentence alerts the reader to notice that here the information moves on from general facts about locusts to something new. The two circumstances positioned in first position in the clauses in sentences 3 and 6 draw the reader's attention to the contrast being set up between two seasons when locusts have particular different behaviours. Compare the following alternative version of the first three sentences.

[1] The young locusts have no wings and <they> are known as 'hoppers'. [2] They live mainly in sandy desert areas. [3] Locusts resemble green grasshoppers in dry years, when vegetation is sparse. [4] They prefer to hunt about by themselves...

You will probably agree that this version is less helpful to readers in terms of foregrounding the shift to more specific information in sentence 3 (and in 4 and 5) which, in turn, is to be contrasted with the information in sentence 6. By structuring the *individual* clauses in the way the original does, the writer has made the information in the *whole* text easy to digest. And while speakers as well as writers utilise variation in the order of elements, it is in writing that an initial circumstance is more common because this monologic mode requires a more planned organisation of one clause in relation to another.

Sometimes, by contrast, a writer wishes to achieve continuity with what went before by beginning the new clause with something mentioned at the end of the previous one, as shown by the underlining in the following example from *Talk About Sound*.

Whenever you hear a sound, there is <u>something moving</u>. <u>This movement</u> is called a vibration...

In order to achieve this smooth flow here, the writer has used a passive voice structure in the second clause. (Compare the effect of the active voice alternative: *We call this movement a vibration.*) The passive structure is much more frequent in written than spoken English. One major reason is that achieving a 'flow' in monologue (without intonation or situational context to help) requires writers to exploit more fully the possibilities for varying the organisation of elements in an individual clause. Despite the limitations imposed by context, the written mode does have the compensating advantage of time for planning and opportunities for editing, so written texts can be constructed with greater attention to information packaging than spoken ones. We have already suggested that this is one reason for the extended noun phrases found in written texts. It is also one reason for the higher proportion of passive clauses in written English reported in Biber et al. (1999, p. 476), since this grammatical structure exploits the possibility of choosing a participant other than the agent to initiate the clause.

Now let us turn our attention more directly to spoken conversational English. Your reference grammar (Chapter 13) describes three principles that govern the structuring of spoken grammar: keep talking, limited planning and qualification of what has been said. The first principle of 'keep talking' expresses the ideal of avoiding silence and leads to hesitations and fillers and to repetitions and reformulations of the clause as four strategies to achieve this. Here are some examples from the LSWE corpus, given in Biber et al. (1999, pp. 1053, 1062). (Pauses and hesitations are indicated by –.)

> That's a very good – er very good precaution to take, yes.
>
> So before we issue – before we hand over the B one what do we do?
>
> Dad, I don't think you sh –, I think you should leave Chris home Saturday.

The second principle is that of 'limited planning' and refers to the essential constraint on speech – it involves the production of meaning without the opportunity of preplanning or rehearsing what we want to say. (And of course, conversely, the hearer does not have the opportunity to scan back over what was said if anything was missed or misunderstood.) One result of limited planning is the creation of constructions that do not neatly conform to our standard descriptions of the clause.

A CTIVITY 10   (allow about 10 minutes)

Look at the following LSWE corpus conversation (CONV) examples from Biber et al. (1999).

(1)   What do you find unusual in their patterning?

(2)   How would you have worded the clauses as a writer?

(3)   Why do you think speakers, but not writers, use this pattern?

> North and south London, they're two different worlds (CONV) (p. 1072)
>
> This little shop, it's lovely (CONV) (p. 1074)
>
> That picture of a frog, where is it? (CONV) (p. 957)
>
> Those Marks and Sparks bags, can you see them all? (CONV) (p. 1074)

COMMENT

From our descriptions of the English clause, you would have expected the speakers to have said simply:

> North and south London are two different worlds
>
> This little shop is lovely
>
> Where is that picture of a frog?
>
> Can you see all those Marks and Sparks bags?

The actual spoken examples include an extra constituent, a noun phrase that precedes the clause proper. This noun phrase is 'referred to' by a pronoun inside that clause. Why do we find these structures in spoken English and not in written? There are probably two converging reasons. One has to do with limited planning time – the speaker can get on with announcing the topic (often a new one) and claiming a turn to speak before having to formulate a well-structured grammatical declarative or interrogative. At the same time, the speaker can mark out this topic as key information to be attended to by giving it its own intonation contour. Having achieved all that, i.e. having 'tuned in' the hearer with this '**preface**', the speaker can get on with constructing a regular clause using a pronoun to link back to the start of the conversational turn.

See Unit 1 for a discussion of 'preface' – also called 'head'.

ACTIVITY 11 (allow about 10 minutes)

Now look at some further examples from the spoken corpus cited in Biber et al. (1999, p. 1080) and answer the following questions.

(1) How does the section in bold seem to relate to the rest?

(2) Why do you think speakers sometimes structure information in this way?

> I mean it was the only one with its own kitchen, **the one I was gonna have**. (CONV)
>
> I just give it all away didn't I Rudy **my knitting**? (CONV)
>
> Oh I reckon they're lovely, I really do **whippets**. (CONV)

COMMENT

This time we have readily recognisable clause structures with a pronoun (*it, they*) as one participant, but now a noun phrase has been added at the end as a kind of **tag** or 'tail' (shown in bold), even following a question tag like *didn't I*. These examples may look quite strange written down, but are perfectly normal grammatical structures in speech. Limited time for planning is again the explanation for these structures according to Biber et al. (1999, p. 1081). Speakers launch into their statements using a pronoun, but by the end of the clause may feel that its reference was not clear and so they need to clarify matters by tacking on a noun phrase.

There are a number of other kinds of added-on ending which enable a speaker to adjust the meaning that has just been uttered, and these (like the above examples) exemplify a third constructional principle of spoken grammar referred to in Chapter 13 of your reference grammar – 'qualification of what has been said'.

ACTIVITY 12 (allow about 10 minutes)

Have a look at the following examples from Biber et al. (1999, pp. 1080–1) and think about what kind of meaning the tag (in bold) achieves. Are all the tags doing similar work?

they're two different worlds aren't they **in a way**? (CONV)

I wouldn't go to Amanda Close **I don't think**. (CONV)

I mean she never liked that car. **Ever**. (CONV)

I don't care about work and them being in a muddle, **no not at all**. (CONV)

COMMENT

The 'added-on' tags seem to be adjusting the meaning of the main statement that has just been made. The first two examples do this by 'hedging' or qualifying the statement, making it rather less definite, less absolute and less assertive than it would otherwise be. The second two examples, on the other hand, work to 'amplify' or emphasise something in the message that has just been uttered, making it more definite, more absolute and more assertive. What the tags have in common is that they allow the meaning of the clause to be 'fine-tuned' after it has been uttered, since it could not be carefully planned. Question tags, too, are said by your reference grammar to be a way of retrospectively changing or emphasising the meaning – this time of the speech-act function of the clause, as in:

Well that little girl's cute isn't she? (CONV) (Biber et al., 1999, p. 1080)

Oh is it tonight is it? (CONV) (Biber et al., 1999, p. 210)

When we look at these examples, we can see that, despite the presence of unfinished structures, filled pauses, repetitions and reformulations which make a transcript of speech look very disorganised, spoken English is not disorganised at all. On the contrary, as well as exploiting the clause structures used in writing, it has additional patterns that allow a speaker to make meaning 'on the run'. These include prefaces or heads to clauses used (in conjunction with intonation) both to claim a turn and to announce a topic. They also include a range of tags or tails to clarify and refine meaning flexibly by adding adjustments after the body of the clause has been uttered. The three principles of 'keep talking', 'limited planning' and 'qualification of what has been said' can thus produce distinctive grammatical patterning as a way to manage the 'online' production and processing of information.

Biber et al. (1999, p. 1082) provides the following example where these principles result in an extended construction composed of three parts, as shown below.

Preface(s)	Body	Tag(s)
North and south London	they're two different worlds	aren't they? in a way

As you can see, a grammar of English that concerns itself with only written language will miss much of the complexity and variety of the language as it is actually used by native speakers. While the major units of grammar are shared across the two modes, there are considerable differences in the frequencies of different forms in the two modes. Some particular constructions have evolved in speech to take account of the contextual constraints of its production.

ACTIVITY 13   (allow about two hours)

To consolidate your understandings of some of the special characteristics of spoken English, read Chapter 2 'Grammar and Spoken English' (Sections 2.1–2.5 only) by Ron Carter in the course reader *Applying English Grammar*. As you do so, note down your answers to the following questions.

◆ Why is the notion of 'sentence' difficult to apply to conversational English?

◆ What are the 'basic forms of spoken grammar' mentioned in the article?

◆ What are the possible reasons for the use of spoken English forms in *written* texts?

◆ How might information about the difference between written and spoken forms of English be of use to you personally?

The following terms introduced in this reading are defined in your reference grammar's glossary: **backchannel**, **antecedent**, **deictic word**, **coordinator**.

C D - R O M S (allow about four hours)

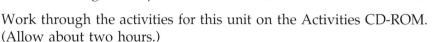

Work through the tasks for this unit on the Concordancer and Corpus CD-ROM using the *Corpus Tasks* booklet. (Allow about two hours.)

Work through the activities for this unit on the Activities CD-ROM. (Allow about two hours.)

In the corpus tasks for this unit you will have noticed that, using the concordancing software, you can pick out words of a particular word class, for instance nouns, from a corpus which has been automatically **tagged** (using a computer program) for parts of speech, like BNC-OU. However, you would not be able to search for a functional category like participant in this corpus because it is not functionally tagged. Such tagging would have to be done manually – a very laborious and time-consuming process for a corpus consisting of millions of words. Halliday explains:

> automatic analysis gets harder the higher up we move along the hierarchy of stratification: it can handle any patterns that are stated in terms of orthographic words and it can handle certain low-ranking patterns within lexicogrammar, but is not able to handle full-fledged systemic functional analysis of clauses, and semantic analysis is also beyond its reach. In lexicogrammatical analysis, it is thus possible to automate the identification of classes of words (handled by [word class] taggers) and grammatical structure stated in terms of classes of words and groups or phrases (syntagms, handled by [formal] parsers); but analysis involving function structures and systemic features is much harder to automate [...]
>
> (Halliday and Matthiessen, 2004, p. 49)

Hence it is more challenging to produce a corpus-based *functional* grammatical description of a language than to produce a corpus-based *structural* grammar, like your reference grammar.

Conclusion

We have begun to explore the way English clauses are structured into smaller units: phrases, words and morphemes. At different ranks, semantic functions are realised by *typical* forms. But a single function is not restricted to a single form and a single form is not restricted to a single function. A clause is structured so that it can function as a representation of experience, as a speech act and as a connected part of a larger discourse. While the essential forms and functions of grammar are common to both spoken and written modes of English, we have seen that they are distributed differently between the two modes due to the particular limitations and advantages peculiar to each mode. Spoken texts in particular may favour abbreviating or extending the basic clause form in various ways as a means of managing the dynamic ongoing production of meaning in conversation.

Learning outcomes

After completing this unit, you should have developed your knowledge and understanding of:

◆ the basic constituents of a sentence: clause, phrase, word and morpheme

◆ the functional parts of a clause – participants, processes and circumstances

◆ how different functions (e.g. circumstance) can be realised by different forms (e.g. adverb phrase or prepositional phrase)

◆ some differences between speech and writing with regard to processes and participants

◆ something of the distribution of clause types in spoken and written English

◆ how corpus studies throw light on the nature of spoken grammar and its differences from written grammar.

In the light of your increased understanding, you should be able to:

◆ identify the basic constituents of a sentence: clause, phrase, word and morpheme

◆ identify the functional parts of a clause: participants, process and circumstances.

Key terms introduced and revisited

active voice	morphology
adverb phrase [adverbial group]	noun phrase [nominal group, noun group]
agent	participant
antecedent	passive voice
backchannel	phrase [group]
circumstance [circumstance adverbial]	preface [head]
clause	prepositional phrase
command	process
concord	question
constituent	rank
coordinator	rank system [rank scale]
declarative	realised by
deictic word	speech act [speech function, speech-act function]
discourse marker	statement
head [central element]	subject [grammatical subject]
imperative	subordinator
interrogative	tag [tail]
lexical density	verb phrase [verbal group, verb group]
morpheme	

Near equivalents are given in [ ].

Answers to the activities

ACTIVITY 2

Rank	Example
Clause	The discomfort of internal gastrointestinal examination may soon be a thing of the past
Phrase	l The discomfort of internal gastrointestinal examination l may < > be l soon l a thing of the past l
Word	l The l discomfort l of l internal l gastrointestinal l examination l may l soon l be l a l thing l of l the l past l
Morpheme	The - dis - comfort - of - internal - gastro - intestine - al - examine - ation - may - soon - be - a - thing - of - the - past

In the phrases, 'may soon be' has been divided into a process 'may be' and a circumstance 'soon'. The < > indicates the position of 'soon'. You will notice that the morphemes have variant spellings with or without an -e, e.g. intestin and intestine. In English this is common. It does not matter if you did not add any -e's when you divided the text into morphemes as this is a matter of personal preference.

ACTIVITY 3

1b, 2c, 3f, 4a, 5e, 6d.

ACTIVITY 4

Processes are in bold, participants underlined and circumstances as plain text. Conjunctions are in parentheses.

1   We **sat** on a hill

2   (and) **observed** the plants.

3   We **saw** bushes and grass

4   (but) we **didn't see** many plants because of the pollution.

5   We **climbed** on the bus again

6   (and) **went** to Mt. Kiera rainforest.

7   We **got** off the bus

8   (and) **ate** our little lunch in the clearing area.

9   We **saw** many different types of plants and trees.

10   We **saw** wattle trees, tall trees, thin trees and rock plants.

11   We **returned** to school at 12 o'clock.

12   (Then) <u>we</u> **went** into school

13   (and) **talked** about our excursion.

Notes

Clause 1   *on a hill* tells us where the process takes place; it is a circumstance. Although it contains a noun phrase (*a hill*), this is part of the prepositional phrase *on a hill* which tells us where the process happened, rather than functioning as a participant in the clause.

Clause 2   In this clause and in clauses 6, 8 and 13, the *we* is ellipted following the conjunction *and*.

Clause 3   Here is an example where a participant (*bushes and grass*) is realised by two noun phrases joined by the conjunction *and*.

Clause 4   *many plants* is a participant, it is <u>what</u> we didn't see, whereas *because of the pollution* is the optional circumstance telling us <u>why</u>.

Clause 5   There are two circumstances here: *on the bus* gives us the location/direction of the process, while *again* tells us something different about the process. You may have taken *climbed on* as the process, in which case *the bus* would be the 'acted on' participant. At this stage we shall not concern ourselves with arguing for one analysis over the other.

Clause 10   The participant (the 2nd one) is realised by more than one noun phrase, in fact there are four.

Clause 11   There are two circumstances, one telling us <u>where</u> (*to school*) and one telling us <u>when</u> (*at 12 o'clock*) the process took place.

Clause 13   You may have regarded *talked about* as the process in which case you should have identified *our excursion* as a participant. Arguments concerning alternative analyses of this kind will be discussed later.

ACTIVITY 5

1   Circumstance: *from the window* is where the process of seeing took place.

2   Not a circumstance: *with matted fur* tells about the cat, not about the process of noticing.

3   Circumstance: *into the pool* tells us where the process of diving took place.

4   Circumstance: *for twenty minutes* tells how long the process lasted.

5   Not a circumstance: *in a raincoat* gives details about the girl, not about the process.

6   Not a circumstance: *with a strong leather handle* tells about the suitcase, not the process of buying.

7   Circumstance: *with his last bit of money* tells how Peter did the process of buying.

8   Circumstance: *by chance* tells how the process of discovering occurred.

9   Not a circumstance: *for advanced students* tells about the class, not the process of cancelling (it wasn't cancelled for the benefit of the advanced students).

10   Circumstances: *at five o'clock* tells us when, and *by the pool* tells us where, the process of having (coffee and cake) took place.

ACTIVITY 6

(1)   The grammatical unit can also function as an agent, a process, a circumstance, a subject (see Section 3) and a question – as well as a participant.

(2)   Other examples of structural forms for this grammatical unit are a noun, a verb, an adverb phrase, a verb phrase, a prepositional phrase and a declarative clause (see Section 3) and a question – as well as a noun phrase.

(3)   A function, e.g. any example given in 1 above.

(4)   A structural form, e.g. any example given in 2 above.

(5)   A function, e.g. any example given in 1 above.

(6)   A structural form, e.g. any example given in 2 above.

ACTIVITY 8

Imperatives	Interrogatives	Declaratives
Strike a triangle with a beater.	What can you feel?	While it is ringing
Touch the triangle	How does someone's voice reach you?	When something stops vibrating, the sound stops.
Throw a stone in a pool of water.		The sound travels through the air as sound waves.
Watch the waves spreading out.		Sound waves move through the air in a similar way.

ACTIVITY 9

Realisations of questions in the LSWE spoken-language corpus

Question realised by clause	
wh-interrogative	****
yes/no-interrogative	*****
declarative	**
Question realised by clause fragment or tag	*********

Key: each * represents 5% of the total number of questions.

(Adapted from Biber et al., 1999, p. 212)

Unit 4
The noun phrase

Prepared for the course team by John Polias

CONTENTS

Materials required

While studying this unit, you will need:

    your reference grammar

    the course reader (at end of unit)

    the Activities CD-ROM (at end of unit).

Knowledge assumed

You should be familiar with the following before starting this unit.

From Foundation Grammar:

    noun phrase, head

    verb phrase, lexical verb

    determiner.

From Unit 1:

    differences in spoken and written texts.

From Unit 2:

    lexical density.

From Unit 3:

    function and form

    circumstance

    participant

    prepositional phrase

    process.

Introduction

A quick puzzle to start with. Where would you normally find the following snippets of English?

    A must-see

    Gripping ... full of pleasure

    A powerful piece with a dark, disturbing secret

    A sprawling, natural crowd pleaser

    A sharp slice of New York life

    A dazzlingly imaginative new version

You may have realised that these are compressed reviews found on posters and advertisements for films and plays. All of them were taken from advertisements in a listings magazine for events in London. They were taken from reviews of the artistic works. Because they have to fit onto posters where the images of the stars who perform in the works take precedence, these reviews must be pithy and thus compressed. If you look a little more closely at these snippets, you'll see that they don't contain verbs. All of them consist of only noun phrases. Despite this, on the advertisements, these reviews communicate perfectly well. These noun-phrase nuggets tell us all we need to know. Verbs aren't really necessary here because the context is clear to us – these are advertisements for artistic performances. The information is being used in an attempt to persuade us to go to this performance. That the people who created the advertisements know they can rely on shared context can be seen with the first one, *A must-see*; the clause 'you must see this film' with a verb phrase is compressed into a noun phrase. The useful capacity of the noun phrase to compress information like this when needed, its capacity to represent the world of things, people and ideas and how this facility is more commonly exploited in the written mode than the spoken mode are our focus in this unit.

① REPRESENTING OBJECTS, PEOPLE AND IDEAS

Objects, people and ideas can be represented by noun phrases.

A CTIVITY 1 (allow about 15 minutes)

Read the texts. Which text do you think is spoken and which written? What things did you focus on to identify the spoken text and the written text? Draw on the grammatical knowledge you will have built up in Units 1–3 and be as precise as you can.

Text 1

I bought a dog as a pet but I wanted a good one so I bought a show quality dog and the lady I bought the dog from worked at the same place as my father and I used to call in and see Dad in the office fairly often once I bought the dog and she got me along to a couple of dog shows and I got interested in it that way and started showing the dog that she'd bred and it sort of snowballed from there.

(Plum, 1988, p. 33)

Text 2

Later on, in 1872, Monet painted that picture called *Impression, Sunrise*, which unintentionally gave its name to the movement. Measuring only 50 cm × 65 cm, it can be seen today by artificial light in the Musée Marmottan in Paris. A blue haziness makes up the whole picture and surrounds the red ball of the sun above ships and harbour buildings. The idea was born at a particular hour out of a natural atmospheric effect, dashed off by his scurrying brush in a personal, almost private pictorial note.

(Adapted from Keller, 1980)

COMMENT

You should have found, as you did in a similar activity in Unit 1, that Text 1 has more pronouns (especially *I*), more lexical verbs and more clauses. Text 2, on the other hand, has fewer pronouns, fewer clauses but more information in its fewer clauses. We could say then that Text 1 is a spoken text and Text 2 a written text. Have a look below at the two texts analysed into clauses and the picture is clear.

Text 1

I bought a dog as a pet

but I wanted a good one

so I bought a show quality dog

and the lady I bought the dog from worked at the same place as my father

and I used to call in

and see Dad in the office fairly often

once I bought the dog

and she got me along to a couple of dog shows

and I got interested in it that way

and started showing the dog that she'd bred

and it sort of snowballed from there.

Text 2

Later on, in 1872, Monet painted that picture called *Impression, Sunrise,*

which unintentionally gave its name to the movement.

Measuring only 50 cm × 65 cm,

it can be seen today by artificial light in the Musée Marmottan in Paris.

A blue haziness makes up the whole picture

and surrounds the red ball of the sun above ships and harbour buildings.

The idea was born at a particular hour out of a natural atmospheric effect,

dashed off by his scurrying brush in a personal, almost private pictorial note.

Text 1 has 89 words in 11 clauses, while Text 2 has 87 words in 8 clauses. Another difference is the amount of information each clause provides. Given that the texts are about the same length, which of the two texts do you think has more information? Do the individual clauses in Text 1 give you a lot of information about the dog or about the dog shows? It would appear that if you did want to find out more, you would probably have to keep on listening for a lot longer and/or ask very specific questions of the speaker.

Do the clauses of Text 2 give you comparatively more information in this case about the painting by Monet? In this short text, you have specific times and dimensions for the painting, specific places of exhibition and descriptions of the painting itself. This is more than the first text gave about the dog and the dog shows. We could ask why these texts have the features they have and to answer this we would need to consider the context in which each of the texts is located as the context shapes the features of the text.

Text 1 is constructed by two people who are face to face in a relatively informal situation. They are talking about the interviewee's involvement in the specialised field of dog shows.

Text 2 is written by someone who does not know the reader and hence constructs a more formal text. The writer has time to reflect on what she wants to say and chooses carefully each word. In doing so, the text is full of details about the painting and not organised around the writer herself.

So how is the dense information in the written text expressed through the different elements of the language? In other words, which lexicogrammatical tools or resources has the writer of the written text used to 'pack' a lot of information into a text with fewer words? What we can identify is that one of the major resources in the language which has the potential for doing this is the noun phrase.

You would have already become aware of this when, in Unit 2, we introduced the notion of lexical density – a measure of how much information (through lexical words) is packed into a text. You would have found in the activities set to determine lexical density that the lexical words that contribute most to the density come in the noun phrases. We shall see in the next section how we can pack more information in by expanding noun phrases.

❷ FORM AND FUNCTION

In the discussion on form complementing function in Unit 3, you were introduced to the functional groups participant, process and circumstance. Let us reconsider these so that we can see how they are linked to noun phrases and verb phrases.

We already know that clauses are made up of one process, expressed by the verb phrase, and that these verb phrases usually have one lexical verb (e.g. *am listening*) although they may have more than one (e.g. *am trying to listen*).

We also know that, apart from imperative clauses like *Stop*, there are one or more participants in a clause and that these are usually realised by noun phrases. So if a clause has three participants, we could have three noun phrases.

And, lastly, we know that a clause can also have circumstances, although these are optional elements. If there is a circumstance, then there is a good chance that it will be realised by a prepositional phrase and a prepositional phrase, in turn, is made up of a preposition and a noun phrase.

Hence, it is clear that the noun phrases in a clause play a large role in two of the three functional groups of a clause that represent experience: participant and circumstance.

In the examples below, a clause from Text 1 and two clauses from Text 2 have been analysed to show the links between noun and verb phrases, and participants, processes and circumstances. The noun phrases are in bold.

I	bought	**a dog**	as **a pet**
participant	process	participant	circumstance
noun phrase	verb phrase	noun phrase	preposition + noun phrase (prepositional phrase)

A blue haziness	makes up	**the whole picture**
participant	process	participant
noun phrase	verb phrase	noun phrase

The idea	was born	at **a particular hour**	out of **a natural atmospheric effect**
participant	process	circumstance	circumstance
noun phrase	verb phrase	preposition + noun phrase (prepositional phrase)	preposition + noun phrase (prepositional phrase)

We can see from the above analyses that the examples from Text 2, the written text, have longer noun phrases. This increased length represents increased density of information. As noun phrases function both as participants in the text and as part of the circumstances, they account for much of the length of the clause.

Biber et al. (1999, p. 65) state: 'in conversation, nouns and verbs are about equally frequent; in news reportage and academic prose, there are three to four nouns per lexical verb.' Also, 'single pronouns abound in ... conversation ..., while longer and more complex structures (noun-phrase structures) are predominant in the written registers' (Biber et al., 1999, p. 231).

This last conclusion in Biber et al. (1999) is important in that it is the longer and more complex noun phrase that plays a significant role in written texts. The power of the noun phrase is that it is a tool for forming technical categories (e.g. *artificial light, natural light, fluorescent tubes*), for describing (e.g. a *blue haziness, his scurrying brush, dirty fluorescent tubes*) and for quantifying (e.g. *hundreds of fluorescent tubes*). It is this potential for quantifying, describing and classifying (among other things) that makes the expansion of noun phrases an important tool in writing.

How are noun phrases made longer and more complex? In other words, how do we 'expand' noun phrases? In order to understand this, it is necessary to understand the structure of the noun phrase. This unit will take you through the different elements that make up the noun phrase. Although reference will be made to the word classes, the focus will be on the functional elements that constitute the noun phrase. And as we move through the sections of this unit, we shall continually make reference to the corpus findings as detailed in your reference grammar.

③ MODIFYING THE HEAD NOUN

The noun phrase must have, at the very least, a noun or a pronoun that functions as the head word. This head word identifies the entity represented by the noun phrase.

ACTIVITY 2 (allow about 10 minutes)

Identify the head word in the following underlined noun phrases (sometimes called nominal phrases or nominal groups). (Try replacing the underlined noun phrase with a pronoun. Then ask yourself which one word in the noun phrase the pronoun has essentially replaced. This word is the head word. Or you could ask 'who' or 'what' in relation to the verb phrase, e.g. Who started calling Monet an Impressionist? The one-word answer will be the head of the noun phrase.)

1   After that, the art critics started calling Monet an Impressionist.
2   Monet painted his impression of sunlight reflected in the water.
3   The art critics (the ones who wrote about art in the newspapers) started calling Monet an Impressionist.
4   It appeared on the cover design of the catalogue at the Centenary Exhibition of Impressionism staged in Paris in 1974.

See 'Answers to the activities' for feedback.

The term **nominal** refers to any word, phrase or clause that fills a noun phrase slot.

The head word can be modified by elements coming before it and elements coming after it. Together with the determiner, we could have **premodification**:

a	natural atmospheric	effect
determiner	premodification	head word

or **postmodification**:

The	lady	I bought the dog from
determiner	head word	postmodification

Sometimes there will be both premodification and postmodification:

an	important	painting	in art history
determiner	premodification	head word	postmodification

Now let us see if there is a discernible pattern between how premodification and postmodification are used in spoken and written texts.

ACTIVITY 3 (allow about 10 minutes)

Underline the noun phrases of each of the following four clauses from Texts 1 and 2. Circle or highlight the head word of each noun phrase so that the premodification and/or postmodification stand out.

Text 1

I bought a dog as a pet
but I wanted a good one
so I bought a show quality dog
and the lady I bought the dog from worked at the same place as my father

Text 2

A blue haziness makes up the whole picture
and surrounds the red ball of the sun above ships and harbour buildings.
The idea was born at a particular hour out of a natural atmospheric effect,
dashed off by his scurrying brush in a personal, almost private pictorial note.

See 'Answers to the activities' for feedback.

Once the noun phrases have been analysed, is it possible to distinguish between texts according to whether one features more or lengthier premodification or postmodification, or if, perhaps, one text features more and lengthier examples of both?

Biber et al. (1999) outline the corpus findings of the register distribution of noun phrases with premodifiers and postmodifiers. They state that noun phrases with a modifier are relatively rare in the spoken mode in contrast to the written mode. Did your findings concur?

Here is the analysis of the noun phrases of Texts 1 and 2 according to modification.

Table 1 Comparing modification in the noun phrases of Texts 1 and 2

	Noun phrases	No modification	Premodification only	Postmodification only	Pre- and post-modification
Text 1	9	5	2	2	0
Text 2	8	1	6	0	1

The results above give similar numbers to those you would have found in corpus analyses, especially the differences in the 'no modification' column. This is where the contrast seems to be greatest: over half the noun phrases of the spoken text are without any modification at all, while the written text has almost all its noun phrases with some modification.

Text 2 has longer noun phrases than Text 1. We can see this if we calculate the average number of words involved in modification in each text and compare them. For Text 1 the average number is approximately 1.3, whereas for Text 2 it is approximately 2.4 – twice as many.

Prior to looking more closely at what constitutes premodification and postmodification, we need to examine the element of the noun phrase that comes at the front, the determiner. Sometimes some kind of numeral will come before the determiner as in *one of* in *one of those chairs* but, on the whole, we expect determiners to come at the front of a noun phrase.

DETERMINERS

Determiners are 'pointers' in a noun phrase, i.e. a **determiner** points to the entity that the head word is referencing.

The determiner functions to reduce what the head word refers to, so that the entity can be identified in some way. The function of the determiner can be performed by a range of different word classes, most commonly by

- articles (**the** lady I bought the dog from, **a** pet, **an** apple)

The indefinite article, *a* and *an*, narrows down the reference to a single member of the class (*a* car). The definite article *the* does not identify the entity but instead tells us that the identification of the head word is found somewhere else in the text or within the context: '*the* car' means that the listener or reader must retrieve the identity of the car from somewhere else in the text; '*the* television', '*the* sun' expect you to retrieve the meaning from shared knowledge.

- demonstratives (**this** article; **that** picture called *Impression, Sunrise*)

The demonstratives refer to the proximity of the entity. *This* book, *these* books mean that they are 'near me'; *that* book, *those* books mean that they are 'not near me'.

- possessives (**my** father, **his** scurrying brush)
- possessives (genitive) (**the driver's** name, **Geoff's** exam stuff)

Possessive determiners refer to the standpoint of the speaker or writer (*my* book, *your* book, *Tom's* book).

ACTIVITY 4 (allow about 30 minutes)

Read section 4.5, 'Determiners', in your reference grammar for a more detailed description and the first part on section 4.6 for corpus findings on the use of the definite article in written texts compared with conversation. Make some notes as you read these sections.

COMMENT

Your reference grammar gives some general names for elements of determiner and pronoun classes – **possessives**, **demonstratives**, **quantifiers**.

⑤ PREMODIFIERS

Let us now look more closely at the constituent parts of premodification. Under traditional grammatical approaches, items such as articles, pronouns, adjectives and nouns would typically be listed as acting to premodify nominal (noun phrase) heads. So, in the following noun phrases taken from a text on flooding in Prague, the analysis would be given as follows.

1		spiralling	estimates
2	the	hastily* erected	defences
	determiner	premodification	head
	article	adjective(s)	noun

hastily is an adverb and does not function to modify the head word (*defences*). Instead it modifies the participial adjective it is adjacent to (*erected*), hence we do not classify *hastily* as a separate constituent of the premodification.

In the next examples, we see that nouns are also used to modify the head word, which is a noun.

3			emergency	crews
4		minor	water	damage
5	the		clean-up	operation
	determiner		premodification	head
	article	adjective	noun	noun

If we have a closer look at these noun phrases, we can see that there is something different in the meaning of (1) and (2), where the modifiers are only participial adjectives, compared with (3), (4) and (5), where most of the modifiers are nouns. Can you work out what the difference is? Both are premodifying but the kind of modification is different.

What you might have found is that the modifying elements in (1) and (2) express some sort of descriptive meaning, whereas examples (3), (4) and (5) express some kind of classification. By descriptive, we mean that the element is giving some sort of quality to the head word, such as its behaviour, size, age or colour. By classification, we mean that the element is classifying or categorising the head word so that we know, for example, what kind of crew (in this case, emergency and not flight or ship crews). The kinds of question we could ask that would indicate the difference are 'What like?' and 'What kind?', respectively. These questions have now been inserted into the table below as questions about 'function'.

	determiner (article or possessive) — Which?	premodification (adjective) — What like?	noun — What kind?	head (noun) — What?
1	the	hastily erected		defences
2	the		clean-up	operation
3			emergency	crews
4	the		Prague subway	system
5		minor	water	damage
6	Parliament's		budget	committee
7	the	cash-strapped		government
8		aggressive or violent		driving

This perspective, where we are looking at the role the word has (apart from the more general modifying role) in the noun phrase, is a functional perspective. So we can now identify the elements of the noun phrase according to the function they perform inside the noun phrase as well as identifying their word class.

In (4), we can see that there is more than one noun functioning in the same way – to express what kind – and in (8) more than one adjective is functioning to describe. These possibilities will be taken up again later in this section when we elaborate on those functional roles.

The last example to be introduced here is one which has an adjective functioning to express 'What kind?' or 'What class?':

	determiner (article) — Which?	premodification (adjective) — What like?	(adjective) — What kind?	head (noun) — What?
	the	ancient	Old	Town

This example illustrates that a word class can have more than one function – a notion introduced in Unit 3. Here the adjective 'old' has the function of classifying the specific town – the writer has been forced to use a synonym of 'old' (*ancient*) as the describer because it would seem strange to have *the old Old Town*. Even the use of the upper case in 'Old Town' indicates its classifying function.

5.1 Classifiers and describers

We can now categorise the elements that premodify according to their function. The two functional categories we have already met can now be labelled as 'describer' (known also as 'epithet') and 'classifier'. These terms come from the Hallidayan perspective on the noun phrase.

The **describer** functions to describe the head word by attaching to it some attribute or quality; it provides an answer to the question 'What is it like?' Describers are typically realised by adjectives (*this nebulous picture, a blue haziness*) and can almost always be compared or intensified (*a more important painting, the largest increase*).

The **classifier** acts to indicate the class or category of the entity (head word). It answers the question 'What type is it?' Classifiers are usually realised by adjectives (*artificial light, solar energy*) and nouns (*an oil painting, the art critics*). A noun used as a premodifier is nearly always a classifier.

So the above example can now be labelled as follows.

	the	ancient	Old	Town
Function question	Which?	What like?	What kind?	What?
	determiner	describer	classifier	head

ACTIVITY 5 (allow about 10 minutes)

To practise identifying the describers and classifiers in a noun phrase, analyse the words in bold in the list which appears below Texts 3 and 4. Write an E under the words functioning as describers (epithets) and a C under the classifiers.

Consider why the authors make the choices they do. Are they choosing more describers than classifiers? What events, experiences, observations and emotions are they representing in their choices of describers and classifiers? The first extract is from John Irving's novel *The Hotel New Hampshire* and is preceded by the man overhearing a song being played inside a building. The second extract is from Tim Park's book *Italian Neighbours* and describes a typical Italian scene.

Text 3

The song was not a Christmas carol, and it struck me as inappropriate to the decorations all over the city of New York, but Christmas decorations are seasonal and the song I heard just a snatch of was one of those universally bleeding-heart kind of Country and Western songs. Some trite-but-true thing was being tritely but truthfully expressed. I have been listening, for the rest of my life, for that song, but whenever I think I'm hearing it again, something strikes me as not quite the same.

(Irving, 1981, p. 340)

Text 4

In the smaller farms on the hill slopes above, the rows of vines are often supported by the cherry trees. A horizontal wooden slat is strapped to the tree; four or five wires are stretched from one slat to the next, one tree to the next, and the vines, twisting and splintery, cling on between. When winter comes and the luxuriant summer foliage of pergola and cherry leaf is gone, the rude peasant mechanics of these slats and wires is left stark in the bright light, like the tangled rigging of some bleached clipper.

(Parks, 1992, p. 194)

1   a **Christmas** carol
2   one of those **universally bleeding heart kind of Country and Western** songs
3   Some **trite-but-true** thing
4   the **cherry** trees
5   A **horizontal wooden** slat
6   the **luxuriant summer** foliage of pergola and cherry leaf
7   the **rude peasant** mechanics of these slats and wires
8   the **tangled** rigging of some bleached clipper

See 'Answers to the activities' for feedback.

These two extracts from fiction texts illustrate that writers of fiction generally describe events, experiences and emotions rather than classify them. We see that the writers do this by choosing describers more frequently than classifiers and, especially in Irving's case, choosing describers that are complex (*trite-but-true*) or that allude to something else in the culture (*universally bleeding heart kind of*).

5.2 Numeratives

Apart from determiners, describers and classifiers, there is another functional group that acts as a premodifier and that is the numerative.

Numeratives quantify and order items numerically.

Numeratives premodify the head by indicating some numerical feature of the noun, such as number, quantity or order.

How many: (exact) **three** categories of offence; (inexact) **several** really useful touches, **a few** really useful touches, **a lot of** really useful touches.

In what quantity: (exact) **a pound of** apples, **a gallon of** water; (inexact) **around a kilogram of** cheese.

Where the noun comes in a counting or numerical sequence: (exact) the **third** insect, the **first** insect, the **last** insect; (inexact) the **subsequent** train, the **preceding** train.

Note that some words may function as either determiners or numeratives in different contexts. For example, in *I had some butter and jam on my toast*, 'some' is a determiner, while in *I only had some butter on my toast – not very much*, 'some' quantifies the head noun and is a numerative.

ACTIVITY 6   (allow about five minutes)

Read the following text which is an article from a science magazine on a news item (current at the time of writing), the flooding of the River Elbe. Look for the language elements that express some numerical aspect and underline them.

Once you have underlined the numerical elements, consider the question: Why would a text like this tend to have the amount and type of inexact numeratives that this text has?

Text 5

The tests did find a large increase in levels of arsenic and lead, probably from slag heaps and waste deposits. The Elbe has also flooded hundreds of sewage plants and picked up many animal carcasses. Toxic substances that lay hidden beneath the riverbed may also have been disturbed, says Volkhard Wetzel, head of the Koblenz Institute.

The water may also be spreading bacteria such as *Salmonella*. 'There is no reason for panic, but we are scrutinizing the situation,' says Axel Hofmann, a medical microbiologist at the Saxonian Institute for Health and Veterinary Medicine in Leipzig. Thousands of inhabitants of Prague and Dresden have been vaccinated against hepatitis A, which can be spread by faeces leaking into drinking water.

Dioxin contamination of the Elbe may also hamper efforts to tackle pollution from various industries during the communist era. Ironically, thousands dived into the Elbe in Dresden only last month to mark its recovery from pollution.

(Schiermeier, 2002, p. 905)

COMMENT

Apart from the words *a* and *no* you probably have identified the words *hundreds of, many, thousands of, thousands, various, last*. You might even have identified *increase*. For our purposes here, let us not focus on *a* and *no* (determiners) and *increase* (head) so that we can focus on all the other listed words, which are numeratives.

The answer to the question about the amount and kind of numeratives lies in the fact that this text is a news article. It deals with a phenomenon, a flood, and is extremely broad in scope as it is impossible to be specific about damage in a flood. Without exact figures, the reporter has had to use numeratives that range from the hundreds to the thousands. The inexactness is continued in choices such as the non-specific *many* and *various*.

5.3 Summarising premodification

Revisiting the examples, we can now see all the functional groupings of premodification.

the		hastily erected			defences
the				Prague subway	system
		minor		water	damage
Parliament's				budget	committee
		aggressive or violent			driving
the		ancient		Old	Town
the	four	small		oil	paintings
	several				men
Which?	How many?	What like?		What kind?	What?
determiner	numerative	describer(s)		classifier(s)	head

Is there a usual order to these functional categories? Look at the three examples which have describers and classifiers. They are organised in the examples in such a way that the describers are to the left of the classifiers. Is this the usual order? Is there another order that retains the same meaning? Collect a few examples from a text you have handy. Is the order that we have here maintained in that text? Does this order include the numerative and the determiner as well?

The three examples from above are presented again.

		minor	water	damage
the		ancient	Old	Town
the	four	small	oil	paintings

You should have seen that this is the usual order in English for these functional groups. In other words, if there is a classifier, it will be immediately before the head and, if a describer is added, it will be immediately before the classifier. So, in the above, because the words *small* and *oil* are describer and classifier respectively, we cannot have *the oil small paintings*, nor can we have *water minor damage*.

Similarly, the numerative will come before the describer (we cannot have *the small four oil paintings*) and the determiner will come before the numerative (we cannot have *four the small oil paintings*). However, there is a situation where a quantifying element will come before the determiner (*one of the four small oil paintings*). In that case, *one of* can be called a **pre-numerative**.

A CTIVITY 7 (allow about 10 minutes)

To conclude this section on premodification, analyse the following emboldened noun phrases. Identify the head and then all the premodifying elements (determiners, numeratives (and pre-numeratives), describers and classifiers).

1　**The world's motoring press** has applauded the latest model.
2　It is **the ultimate luxury car**.
3　The clock has **a classic, champagne-coloured design**.
4　We took it for **a rather refined test drive**.
5　Go to **your nearest MG Rover dealer**.
6　It just has to be **one of the most versatile off-road vehicles**.

See 'Answers to the activities' for feedback.

⑥ POSTMODIFIERS AND QUALIFICATION

We have already introduced postmodification with the following examples.

determiner	premodification	head	postmodification
an	important	painting	in art history
a	large	increase	in levels of arsenic and lead
Thousands of		inhabitants	of Prague and Dresden
Dioxin		contamination	of the Elbe

The postmodifying element is one whose function is to further qualify the head (to the right of the head) and so its functional label is **qualifier**.

Qualifiers can be realised by either prepositional phrases or clauses or both. The above examples have prepositional phrases functioning as qualifiers while the following examples have clauses functioning as qualifiers.

determiner	premodification	head	postmodification
the		lady	I bought the dog from
	Toxic	substances	that lay hidden beneath the riverbed
		faeces	\<that are\> leaking into drinking water

It is possible to have multiple qualifiers. In the following example, the head word is *efforts* and after it are several qualifiers. To illustrate this, each new qualifier is introduced on a separate line. If the new qualifier is a prepositional phrase, it is shown with single square brackets [ ]. If the new qualifier is a clause, it is shown with double square brackets [[ ]].

> ...may hamper efforts
>
> ...may hamper efforts [[to tackle pollution]]
>
> ...may hamper efforts [[to tackle pollution [from various industries]]]
>
> ...may hamper efforts [[to tackle pollution [from various industries] [during the communist era]]]

Embedded clauses are usually denoted by [[ ]].

The complexity in the above example comes from the fact that the qualifiers are being qualified themselves by other qualifiers. This phenomenon is referred to as **embedding** (or 'nesting'), so we can have multiple **embedded clauses** and embedded prepositional phrases. According to the corpus findings in your reference grammar (p. 267), this phenomenon of complex postmodification is rare in the spoken mode.

The following three examples from texts used in this unit show further illustrations of complex embedding. Embedded clauses are surrounded by double square brackets [[ ]] and prepositional phrases by single square brackets [ ].

determiner	premodification	head	postmodification
His		impression	[of sunlight [[reflected in the water]]]
	news media	accounts	[of a 'new' phenomenon [[involving crime]]]
The	cover	design	[of the catalogue [at the Centenary Exhibition [of Impressionism] [[staged in Paris in 1974]]]]

At this point, let us have a look at a student's history text on causes of the First World War. Several of the noun phrases from the extract have been listed and analysed to show whether there is anything characteristic about the qualifiers in a written text such as this. You could, of course, also analyse one of the texts you have written for an assignment in this or any other tertiary-level course.

Text 6

(From a student's history text)

The final element in the war's outbreak was the dominance of militarism in the thinking of European leaders. All the major European nations had been improving their armies in size and technology, creating an impatience for war. There was also a dangerous reliance on single inflexible war plans. For example,

Russian militarists had created a plan to mobilise forces to the borders of Austria-Hungary and Germany simultaneously. Likewise, Germany had only one plan for war, the Schlieffen plan, and this involved attacking France before concentrating on its eastern front with Russia. This plan relied on the six-week period required by Russia to mobilise, which would allow for Germany to cope with a two front war. This buffer period was shrinking every year because of increased railway construction in Russia and this contributed to German militarists wanting war as early as possible. So, these factors lead many historians to blame Germany's militarists for leading Europe into war.

(Carl Nilsson-Polias © 2001 Lexis Education)

The final **element** [in the war's outbreak]

the **dominance** [of militarism] [in the thinking [of European leaders]]

All the major European **nations**

an **impatience** [for war]

a dangerous **reliance** [on single inflexible war plans]

Russian **militarists**

a **plan** [[to mobilise forces [to the borders [of Austria-Hungary and Germany]]]]

In this written text, many of the noun phrases not only have qualifiers but have complex embedding, where there are qualifiers inside other qualifiers.

⬧ PREPOSITIONAL PHRASES

A prepositional phrase can qualify the head word in a noun phrase or act as a circumstance in a clause.

We have seen already that a prepositional phrase typically consists of a preposition and a noun phrase (in bold in the next examples). For example:

in **the morning**

in **the house**

behind **me**

to **London**

Also, our exploration of noun phrases has shown that prepositional phrases can perform a number of functions in the clause.

One function for a prepositional phrase is as qualifier of the head in a noun phrase. The contrasting function introduced earlier in this unit is as a circumstance in the clause. For example, let us compare the following two clauses.

1   Alice was reading a book near the window.

2   Alice picked up the book near the window.

What role does the prepositional phrase *near the window* play in each clause?

In (1), *near the window* functions as a circumstance, telling us where the reading took place.

In (2), *near the window* functions to qualify the book, telling us which book in particular was picked up.

Looking at these more closely:

(1) as circumstance

Alice	was reading	a book	near the window
participant	process	participant	circumstance

(2) as qualifier

Alice	picked up	the	book	near the window
participant	process		participant	
		determiner	head	qualifier

ACTIVITY 8 (allow about five minutes)

Identify whether the prepositional phrase (in bold) is acting as a qualifier or circumstance. Write a Q for qualifier and a C for circumstance next to each clause.

1   The image I remember is of a man **with a rifle**.

2   The accused is supposed to have shot the victim **with a rifle**.

3   He followed the dog **down the road**.

4   And then the dog **down the road** joined in the race.

See 'Answers to the activities' for feedback.

ACTIVITY 9 (allow about one hour)

Read Section 2.6 of Chapter 2 'Grammar and Spoken English' by Ron Carter in the course reader *Applying English Grammar*. In Unit 3 you read the first five sections. Reading Section 6 will help focus your understanding of the noun phrase in English and in relation to its realisation in speech and writing. Before you start reading, consider the following questions to which you will find answers in Carter's Section 2.6.

Terms introduced in the reading: **attributive adjective**, **nominalisation**.

(1) Which part of speech cannot be premodified or postmodified – adjectives, verbs or pronouns?

(2) If you go back to some of the written texts presented in this unit, you will see a number of complex noun phrase (NP) patterns in English, for example:

his impression of sunlight reflected in the water (NP + of + NP)

the ones who wrote about art in the newspaper (NP + wh-clause).

What others do you find? Are these the ones that Carter's corpus-based research shows are the common ones in written English?

(3) Why does the process of 'nominalisation' enable more formality in written English?

ACTIVITIES CD-ROM (allow about two hours)

Now work through the activities for Unit 4 on the Activities CD-ROM.

Conclusion

The focus of this unit has been on the noun phrase. You have begun to see the relationships between the form of a noun phrase and its function. You have developed an understanding of how the noun phrase is used in spoken and written texts.

Learning outcomes

After completing this unit, you should have developed an understanding of:

◆ the differences between speech and writing through a knowledge of the noun phrase

◆ how English can be organised at the level of the noun phrase according to function.

In the light of your increased understanding, you should be able to:

◆ identify the functional and structural elements of noun phrases.

Key terms introduced and revisited

adjective	noun
article	noun phrase [nominal group]
attributive adjective	numerative
circumstance	participant
classifier	possessive
demonstrative	postmodification
describer [epithet]	premodification
determiner	pre-numerative
embedded clause	prepositional phrase
embedding	process
head	pronoun
lexical density	qualifier
lexical verb	quantifier
nominal	verb phrase
nominalisation	

Near equivalents are given in [ ].

Answers to the activities

ACTIVITY 2
Head words are in bold.

1   After that, the art **critics** started calling Monet an impressionist.

2   Monet painted his **impression** of sunlight reflected in the water.

3   The art critics (the **ones** who wrote about art in the newspapers) started calling Monet an impressionist.

4   It appeared on the cover **design** of the catalogue at the Centenary Exhibition of Impressionism staged in Paris in 1974.

ACTIVITY 3
The noun phrases are underlined. The head words are in bold.

Text 1

I bought a **dog** as a **pet**

but **I** wanted a good **one**

so **I** bought a show quality **dog**

and the **lady** I bought the dog from worked at the same* **place** as my father

*'same' is analysed here as a determiner.

Text 2

A blue **haziness** makes up the whole **picture**

and surrounds the red **ball** of the sun above ships and harbour buildings.

The **idea** was born at a particular **hour** out of a natural atmospheric **effect**,

dashed off by his scurrying **brush** in a personal, almost private pictorial **note**.

'above ships and harbour buildings' is analysed here as postmodifying *ball* (or *sun*, as an instance of complex embedding within a long noun phrase, explained on p. 118).

ACTIVITY 5
The describers [E] and classifiers [C] in the noun phrases have been identified in bold.

1   a **Christmas** [C] carol

2   one of those **universally bleeding heart kind of** [E] **Country and Western** [C] songs

3   Some **trite-but-true** [E] thing

4   the **cherry** [C] trees

5   A **horizontal** [E] **wooden** [C] slat

6   the **luxuriant** [E] **summer** [C] foliage of pergola and cherry leaf

7   the **rude** [E] **peasant** [C] mechanics of these slats and wires

8   the **tangled** [E] rigging of some bleached clipper

ACTIVITY 7

The functional elements in the nominal groups have been identified in bold as determiners [D], numeratives [N] and pre-numeratives [pre-N], describers [E], classifiers [C], and head [H].

1   **The world's** [D] **motoring** [C] **press** [H] has applauded the latest model.

2   It is **the** [D] **ultimate** [E] **luxury** [C] **car** [H].

3   The clock has **a** [D] **classic**, [E] **champagne-coloured** [E] **design** [H].

4   We took it for **a** [D] **rather refined** [E] **test** [C] **drive** [H].

5   Go to **your** [D] **nearest** [E] **MG Rover** [C] **dealer** [H].

6   It just has to be **one of** [pre-N] **the** [D] **most versatile** [E] **off-road** [C] **vehicles** [H].

ACTIVITY 8

1   The image I remember is of a man **with a rifle**. [Q]

2   The accused is supposed to have shot the victim **with a rifle**. [C]

3   He followed the dog **down the road**. [C]

4   And then the dog **down the road** joined in the race. [Q]

Unit 5

The verb phrase, adjective phrase and adverb phrase

Prepared for the course team by John Polias

CONTENTS

Materials required

While studying this unit, you will need:

    Unit 4 (in Activity 4 and Section 5)

    the course reader (at end of unit)

    the Activities CD-ROM (at end of unit).

Knowledge assumed

You should be familiar with the following before starting this unit.

From Foundation Grammar:

    adverb phrase

    circumstance and stance adverbials

    verb phrase

      aspect, tense, modality

      temporal and modal auxiliaries.

From Unit 2:

    coordination

    function word

    lexical word

    lexicogrammatical pattern.

From Unit 3:

    adverb phrase

    interrogative clause

    participant, process, circumstance

    prepositional phrase

    question tag.

Introduction

See if you can understand completely what's being reported in the following news text about a 'road rage' incident. ('Road rage' refers to the serious conflict that can arise between people driving on the roads.)

Road rage causes fatal accident

Death of a teenage passenger in a pickup truck – off the road by another pickup in a case of road rage.

Death of Jermaine Reid 17, of Jacksonville early Thursday when he from the bed of a pickup off the north lane of Interstate 295 near the suburb of Orange Park.

A confrontation between several men in two pickups near a service station.

North on I-295, a Toyota pickup, the left rear of a Chevrolet pickup. The driver – no control and then into trees.

The Toyota driver later at Jacksonville Police station.

(Adapted from The National Institute for the Prevention of Workplace Violence, 2000)

Any ideas about the train of events happening here? Hard work isn't it, trying to work it all out, to connect up events and things and people? With some effort, it's possible to do it, to work out that the Toyota pickup bumped the Chevrolet pickup which led to it crashing into trees and the teenager being killed. But surely there's a better way of representing the events which places fewer demands on the reader, a more explicit way of representing events so that we feel more comfortable in our reading? Besides, why was the Toyota driver later at Jacksonville police station? Did the police catch him? It's not too clear. What do we need to 'join up the dots', to make connections between people and things? Verb phrases are the answer, as you will see in the following version which contains them (in bold).

A single-word verb is regarded as a phrase.

Road rage causes fatal accident

A teenage passenger in a pickup truck **was killed** *when it* **was forced** off the road by another pickup in a case of road rage.

Jermaine Reid 17, of Jacksonville **died** early Thursday when he **was thrown** from the bed of a pickup forced off the north lane of Interstate 295 near the suburb of Orange Park.

A confrontation between several men in two pickups **began** near a service station.

While **driving** north on I-295, a Toyota pickup **bumped** the left rear of a Chevrolet pickup. The driver **lost** control and **veered** into trees.

The Toyota driver **kept going** but later **turned** himself **in** to Jacksonville Police.

We saw at the start of Unit 4 with the short review pieces such as *a must-see* and *a dazzlingly imaginative new version* that communication can take place without verb phrases. But this tends to be the case only where the context is very clear. If we're reading a listings magazine which contains information about plays and films, then we can get the message from the noun phrase alone. But for a news report of an event that happened in Jacksonville, Florida where you're very unlikely to have any background information on the event from other sources such as friends, relatives and your own country's news media, and where the relations between cause and effect are significant, you're going to have comprehension problems. Understanding cause–effect relations will require processes realised by verb phrases. We could probably survive without verb phrases, but life would be an awful lot harder, certainly involving a lot more effort, sweat and frustration. They make communication much easier particularly when we're trying to communicate ideas to people who do not share our context. A report of an event in Jacksonville, Florida becomes comprehensible because verb phrases help to make the connections between the events and people concerned.

In this unit we shall again build on basic concepts you have worked with in Unit 3. We shall explore how we represent our knowledge and experience of the world around us and we shall see how we use verb phrases especially to do that. We shall look at the role of the verb phrase in representing the 'goings on', or the processes, in our world. The verb phrase allows us to express more than just these processes and we shall also see how we can express aspects of time and uncertainty in the phrase. By the end of the unit, you will have gone through a thorough exploration of the verb phrase and thus be in a more knowledgeable position as to what it can do in written and spoken communication.

In addition, we will also consider the role of adjective and adverb phrases.

1 REPRESENTING 'HAPPENINGS'

'Happenings' are processes, which can be represented through verb phrases.

In Unit 4 you were asked to consider some texts according to the patterns of the noun phrases. In this unit, instead of participants and the noun phrase, our interest is focused on the kinds of process that are going on in the texts. These processes construe the doing, thinking, saying and relational experiences of people and other entities. These processes are realised by the verb phrase.

Following Halliday's functional approach to grammar, we can group these processes according to their semantic categories. Are these processes ones that deal with external actions, are they concerned with non-visible mental processes that go on inside the head, do they show that people are saying things, or are they processes which relate participants to each other?

ACTIVITY 1 (allow about 10 minutes)

Identify the kind of process going on in each of the given examples. Consider only the verb phrases in bold and use the given codes to represent the four semantic categories of action (A), mental (M), saying (S) and relational (R). The lower-case letters with the numerals (e.g. 1a and 1b) indicate that the clauses belong to the same sentence.

1a A teenage passenger in a pickup truck **was killed**

1b when it **was forced** off the road by another pickup in a case of road rage.

2a I **bought** a dog as a pet

2b but I **wanted** a good one.

3a Police **don't know**

3b if the men **knew** each other.

4 And the motoring press **is** once again euphoric.

5 There **are** driver and front passenger SRS airbags.

6 No one was wearing a seat belt, and alcohol wasn't involved, Leeper **claimed**.

7a While **driving** north on I-295,

7b a Toyota pickup **bumped** the left rear of a Chevrolet pickup.

8 Chief among these **is** the tailgate.

9 'There is no reason for panic, but we are scrutinizing the situation,' **says** Axel Hofmann.

COMMENT

In the above examples, 1a, 1b, 2a, 7a and 7b construe actions, 2b, 3a and 3b construe mental processes, 6 and 9 construe 'saying' and 4, 5 and 8 construe relational processes.

Following Halliday we can label, define and exemplify each of these four process types as follows.

Material processes construe external action, both concrete (catch, play, run) and abstract action (resign, dissolve (committee), close (meeting)).

Mental processes construe processes that go on inside the head, such as thinking and sensing – intellectual action. They include cognition (*I don't believe you*), affection (*I hate injections*) and perception (*I saw the accident*).

Verbal processes construe the saying and reporting of things – verbal action. They include saying and all its many synonyms, e.g. tell, ask, state, whisper, retort.

Relational processes construe the many different ways of being and having and they relate participants to each other. There are relational processes that relate a quality with another entity (*She was so small*), ones that identify (*She is the biology lecturer*) and ones that show possession (*She has a piano*).

Your reference grammar (section 5.3) has seven major semantic categories of **lexical verb**: activity verbs, communication verbs, mental verbs, causative verbs, verbs of occurrence, verbs of existence or relationship and verbs of aspect. It is clear that there are similarities with the four broad domains used by Halliday. For our purposes, we can say that 'material processes' are equivalent to 'activity verbs', 'mental processes' and 'mental verbs' are the same, 'verbal processes' and 'communication verbs' are the same and 'relational processes' are equivalent to the other verb domains 'causative', 'simple occurrence', 'existence', 'relationship' and 'aspectual'.

Processes are classified in slightly different ways by linguists, according to their theoretical approach and the purposes of their research. In Unit 20 of Book 4 we shall use a classification which includes **existential** processes as well as the four types outlined here. The topic of process types will also be revisited in Sections 5 to 7 of Unit 11 in Book 2 and in Unit 13 of Book 3.

ACTIVITY 2 (allow about 10 minutes)

Identify the semantic domain of the processes that have been underlined. It is the last word in the verb phrase, the lexical verb, that determines the process type. Use the same codes as in the previous activity.

1a   'Come over here, Linnea,'

1b   said Mr. Bloom.

2a   'Why? I asked,'

2b   because I hadn't noticed *that* little picture before.

3a 'This <u>is</u> an important painting in art history,'

3b <u>explained</u> Mr. Bloom.

4 'It<u>'s called</u> Impression–Sunrise.

5 Monet <u>painted</u> his *impression* of sunlight reflected in the water...

6a They <u>thought</u>

6b painting impressions of the moment <u>was</u> a waste of time.

7 Paintings <u>should be</u> precise.'

See 'Answers to the activities' for feedback.

To see more widespread patterns of the use of processes, it is useful and interesting to compare two texts. By comparing processes, we can see how the speaker or writer is representing experience.

◆ A CTIVITY 3 (allow about 20 minutes)

Read the two extracts below on 'road rage'. As I said earlier, 'road rage' refers to the serious conflict that can arise between people driving on the roads, perhaps because they got 'cut up' by another driver or perhaps because the person in front of them is driving too slowly.

Analyse the texts by identifying what kinds of process the verb phrases in bold are realising. What is the frequency of the different process types in each text? Consider then how differently the two texts are construing the phenomenon of road rage.

Text 1

Road rage causes fatal accident

A teenage passenger in a pickup truck **was killed** when it **was forced** off the road by another pickup in a case of road rage.

Jermaine Reid 17, of Jacksonville **died** early Thursday when he **was thrown** from the bed of a pickup forced off the north lane of Interstate 295 near the suburb of Orange Park, the Florida Highway Patrol **said**.

A confrontation between several men in two pickups **began** near a service station, **said** Lt. Bill Leeper. Police **don't know** if the men **knew** each other or who **started** the argument, but threats **were made**.

While **driving** north on I-295, a Toyota pickup **bumped** the left rear of a Chevrolet pickup. The driver **lost** control and **veered** into trees.

The Toyota driver **kept going** but later **turned** himself **in** to Jacksonville Police. His name **was not released**. No charges **have been filed**.

Police **said** the other driver Jeffrey Ferrell, 20, of Jacksonville and two passengers, Joshua Register, 17, of Jacksonville and Clyde Forgrave, 21, of St. Marys, Ga., **were taken** to Shands Jacksonville hospital.

Ferrell **was** in fair condition and Register and Forgrave **were treated** for their injuries and **released**.

No one **was wearing** a seat belt, and alcohol **wasn't involved**, Leeper **said**.

(Adapted from The National Institute for the Prevention of Workplace Violence, 2000)

Text 2

Constructing 'road rage' as news

This article **deals** specifically with news media accounts of a 'new' phenomenon involving crime: 'road rage'. Road rage **is** particularly interesting to study because the news media **played** an important role in using and defining this new term for their audiences. The term **emerged** in the mid 1990s **to describe** a constellation of behaviours related to aggressive or violent driving and other socially undesirable reactions to other drivers using the same road space, such as rude gestures and verbal abuse. Some of these behaviours (such as homicide and assault) **were** already **defined** as criminal at the time the term emerged, while in some jurisdictions others **have** since **been** specifically **designated** as criminal. For example, legislation **was introduced** in the New South Wales State Parliament in May 1997 **to punish** road-rage-related behaviour. The laws **introduced** three categories of offences: menacing driving, driving with intent to menace, and predatory driving.

(Lupton, 2001, pp. 23–5)

COMMENT

In Text 1, the processes are concerned with actions and thus material processes (*killed, forced, died, thrown, began, started, going, lost, veered, bumped*) by people and concrete objects (*pickup truck*). Although the main processes are material ones, there are also other processes, such as mental processes (*know, knew*) and verbal processes (*said*). So in this news text, 'road rage' is made up of the actual people and objects involved in the carrying out of the road rage, as well as the people arresting those involved, hence the use of material processes. Since the writer of the text is dependent on the police to give him/her the information about the incident, there is also the use of verbal processes. And furthermore, because the police are uncertain about all the facts, there is the use of mental processes to express those uncertainties.

With Text 2, we can see that the processes are no longer ones focusing on doing things. Instead there is a focus on setting up relationships between things (*deals, is, defined, designated*). Many of the participants in these relationships are abstract actions (*crime, abuse, behaviour*). This text still represents the actions of road rage but not as physical processes with human and concrete 'actors' doing the actions as in Text 1, but rather as abstract participants realised through noun phrases. And since the actions are now realised through the participants, the processes that are used to link these abstract participants are generally relational processes.

In summary, then, we can see how the choice of processes construes the phenomenon of road rage in entirely different ways: one text is focused on reconstructing the external activities of the human and concrete participants, while the other is focused on the issues that emanate from or are associated with the phenomenon.

The next section will explore the constituent elements of the verb phrase – these elements were introduced to you in Unit 3. We shall see that not only can the verb phrase express some process but it can also express tense, aspect and modality as well.

See Foundation Grammar for an introduction to tense, aspect and modality of verb phrases.

❷ STRUCTURE OF THE VERB PHRASE

The verb phrase may consist of two major elements: the lexical part of the verb phrase and the auxiliaries.

2.1 Lexical verb

The verb phrase always contains a 'central' verbal element that expresses the process. This can be referred to as the **lexical verb**. In the following, the verb phrases (in bold) have their lexical verb underlined.

See Foundation Grammar for an introduction to lexical and modal verbs.

They **<u>meant</u>** it as a compliment.

They **did <u>mean</u>** it as a compliment.

They **might have <u>meant</u>** it as a compliment.

As we can see, the lexical verb is the last element of the verb phrase and expresses some kind of process. Additionally, as we can see in the examples above, the verb phrase may contain one or more other elements, called **auxiliary verbs**. There are auxiliaries that express tense or aspect and auxiliaries that express modality.

2.2 Temporal finite and modal finite

The first auxiliary in the verb phrase can have a label of its own: it can be referred to as the **finite**. The finite together with the subject allows negotiation by the speakers (*They didn't mean it; Yes, they did; No, they didn't*). The finite is either a **temporal finite** (expressing tense) or a **modal finite** (expressing **modality**). We have decided to use the term 'finite' here because it relates to something you will deal with in the next unit, the notion of finite and non-finite clauses.

The temporal finite often helps to anchor the verb phrase in terms of person (*I, you, he, she, it, we, they*) and number (plural or singular). For example, *I don't think so* shows through *don't* that it is the first person and is singular, whereas with *She doesn't think so*, it is clear through *doesn't* that it is third person and singular.

The modal finite (*may, might, could, should, must, will*) expresses a degree of certainty (*It might snow later; It must be them, mustn't it?*) or obligation (*You must sign before you enter; You might want to register first*).

In the following examples from the texts in this unit and Unit 4, the finites have been analysed as either temporal or modal.

Legislation	was	introduced	in the NSW State Parliament
Others	have	been designated	as criminal
They	didn't	mean	it as a compliment
	temporal finite		

The water	may	be spreading	bacteria such as *Salmonella*
Paintings	should	be	precise
	modal finite		

The finite is also the component of the verb phrase that comes at the front of a clause to form an interrogative clause – as in the following examples.

(1) To form an interrogative, the finite is placed before the subject of the clause:

Did they mean it as a compliment?

Might the water spread bacteria?

It can also be used for three other important reasons.

(2) To form question tags or mood tags:

They meant it as a compliment, **didn't** they?

The water **might** spread bacteria, **mightn't** it?

(3) To form a negative statement:

They **didn't** mean it as a compliment.

The water **mightn't** spread bacteria.

(4) To form the stressed form of a positive statement:

They **did** mean it as a compliment.

2.3 Tense and modality

The temporal finites vary according to whether they express *past*, *present* or *future time*.

Temporal finites

past	present	future
did, was, ...	does, is, has	will, would, ...
didn't, wasn't, ...	doesn't, isn't, ...	won't, wouldn't, ...

The modal finites vary according to whether they express low, median or high degrees of certainty or obligation.

Modal finites

low	median	high
can, may, might, ...	will, would, should, ...	must, ought to, has to, ...
needn't, doesn't have to, ...	won't, wouldn't, shouldn't, ...	mustn't, oughtn't to, can't, ...

Note that *will* and *would* can function as either temporal or modal finites, using this grammatical model. For instance, in *Dan <u>will</u> know the truth when he reads the paper*, the finite expresses future time; however, in *Dan <u>will</u> know the truth because he was there at the time*, it expresses probability that something is the case.

In your reference grammar and in the Foundation Grammar a rather different definition of *tense* is used, which only counts present and past as tenses in English (these are indicated by inflection of the first word in a finite tensed verb phrase e.g. *she <u>eats</u>* vs. *she <u>ate</u>*; *he <u>is</u> coming* vs. *he <u>was</u> coming*). Non-inflecting auxiliaries like *must*, *should* and *will* typically express other meaning distinctions than the time at which an event occurs: see Sections 6.2 and 6.9 of the reference grammar for more detail on this model.

ACTIVITY 4 (allow about five minutes)

Reread Text 2 (p. 132) and decide which tense the temporal finites are realising.

Consider why it is possible for the writer not to have chosen any modal finites in the short extract that makes up Text 2.

Reread Text 5 in Unit 4 (p. 115) and determine the level of modality chosen and expressed through the modal finites. Can you suggest why that level of modality was appropriate for the text?

COMMENT

In Text 2 you should have found that, although there are some examples of the present tense which state how interesting it is to study the phenomenon of road rage, most of the finites are expressing the past tense (*were defined, was introduced*). That is because the writer is recounting events.

The lack of modality, which in this case refers to the lack of uncertainty, is attributable to the fact that this paragraph deals with specific times and specific events, events that can be tracked back to a specific date because they are on public record. For example, parliamentary decisions are recorded carefully for all to look up. With clear evidence to justify statements being made, the writer does not have to express any uncertainty in this paragraph.

Modality, in Halliday's terms, will be explored in Sections 1.1 and 1.2 of Unit 10 in Book 2.

An analysis of Text 5 in Unit 4 shows that there are four examples of modal finites, three *may* and one *can*, which express a low degree of certainty (see the table of modal finites above). The four examples are repeated below.

> Toxic substances that lay hidden beneath the riverbed **may** also have been disturbed, says Volkhard Wetzel, head of the Koblenz Institute.

> The water **may** also be spreading bacteria such as *Salmonella*.

> Thousands of inhabitants of Prague and Dresden have been vaccinated against hepatitis A, which **can** be spread by faeces leaking into drinking water.

> Dioxin contamination of the Elbe **may** also hamper efforts to tackle pollution from various industries during the communist era.

Not all of Text 5 in Unit 4 is similarly uncertain, but the text is trying to identify the cause of the high toxic levels in the water and this creates a degree of uncertainty. The writer, and the scientists included in the article, can be certain that there are high toxic levels because they have carried out tests but they are not sure why the levels are high. To make that meaning, they have chosen to use modal finites of a low degree, such as *may*.

A CTIVITY 5 (allow about 30 minutes)

Read section 5.2 of your reference grammar, which looks at the frequency and distribution of lexical verbs, modal finites and temporal finites across the written and spoken modes in the LSWE corpus. You may also want to read section 6.2.4 on the distribution of tense and modality.

 VERB PHRASE COMPLEX

Can a verb phrase have more than one lexical verb? In order to expand or further specify the nature of the process, additional lexical verbs can be used in a verb phrase. The verb phrase is then made up of two or more lexical verbs constituting one process, thus forming a **verb phrase complex**.

> The Toyota driver **kept going**.

> The art critics **started calling** Monet an Impressionist.

Here, the verb phrases are complex. It is not just that the driver was going, but that he '*continued*' going. This is expressed by joining *kept* with *going*. Similarly, it is not simply that the art critics called Monet an Impressionist, but that they '*began* to call' him that.

So, in these examples, the *started* and *kept* elaborate the *calling* and *going*, respectively. Accordingly, we do not analyse *kept* or *started* as separate lexical verbs.

Note that your reference grammar does not use the term 'verb phrase complex', and analyses such clauses differently (see Sections 8.16.1-2, 10.13 and 10.21).

The Toyota driver	**kept going.**		
The art critics	**started calling**	Monet	an Impressionist.
participant	process	participant	participant
noun phrase	verb phrase complex	noun phrase	noun phrase

There are numerous items which can play supporting roles in specifying, elaborating or modulating the nature of the process. Your reference grammar calls these verbs 'controlling verbs'. For example:

> The critics **ended up calling** Monet an Impressionist.

> The critics **regretted calling** Monet an Impressionist.

The critics **insisted on calling** Monet an Impressionist.

The critics **tend to see** things differently.

The driver **appeared to stop**.

It is also possible to have more than two lexical verbs making up a single process. For example:

The driver **tried to keep going**.

The driver **managed to keep going**.

It is important to be aware of the existence of complex verb phrases with a possible range of elements. The key is to identify instances where the additional lexical verbs (e.g. *try, manage, end up, happen, succeed in*) would make no sense in isolation – they take on a meaning only in combination with the lexical verb and any auxiliaries. In the above example *The driver tried to keep going*, *tried* modulates the process that follows, i.e. *to keep going*. 'Tried' is not separate from 'going' so the two lexical verbs *tried* and *to keep going* are one process.

◢ **A CTIVITY 6** (allow about five minutes)

In the sentences below, determine whether the verb phrases constitute a single process and hence a single clause (e.g. *She stopped listening to the radio*), or whether they constitute two processes (e.g. *She stopped to listen to the radio*) and hence make up two separate clauses.

1   I kept watching the film.

2   I started watching the show.

3   I went to find my sister.

4   I managed to find my sister.

5   I stayed up to see the film.

6   I remembered to see the film.

7   I tried to find my sister.

See 'Answers to the activities' for feedback.

Processes of cause (the first two examples below) or enablement (the third example below) can also be expressed by two lexical verbs acting as a single process. The participants 'taxes', 'us' and 'the children' interrupt the processes.

1	The new law	**caused**	taxes	**to increase**
2	His comments	**made**	us	**laugh**
3	My parents	**allowed**	the children	**to stay up**
	participant	proc ...	participant	... ess
	noun phrase	verb phrase ...	noun phrase	... complex

Even though the complex verb phrases are discontinuous (interrupted), each of these clauses is analysed as having one single process: *caused + to increase*; *made + laugh*; *allowed + to stay up*. The reasons for analysing these multiple elements as constituting a single verb phrase and, hence, as a single process are similar to those with elements such as *try* and *manage* (see page 138). However, in contrast to those, a verb phrase with a causative element is typically broken up by a participant – *us* comes between *made* and *laugh* and *the children* comes between *allowed* and *to stay up*.

Another type of complex verb phrase has two lexical verbs linked with a coordinator or subordinator as well as a modifying lexical verb, all acting as one process. For example:

> She **started folding and kneading** the dough.

> The driver **appeared to stop and check** a map.

In both these examples, the coordinator *and* is linking two lexical verbs. In the first example the modifying lexical verb is *started* and in the second it is *appeared*.

An analysis of the texts presented in Unit 4 and in this unit, found only three examples of modifying lexical verbs. Two come from a spoken text and one from a written text (on road rage). The examples are presented again here.

Text 1 (Unit 4)

...and I **used to call in and see** Dad in the office fairly often once I bought the dog ... and **started showing** the dog that she'd bred and it sort of snowballed from there.

Text 1 (this unit)

The Toyota driver **kept going** but later turned himself in to Jacksonville Police. His name was not released. No charges have been filed.

4 PHRASAL VERBS

A preposition or an adverb can work together with a verb to form a verb phrase. These verb phrases are termed **phrasal verbs**. In the following examples, the verb phrases are underlined and the phrasal verb is in bold.

> The Toyota driver <u>**turned**</u> himself <u>**in**</u> to Jacksonville Police.

> A blue haziness <u>**makes up**</u> the whole picture.

See your reference grammar for 'coordinator' and 'subordinator'. Also see Unit 2 for coordination.

Your reference grammar terms such adverbs **adverbial particles** (Section 2.4.5), a subclass of function words. This difference of classification could affect a calculation of lexical density, for instance, so it is important to specify clearly which analytical approach you are following in your work.

The idea <u>was</u> **dashed off** by his scurrying brush.

In phrasal verbs, the final element of the lexical verb is typically a preposition or adverb of location (*off, up, in*). The final element no longer operates independently as an adverb or preposition but is 'fused' semantically with the other element(s) of the verb. Thus, *dashed off* has a meaning similar to that of the single lexical verb *completed*, although in addition it carries the meaning 'in a hurry':

The idea <u>was</u> **dashed off** by his scurrying brush.

The idea <u>was</u> **completed** hurriedly by his scurrying brush.

4.1 Checks for phrasal verbs

There are various checks to determine whether an item in question does constitute a phrasal verb.

As a first test, ask yourself: Is it possible to find a single word replacement? For example, *makes up* can be replaced by *comprises*.

If the items tend to remain together under certain reorganisations of the clause, then they probably constitute a phrasal verb. For example, the elements of the phrasal verb *called off* remain together in the following clauses.

The meeting has been **called off**.

It was Friday's meeting that they **called off**.

What they **called off** was Friday's meeting.

Be aware that the preposition belongs to the process in the above three clauses. However, in the following examples, *up* is part of a circumstance *up there*, but part of the process in *look up*.

	Look		up there!
I	had to look up	the word	in the dictionary
participant	process	participant	circumstance

Another test is to check that the elements that make up a phrasal verb can be 'interrupted' by a participant, usually in pronoun form. For example:

He **called off** the meeting. He **called** the meeting **off**. He **called** it **off**.

The Toyota driver **turned** himself **in** to Jacksonville Police.

He **looked up** the answer. He **looked** the answer **up**. He **looked** it **up**.

Some phrasal verbs occur only in this discontinuous form, that is, with an 'interrupting' participant. For example:

> He **put** me **up** to it. (Meaning he persuaded or encouraged or challenged me to do it.)

If you had difficulty understanding phrasal verbs, you may find it useful to read sections 5.8 and 5.9 in your reference grammar.

The corpus findings on the register distribution of phrasal verbs (Biber et al., 1999, section 5.3.2.2) are especially useful. To quote:

> Overall, phrasal verbs are used most commonly in fiction and conversation; they are relatively rare in academic prose. In fiction and conversation, phrasal verbs occur almost 2000 times per million words.

> The distribution of phrasal verbs closely matches that for lexical verbs generally, except that academic prose has fewer than would be expected. Thus, rather than being a marked feature of conversation, phrasal verbs are notably rare in academic prose.

> (Biber et al., 1999, pp. 408–9)

5 ACTIVE AND PASSIVE VOICE

In the last two sections we considered how verb phrases can consist of more than one lexical verb to form a verb phrase complex, and a lexical verb plus another element such as a preposition to form a phrasal verb. We now consider, in this last section on the verb phrase, how the verb phrase changes its structure depending on whether it is in the 'active voice' or 'passive voice'.

You are probably familiar with the contrast between clauses which are in the active voice and those in the passive voice. By way of a very brief review, let us examine the contrast using material processes.

See Foundation Grammar for an introduction to active voice and passive voice.

In the **active voice**, the 'doer' of the action occurs before the verb, as the subject, and the 'done-to' occurs after the verb. For example:

The police	didn't release	the driver's name
'doer' (participant)	material process	'done–to' (participant)
subject	verb phrase	

In the **passive voice**, the 'done-to' is the subject of the clause, as in the following example:

The driver's name	was not released	by the police
'done–to' (participant)	material process	'doer' (participant)
subject	verb phrase	

The structure of the verb phrase in a passive voice clause differs from that in an active voice clause. The structure of the verb phrase in the passive voice usually contains a temporal finite (almost always a form of the verb 'to be') plus the past participle of the lexical verb. So, from the examples above:

The driver's name	was	released	by the police
	temporal finite	lexical verb	

ACTIVITY 7 (allow about 10 minutes)

Identify each of the following clauses as active or passive.

1   The exam supervisor came running over.

2   Genes do influence the rate of ageing.

3   Genetic effects on ageing can be understood only as a side-effect of something else.

4   Ageing is caused by the accumulation of damage.

5   They had the middle seat empty.

6   Birds live longer than comparably sized mammals.

7   There's something on my foot.

8   Many of the genes that slow ageing are involved in the response to changing nutrient levels.

See 'Answers to the activities' for feedback.

If you still find differentiating active clauses from passive clauses difficult, read section 6.6 in your reference grammar for a detailed description.

There appear to be conflicting messages about whether we should use the passive voice or avoid it. It is not possible to pick up and argue these views, but we can outline at least two things that the passive voice allows us to do. One is that it allows us to hide who carries out an action, e.g. 'The swimming pool was shut down' instead of 'The council shut down the swimming pool'. The second is that it allows information in a text to be organised strategically according to the writer's objectives. In other words, does the context pressure us to begin with 'The swimming pool' or 'The council'? These two important aspects, agency and information flow, will be taken up in later units in this course.

At this point, let us return to the different choices made in spoken and written modes to see what happens in terms of active and passive voice. We shall examine two texts to identify the use of the passive voice and the active voice.

ACTIVITY **8** (allow about 20 minutes)

Compare the use of the passive voice in Text 3 and Text 4, i.e. which uses the passive voice more often? Why do you think this is?

Text 3

Ageing is caused by the accumulation of damage, and no gene has evolved specifically to cause damage and debility. Yet genes do influence the rate of ageing. Birds live longer than comparably sized mammals, which suggests that the rate of ageing evolves. And mutations in single genes can increase the lifespans of laboratory animals. Many of these genes have been identified and are known to encode normal constituents of cells and endocrine systems. So why has natural selection favoured the wild-type form of the gene rather than a mutant trait that extends lifespan?

Genetic effects on ageing can be understood only as a side-effect of something else. Genes that slow ageing could exert these effects because they repress the causes of ageing related damage. Reproduction seems to be one of these sources of damage, because fecundity is often reduced both during the evolution of slow ageing and by single-gene mutations that extend lifespan. Food seems to be another damage source, because many of the genes that slow ageing are involved in the response to changing nutrient levels. And reducing food intake slows down ageing in organisms ranging from yeast to mammals.

(Partridge and Gems, 2002, p. 921)

Text 4

S3: Actually, over at Manly along the promenade, if you walk along there at night, they're that big [gesture] – they're huge but they're, they're a different ... um brand

S2: Big roaches, are they?

S3: Yeah, they're big ones, real big ones.

S1: I remember we were sitting for our analytical chemistry exam and it was the final exams and they have sort of like bench desks where there's three to a bench normally and they had the middle seat empty and two sat either side and I was sitting there and I thought 'Geez I can feel something on my foot.'

S2: uuhh

S1: And I thought 'No, no, don't worry about it,' you know 'what on earth is this chemical equation?' and I am trying to think 'but there's something on my foot!' and I looked down and there was this cockroach like this [gesture] – and I just screamed and jumped up on the chair and as I did that I knocked the bench and it went up and all Geoff's exam stuff went into the bin next to him, and I was standing on this chair screaming and the exam supervisor came running over, 'what's going on there?' [laughs] And I said, 'there's a cockroach down there' [laughs] 'cause you're not allowed to speak, sneeze, cough, anything in those final exams, and um, there's me screaming on the chair.

(Eggins and Slade, 1997, p. 228)

COMMENT

Text 3, which belongs to the academic register, has quite frequent use of the passive voice. (See 'Answers to the activities' for an analysis of this text.) There is only one example of a passive construction in Text 4 (*you're not allowed*).

This compares favourably with the findings of the LSWE corpus (Biber et al., 1999, Section 11.3), which describe the academic register as having the greatest frequency of all types of passive construction and conversation as having by far the least.

Was your reason for this contrast based on the differences discussed so far between spoken language and written language? The main aspect to consider is what the writer or speaker chooses to put first in the clause.

In spoken texts, the speaker is presenting his/her perspective, also the speaker is usually the 'doer'. The active voice is therefore the dominant choice.

Last in this unit, we look at two other types of phrase – adjective phrases and adverb phrases.

⑥ ADJECTIVE PHRASES

Adjective phrases have an adjective as the head word, which can be modified in a similar way to the way a noun head word can be modified in a noun phrase.

Adjective phrases are used in noun phrases; these are typically the describers in the noun phrase that we looked at in Unit 4. They can also function as a participant in a relational process. This was touched on in the examples given for relational processes in this unit.

Here are some examples of adjective phrases (a single adjective is regarded as a phrase). The adjective head is in bold:

really **big**

most **obnoxious**

too **cold** to go for a swim

happy to go along

bad enough

Let us look at the two main roles for adjective phrases which we have mentioned above: as describers in a noun phrase and as the second participant in a relational process.

6.1 As describer in a noun phrase

Adjective phrases can take on several of the premodifying functions in a noun phrase: classifier, describer and numerative. Our focus here is on the describer. In the following examples, the noun phrase is underlined and the adjective phrase is in bold:

He gave an **electric** performance.

It was a **natural** way to end the story.

A **rather pot-bellied** man came into the store.

His **white** shirts were well washed but never pressed.

Fiction gives us some interesting examples of the use of adjectives. The following examples are from *The Hotel New Hampshire* by John Irving.

These examples show that adjectives, like other word classes, can form complexes. The second is a very intricate example of a multiple-adjective phrase inside a long noun phrase. (The noun phrases are underlined and the adjective phrases are in bold.)

His **cheap and slightly shiny navy-blue** suit was unusually clean but wrinkled.

He was not the **limp, low-key sort of lazy-weary, sluggish (or at least lethargic)** talker he was when his subject was the revolution.

In this next example, there are adjectives premodifying and postmodifying the head noun (*face*):

He had an **almost athletic** face, **scrubbed, youthful, determined**.

This last example, where describers come after the head word, breaks the usual order of the elements in an English noun phrase. We expect describers to come before the head word. Fiction allows us to play around with some of the elements of the noun phrase whereas non-fiction is less flexible.

6.2 A participant in a relational process

An adjective phrase can take a participant role in a relational process clause.

Relational processes set up a relationship between two participants. They are typically realised by the verbs 'to be' and 'to have' and their synonyms (e.g. *mean, become, consist of, be called*). In the following examples, the adjective phrase is in bold:

That's **right**.

He's **totally crazy**.

The radio was **so loud**.

Once again the motoring press is **euphoric**.

As we have seen above, where the adjective phrase is functioning as a modifier it is possible to have adjective phrase complexes. Again from John Irving's *Hotel New Hampshire*, we have the following examples (adjective phrase complexes are in bold):

His white shirts were **well washed but never pressed**.

His cheap and slightly shiny navy-blue suit was **unusually clean but wrinkled**.

Just as it is possible to premodify the head adjective, it is also possible to postmodify it. In the following examples, the adjective phrase is underlined and the head adjective is in bold:

It's <u>too **hot** to handle</u>.

It's <u>very **close** to the bone</u>.

At this point, having seen several examples of adjective phrases as participants, we consider why an adjective phrase can be regarded as a participant in the relational process, seeing as participants are usually noun phrases.

The answer lies in taking the perspective that the adjective phrase is, in a sense, a 'truncated' noun phrase. For example, 'a happy man' is reduced to 'happy' in:

John is a **happy man**.

John is a **happy one**.

John is **happy**.

Similarly:

The Rover 75 Tourer is **the ultimate car**.

The Rover 75 Tourer is **the ultimate**.

The last example is close to examples of an adjective functioning as the head of a noun phrase, as in the following (noun phrases are underlined and head words are in bold):

Policies like these only support the **rich**.

These people may be the real working **poor**, the **elderly**, the very **young**, the **unemployed** or the **transient**.

The **latter** are known vectors of certain rickettsial organisms.

Labelling the clauses according to the functional groups, i.e. as participants, processes and circumstances, we have the following.

The radio	was	so loud
It	's	too hot to handle
John	is	happy
His white shirts	were	well washed but never pressed
participant	process	participant
noun phrase	verb phrase	adjective phrase

 ADVERB PHRASES

Adverb phrases are used in other phrases – noun phrases and prepositional phrases – and can also be used as circumstance and stance adverbials.

See Foundation Grammar and your reference grammar for adverbials.

An adverb phrase has an adverb as its head word and may have other adverbs to modify it. In each of the following adverb phrases, the head adverb is in bold:

so **beautifully**

hardly **ever**

very **smoothly**

luckily enough

Adverb phrases can play the following roles.

1   Modify another adverb or adjective:

Yeah, they're big ones, **really** big ones.

I used to call in and see Dad in the office **fairly** often.

2   Express some kind of interpersonal meaning through **stance adverbials**:

There's three to a bench **normally**.

The cockroach is **probably** the most obnoxious insect known to man.

Apparently, he was flying through the air with one leg up in the air.

3   Realise circumstances:

Its importance is becoming **more fully** recognised.

She smiled **sweetly**.

I used to call in and see Dad in the office fairly **often**.

4   Modify prepositions:

He was **immediately** behind me.

ACTIVITY 9 (allow about two hours)

Now read Sections 4.1, 4.2 and 4.3 of Jim Martin's article 'Grammatical Structure: What Do We Mean?', which is Chapter 4 in your course reader *Applying English Grammar*.

In much of Book 1, you have been looking at how grammatical form relates to grammatical function. Jim Martin's article takes you through different grammatical traditions which take different approaches to form and function. As you work through the reading, think in particular about the essential difference between class labelling and functional labelling.

You will meet the term **'predicator'** in this article. A short explanation of the term in the context of the reading follows.

A verb phrase is made up of one or more words. Often there is a finite which encodes primary tense or the speaker's opinion, as in the following examples:

Why is he arguing with me? (The temporal finite *is* encodes primary tense.)

He could agree with me now and again. (The modal finite *could* encodes the speaker's opinion.)

The rest of the verb phrase is referred to as the 'predicator'. This is because it is the basis for the predication, i.e. validation, of the rest of the clause.

ACTIVITIES **CD-ROM** (allow about two hours)

Now work through the activities for Unit 5 on the Activities CD-ROM.

Conclusion

The focus of this unit has been on the verb phrase and its function in a clause. In Units 4 and 5, you have seen how phrases can function at different levels, sometimes at the clause level and sometimes within other phrases. In this respect, you have begun to understand the complex links between phrases. You have also begun to see the relationships between the form of a phrase and its function. You have developed an understanding of this by looking at naturally occurring spoken and written texts.

You will be applying your knowledge of these aspects of phrases in later units in this course.

Learning outcomes

After completing this unit, you should have developed your knowledge and understanding of:

◆ differences between speech and writing through a knowledge of the verb phrase

◆ how English can be organised at the level of the verb phrase according to function.

In the light of your increased understanding, you should be able to:

◆ analyse verb phrases with a focus on function

◆ interpret frequency tables in relation to the verb phrase.

Key terms introduced and revisited

active voice	noun phrase
adjective phrase	participant
adverb phrase	passive voice
aspect	phrasal verb
auxiliary verb	predicator
circumstance	prepositional phrase
circumstance adverbial	process
finite	question tag
interrogative clause	relational process
lexical verb	stance adverbial
material process [action process, activity verb]	temporal finite [primary auxiliary]
mental process [mental verb]	verb phrase [verbal group, verb group]
modal finite [modal auxiliary, modal verb]	verb phrase complex
modality	verbal process [saying process, communication verb]

Near equivalents are given in [ ].

Answers to the activities

ACTIVITY 2

1a 'Come <A> over here, Linnea,'

1b said <S> Mr. Bloom.

2a 'Why?' I asked, <S>

2b because I hadn't noticed <M> *that* little picture before.

3a 'This is <R> an important painting in art history,'

3b explained <S> Mr. Bloom.

4 'It's called <R> Impression–Sunrise. ('is called' is a synonym of 'is')

5 Monet painted <A> his *impression* of sunlight reflected in the water.
   ...

6a They thought <M>

6b painting impressions of the moment was <R> a waste of time. (The clause *painting impressions of the moment* is an embedded clause and so functions as a single participant in this clause, i.e. [[*painting impressions of the moment*]] *was a waste of time.*)

7 Paintings should be <R> precise.

Embedded clauses were mentioned in Unit 4 and are discussed further in Unit 6.

ACTIVITY 6

A clause boundary is indicated by ‖.

1 I kept watching the film. <one process>

2 I started watching the show. <one process>

3 I went ‖ to find my sister. <two processes>

4 I managed to find my sister. <one process>

5 I stayed up ‖ to see the film. <two processes>

6 I remembered to see the film. <one process>

7 I tried to find my sister. <one process>

ACTIVITY 7

In the analyses of the passive voice clauses, the part of the verb phrase that is the form of the verb 'to be' is in bold. The remaining part of the verb phrase is, therefore, the past participle.

1 The exam supervisor came running over. <active>

2 Genes do influence the rate of ageing. <active>

3   Genetic effects on ageing **can be** understood only as a side-effect of something else. <passive>

In (3) there is also the modal auxiliary *can*.

4   Ageing **is** caused by the accumulation of damage. <passive>

5   They <u>had</u> the middle seat empty. <active>

6   Birds <u>live</u> longer than comparably sized mammals. <active>

7   There'<u>s</u> something on my foot. <active>

8   Many of the genes that slow ageing **are** involved in the response to changing nutrient levels. <passive>

ACTIVITY 8

Analysis of Text 3 for passive clauses

The passive verb phrases are in bold.

Ageing **is caused** by the accumulation of damage, and no gene has evolved specifically to cause damage and debility. Yet genes do influence the rate of ageing. Birds live longer than comparably sized mammals, which suggests that the rate of ageing evolves. And mutations in single genes can increase the lifespans of laboratory animals. Many of these genes **have been identified** and **are known** to encode normal constituents of cells and endocrine systems. So why has natural selection favoured the wild-type form of the gene rather than a mutant trait that extends lifespan?

Genetic effects on ageing **can be understood** only as a side-effect of something else. Genes that slow ageing could exert these effects because they repress the causes of ageing related damage. Reproduction seems to be one of these sources of damage, because fecundity **is** often **reduced** both during the evolution of slow ageing and by single-gene mutations that extend lifespan. Food seems to be another damage source, because many of the genes that slow ageing **are involved** in the response to changing nutrient levels. And reducing food intake slows down ageing in organisms ranging from yeast to mammals.

Unit 6

Understanding complexity in and around clauses

Prepared for the course team by Brian Dare

CONTENTS

Material required

To study this unit, you will need:

>   your reference grammar (Sections 3 and 4)
>   the course reader (at end of unit)
>   the course CD-ROMs (at end of unit).

Knowledge assumed

From Unit 3:

>   clause
>   grammatical unit
>   participant, process, circumstance
>   rank scale
>   qualifier.

From Unit 4:

>   participant realised by noun phrase
>   circumstance realised by prepositional phrase.

From Unit 5:

>   circumstance realised by adverbial phrase
>   mental and verbal processes
>   process realised by verb phrase.

Introduction

Read the following reports – SUV is an acronym for sports utility vehicle.

> The SUV was speeding up on my bumper as I was trying to get over into another lane and had on no signal and then when I did not get over fast enough the driver sped up went around me cut me off while swearing, cursing, and honking.
>
> (Roadragers, 2003)

> The phenomenon known as 'road rage' emerged and attracted much attention in the news media in the 1990s. This article reports the findings from a study on representations and understandings of road rage in Australia. Over 600 news items published between 1995 and 2000 in the two major Sydney newspapers (the *Sydney Morning Herald* and the *Daily Telegraph*) were analysed using discourse analysis.
>
> (Upton, 2001, pp. 23–5)

If you have ever experienced a sports utility vehicle speeding up on your bumper doing the kinds of thing reported above as you drive along carefully in your own lane, you may be tempted to go to the same Roadragers website and write a report on your particular case of road rage. Your text might look very much like the first text above. However, if you are a university researcher writing up your research on the phenomenon of road rage you are likely to produce something closer to the second text. While these texts are both concerned with road rage, they are very different texts which represent the experience of road rage in very different ways.

Each of the above texts consists of more than a single clause. Both consist of a series of clauses joined in particular ways to construct an angle on the same phenomenon of road rage. What then are the resources for joining one clause to another that these writers draw on, and what role do these choices play in representing this phenomenon? As we shall see later in this unit, these two texts have different kinds of complexity and simplicity which are closely connected to the ways the clauses in each text are combined together.

In Unit 3 you looked at the different ways words can combine to form phrases (groups) and how these in turn combine to form clauses. You were also introduced to the functional groupings participant, process and circumstance. As you saw in Unit 4, participants are typically realised by noun phrases. And in Unit 5 you saw that processes are realised by verb phrases and, in Units 4 and 5, that circumstances are realised by adverbial and prepositional phrases.

The focus in this unit shifts from a close examination of the constituents of these various phrases to the ways in which they can combine to make a clause, and then to how clauses can combine as clause complexes. As we shall see, these more complicated grammatical structures can be achieved in two main ways:

(1) by linking together two or more clauses to form 'clause complexes'

(2) by inserting a clause within the structure of another clause to form an 'embedded clause'.

As with previous units, we shall be considering how these structures vary across spoken and written language. As we shall see, particular patterns in terms of clause combinations will show up in each mode.

◆ FUNDAMENTAL UNIT OF MEANING: THE CLAUSE

Before proceeding to looking at clause complexes, it is important that you are clear about what constitutes a clause and that you can identify individual clauses within texts. The work you did in Unit 3 will be useful here as we revisit the notion of what constitutes a clause. Understanding the make-up of a clause will be helpful in understanding the next part of the unit, where we focus on the ways clauses can combine to form larger stretches of text.

Within the various ranks of grammatical categories (word, phrase, clause and clause complex) the clause has a special status or function. The clause is a fundamental unit in the process of communication because it is the minimal unit which can stand alone as constituting a complete message. Apart from one-word imperatives like 'Go!', 'Stop!' and 'Run!', individual words – 'old', 'man', 'the', 'goes' – do not, in isolation, constitute a complete message; nor do phrases – 'will', 'be going', 'on Monday', 'the old man from the town'. It is only when words are gathered together into phrases and then phrases are gathered together into a clause that we have a complete, potentially free-standing message – 'The old man cut the cake on Monday'. This fundamental unit of meaning structure in English is the clause and it is to that we now turn.

A useful way to begin thinking about a clause is to see it as a unit of meaning built up around a process, a central 'going on', which could be a kind of action (jumping, leaving, giving), some kind of sensing (thinking, seeing, feeling), saying (saying, stating, claiming), having (having, owning, possessing) or being (being, relating, concerning). In Unit 3 we saw how every clause has one such process, which can have participants of one kind or another involved (*people* leave, *the dog* jumped *the fence*, *her thoughts* wandered, *they* owned *several cars*, *the cars* were *rusty*). Clauses can also contain circumstances, which provide additional information as to when, where and how the participants were involved in the process (people leave *early*, the dog jumped the fence *easily*, the cars were rusty *because of the salt water*).

Clauses, then, can range from those with one process only to those with a process and a number of participants and circumstances.

A simple text will illustrate some of these possibilities.

Text 1

Last week Maria and I went to the city on the 311 bus. When we got there we went to 'Toys 'r' Us' to buy some games for my sister's birthday. I bought her a book and a Nintendo and she liked them.

(Adapted from an unpublished student text © Lexis Education)

If we now break this text into its component clauses and identify all the participants, processes and circumstances, we obtain the following analysis.

Last week	Maria and I	went	to the city	on the 311 bus
circumstance	participant	process	circumstance	circumstance

When	we	got	there
conjunction	participant	process	circumstance

we	went	to 'Toys 'r' Us'
participant	process	circumstance

to buy	some games	for my sister's birthday
process	participant	circumstance

I	bought	her	a book and a Nintendo
participant	process	participant	participant

and	she	liked	them
conjunction	participant	process	participant

While these examples represent many of the possible permutations, the list is not exhaustive. However, there is a limited number of possibilities in English in terms of the combinations of the above groupings. As a minimal requirement we need one process. The number of participants can vary from one to three although there is only a small group of processes that can involve three participants (verbs like 'give', 'offer' and 'send', where you can give something to someone, offer someone something and send someone something). We can add a number of circumstances, but once we move beyond three or four it begins to sound very unusual. There is also the possibility of a clause having a conjunction when linking a clause to another clause.

A structural perspective on major clause patterns can be found in section 5.7 of your reference grammar.

Recognising the clause as a combination of these groupings opens up a range of potential understandings about language. It will help us to see, for example, that in any given clause certain elements in the clause can be shifted to the front of the clause and how this affects the meaning. As we have seen in Unit 3, it also allows us to explore patterns across texts as well as aspects such as active and passive voice and the mobility of certain groupings (conjunctions are far less mobile than circumstances, for example).

1.1 Establishing clause boundaries

Where does one clause begin and another end?

Having a strong sense of the composition of the clause and seeing it as the fundamental unit of meaning, made up of the various groupings, will be useful in helping us to identify where one clause ends and the next begins, i.e. the clause boundary. As we work our way through the unit we shall add a number of other identification procedures that will further assist you.

In order to develop your ability to identify clause boundaries, we shall go back to Text 1 used at the beginning of this section. Using the symbol ‖ to indicate a clause boundary, the text would be analysed as follows.

> Last week Maria and I went to the city on the 311 bus. ‖ When we got there ‖ we went to 'Toys 'r' Us' ‖ to buy some games for my sister's birthday. ‖ I bought her a book and a Nintendo ‖ and she liked them.

One of the keys to identifying clause boundaries in this text, as with all texts, is to see that each clause must have a process. You will notice that between each symbol ‖, there is at least one process. So a first step is to identify all the processes within the text. In the above text we would identify the processes *went*, *got*, *went*, *to buy*, *bought* and *liked*.

Once the processes have been identified, a number of other aspects can help you identify the boundaries:

◆ With written language, full stops indicate a clause boundary (strictly speaking, this indicates a clause complex boundary – see later).

◆ Intonation patterns provide a guide.

◆ Commas (which in written language reflect intonation) often, but not always, mark clause boundaries.

◆ We can use conjunctions as one of the key indicators because of their position near or at the beginning of a new clause. In the above text, for example, we can see *When* and *and* (we could include the implicit *in order* in front of *to buy*) as the beginning of new clauses.

◆ Another helpful test is to see if the clause is moveable as a unit. For example, in the clause combination *When we got there ‖ we went to 'Toys 'r' Us' ‖ to buy some games for my sister's birthday*, could (although it sounds a bit awkward) be changed to *We went to 'Toys 'r' Us' when we got there, to buy some games for my sister's birthday.*

Unit 3, Sections 2 to 4 gave three useful perspectives for identifying clauses: the clause as a representation of experience, as an interpersonal move, and as a package of information. Clause identification will be an important foundation for many analytical techniques presented later in the course, especially in Section 4 of Unit 9 and Section 5 of Unit 11 in Book 2; Unit 13 and Section 3 of Unit 14 in Book 3; and Section 2.2 of Unit 17 and Section 2 of Unit 20 in Book 4. These sections contain further illustration of clause division in the example texts.

◆ A further guide to identifying clause boundaries, but not evident in this text, is the presence of grammatical elements like 'who', 'which', 'whose', 'where' and 'when'. These will be explored further on in the unit when we discuss different kinds of clause.

ACTIVITY 1 (allow about 15 minutes)

Using the above guide to identifying clause boundaries, carry out an initial clause boundary analysis of Text 2, a short spoken text from Biber et al. (1999, p. 1069).

Before you start the analysis, read the text aloud and see if you can establish the points at which there is a change in the intonation or where there is a distinct pause.

When you think you have found the boundary, insert the symbol ‖, which we use to mark a clause boundary.

What do you notice about the words that follow a clause boundary?

Text 2

The trouble is if you're the only one in the house he follows you and you're looking for him and every time you're moving around he's moving behind you so you can't find him. I thought I wonder where the hell he's gone I mean he was immediately behind me.

COMMENT

Compare your analysis with the following.

Text 2 (annotated)

The trouble is ‖ if you're the only one in the house ‖ he follows you ‖ and you're looking for him ‖ and every time you're moving around ‖ he's moving behind you ‖ so you can't find him. ‖ I thought ‖ I wonder ‖ where the hell he's gone ‖ I mean ‖ he was immediately behind me.

How did you get on? Don't worry if you didn't get them all right, particularly if this is the first time you have attempted such an analysis. Did you pick up the fact that a number of the clauses begin with a conjunction (*if* you're, *and* you're, *and* every time, *so* you)? The falling intonation at the end of each clause may have been helpful as well. Notice how each clause contains a process.

Identifying clause boundaries, particularly with spoken texts like Text 2, can be quite tricky because of the presence of 'non-clausal units'.

Non-clausal units are defined as structural units that are not composed of clauses. **Non-clausal material** is defined as the parts of the text which do not consist of clauses.

ACTIVITY 2 (allow about 20 minutes)

Read sections 8.1.1, 8.14 and 13.4 in your reference grammar. These sections outline why non-clausal language is more common in conversation than in writing. (Section 13.4 mentions 'independent clauses'. You will be learning about these later in this unit.)

COMMENT

Identifying clause boundaries in written language is more straightforward because clausal units predominate. However, written texts have other kinds of complexities, such as 'embedded clauses'. This will be followed up later in this unit.

② RANK SCALE

The rank scale looks at language hierarchically.

In the previous units, you have been looking at groupings of various kinds: different word classes (e.g. nouns, adjectives, conjunctions), and various functional groupings and their realisations (participants realised through noun phrases, processes realised through verb phrases, circumstances realised through adverbial and prepositional phrases). We saw above how participants, processes and circumstances can combine in certain ways with other groupings such as conjunctions to give a larger grouping: the clause. We now begin to explore the way in which clauses of various kinds can combine together into larger stretches of language known as **clause complexes**.

In order to develop a more thorough picture of how language works to make meaning at all these different levels, we elaborate on the notion of a rank scale introduced in Unit 3. In the scale that we use here, there are four levels: the clause/clause complex level, the phrase level, the word level and the morpheme level. We can work at all these various levels at different times when talking about language. For instance, if you were concerned about which word class a word belonged to, you would be working at the word level. If, as a teacher, you were concerned with a child's spelling, you would be looking at this level and possibly at the morpheme level as well. In Units 3, 4 and 5, you looked at the composition of phrases and so were working at the phrase level. The focus of this unit is on the clause/clause complex level.

We illustrate this notion of a rank scale through a simple example. Consider the following clause complex (see a later discussion on 'clause complex' versus 'sentence').

> Even though every room in the school had an air conditioner, the heat was unbearable.

In separating this clause complex into its various ranks, we can see that this clause complex is made up of two clauses, which in turn are made up of a number of phrases, which in turn are made up a number of words. We can represent this diagrammatically as follows.

Rank	Clause complex						
clause	Even though every room in the school had an air conditioner,‖the heat was unbearable.						
phrase	Even though	every room in the school	had	an air conditioner,	the heat	was	unbearable.
	conjunction	participant	process	participant	participant	process	circumstance
word	Even | though | every | room | in | the | school | had | an | air | conditioner, | the | heat | was | unbearable.						
morpheme	Even-though-every-room-in-the-school-had-an-air-condition-er,-the-heat-was-un-bear-able.						

What we have here are the grammatical constituents of a clause complex ranked hierarchically. At the highest rank, the clause complex is made up of two clauses: *Even though every room in the school had an air conditioner* and *the heat was unbearable*. These clauses are made up of phrases (participants, processes, conjunctions) from the rank below. These phrases (which are at the rank of phrase) are made of words (from the rank of word), which are made up of morphemes (from the rank of morpheme). As we shall see, this rank system will be helpful in understanding how meaning is made at and below the clause level.

You may be wondering why we don't use the term 'sentence' in the place of 'clause complex', since the term 'sentence' is used widely in traditional grammar books. The sentence is essentially a phenomenon of written language – it can be identified as a stretch of words beginning with a capital letter and ending with a full stop. This signalling obviously cannot apply to spoken language. This doesn't mean that there aren't signals in spoken language that indicate boundaries of different kinds. It just means that a more useful unit to be working with in spoken language is the clause complex. So in order to use a unit that is equally applicable to written and spoken language we shall use the term 'clause complex' instead of 'sentence'. A clause complex in these terms is also considered to be at the same rank as a clause.

With this understanding, we now turn to clause complexes.

❸ COMBINING CLAUSES INTO CLAUSE COMPLEXES

In the same way that we looked to see how phrases combined to make up clauses, we now explore how clauses can join together to form clause complexes.

Clause complexes are the highest or broadest-scale rank/level of grammatical constituent. Clause complexes are formed through the linking of individual clauses. Thus the string of words *You can finish your essay now while I organise some food for tonight* is a clause complex made up of two clauses: *You can finish your essay now* and *while I organise some food for tonight*. Each of these units constitutes a clause because each has its own separate process (*can finish* and *organise*) with each process surrounded by its own associated participants and circumstances. Clause complexes, accordingly, are said to be constituted of one or more clauses.

There are two ways that clauses can be linked to form clause complexes:

♦ **coordination** – where two potentially independent grammatically equal clauses are linked, generally through conjunctions like 'and', 'but' and 'or'.

♦ **subordination** – where a potentially independent primary clause is linked with a dependent or secondary clause which could not operate independently. This kind of linking is generally achieved through conjunctions like 'while', 'because' and 'although' and through relative pronouns like 'who' and 'which'.

The terms 'independent', 'dependent', 'primary' and 'secondary' are explained below.

An **independent clause** is one which stands by itself and has equal status to the other clause or clauses it is being linked with. A **dependent clause** (subordinate clause), on the other hand, is not able to stand alone.

3.1 Combining independent clauses through coordination

Consider the following text where someone is talking about a dog that they have recently bought. The clause boundaries are included and are indicated by ‖.

Text 3

I bought a dog as a pet ‖ but I wanted a good one ‖ so I bought a show quality dog ‖ and the lady [[I bought the dog from]] worked at the same place as my father ‖ and I used to call in and see Dad in

The clauses in square brackets are 'embedded clauses'. They are discussed later in this unit.

the office fairly often ‖ once I bought the dog ‖ and she got me along to a couple of dog shows ‖ and I got interested in it that way ‖ and started showing the dog [[that she'd bred]] ‖ and it sort of snowballed from there.

(Plum, 1988)

Does this text sound like someone speaking or writing about their experiences? What do you think makes it easy to identify it as a spoken text? Did you notice the way one clause is added to the next clause, which is added to the next? What sort of conjunctions are prevalent in this text? How do you think this text would be different if it were a written text?

This text displays some of the typical features of spoken language. Note the way the clauses are added on through the conjunctions *and, so* and *but*. We can see how the speaker is using a number of very short clauses which are closely aligned with the flow of events that is unfolding here. A written version would construct the same set of events differently – we would be unlikely to see a sentence with the same number of clauses in it, for example.

A C T I V I T Y 3 (allow about 10 minutes)

From Text 3, you might predict that 'and' is used more frequently in spoken language. For an interesting discussion on the distribution of coordinators such as 'or', 'but' and 'and' across the registers and their use as phrase level coordinators (as in 'John and Gina' and in 'her commitment and enthusiasm') read section 8.4.1 of your reference grammar.

In both Text 2 (p. 160) and Text 3, the principal means by which the clauses are linked to each other is by coordination, where one independent clause is linked to another to form a clause complex. In both texts, a series of independent clauses are linked primarily through the coordinating conjunctions *but, and, or* and *then*.

Consider these following further examples of independent clauses linked in this way:

1   Mary plays the piano ‖ and John learns origami.
2   You can watch television ‖ or you can have a swim in the pool.
3   My brother loves performing ‖ but he hates practising.

We say that these are all independent clauses for the following reasons:

♦   They are all finite. This means that the verb phrases are marked for tense, which can be tested by the presence of a temporal finite or auxiliary (*are, will, does, didn't, has, is, shall*), or a modal finite or auxiliary (*may, might, can, could, ought to, should, won't, need*) in the verb phrase. A verb phrase which has the simple present (*I leave early, we wait at the bus stop*) or the simple past (*I left early, we waited at the bus stop*) is also finite.

◆ Each is capable of standing on its own without reference to the material to which it is linked.

The independent grammatical status of a clause is indicated by the possibility of reorganising the sequence of the clauses without significantly changing the meaning or rendering the clause complex ungrammatical. Thus these clause complexes could easily be reordered as follows.

1 John learns origami ‖ and Mary plays the piano.

2 You can swim in the pool ‖ or you can watch television.

3 My brother hates practising ‖ but he loves performing.

This is not always possible, even where the clauses are independent. Take the following example (where < > indicate an ellipsis).

4 He woke up ‖, < > rubbed his eyes ‖ and < > jumped out of bed.

These are still independent clauses even though the order cannot be changed. It cannot be changed because these clauses are linked closely to the unfolding events in the real world: he didn't get out of bed and then wake up. As well, the fact that two of the clauses have ellipted subjects makes it difficult to see them as independent because, in a sense, the second and third clauses are relying on the first to complete the meaning.

If we restore the ellipted items, they could, however, be written as three separate sentences:

He woke up. <He> rubbed his eyes. <He> jumped out of bed.

Another less common example of joining clauses through coordination is demonstrated in the following examples.

5 It was a small issue ‖: it never really bothered her.

6 Dogs are like humans ‖ – they have feelings.

Here the second clause further specifies the first clause and the link, at least in a written text, is provided by a colon or a dash.

3.2 Combining clauses through subordination

Now we turn to a further way of combining clauses into clause complexes: through subordination.

Consider the following extract from a film review of *Harry Potter and the Sorcerer's Stone*, based on J. K. Rowling's book. The review was written by David Ansen for *Newsweek* magazine.

Text 4

Chris Columbus's 'Harry Potter and the Sorcerer's Stone' may have made many hundreds of millions of dollars, but only kids seemed to be genuinely enthusiastic about it. (A lot of kids, to be sure.) Grown-ups, who were equally bewitched by J. K. Rowling's book, felt let down by the movie: it followed the letter of the tale but missed the spirit, mistaking special effects for magic. Would the filmmakers learn from their mistakes in the second instalment? Wanting to give the movie the benefit of the doubt, I avoided reading 'Harry Potter and the Chamber of Secrets' before I saw Columbus's follow-up. This time the twists and turns of Harry's adventures at Hogwarts – where he encounters even greater perils – could take me by surprise.

(Ansen, 2002)

Here the clauses are linked in a number of different ways. See if you can identify the two examples of clauses joined by coordination. The kinds of conjunction that are associated with coordination are *and*, *but*, *so* and *or*.

You would have found that there are two examples in this text, both involving the use of the conjunction *but*:

Chris Columbus's 'Harry Potter and the Sorcerer's Stone' may have made many hundreds of millions of dollars, **but** only kids seemed to be genuinely enthusiastic about it.

...it followed the letter of the tale **but** missed the spirit...

Focus now on the second sentence beginning *Grown-ups, who were...* . There are five processes in this sentence and so there are five clauses. One of the clauses, the one beginning *who were...* could easily be taken out of the sentence. Clauses like this are known as **interrupting** or **included clauses** and we use double chevrons << >> to mark the beginning and end of such clauses. We shall say more about these kinds of clause when we look at embedded clauses later in the unit.

Before looking at the analysis below, see if you can locate the five processes and then the clause boundaries in the second sentence.

The five clauses (with the processes in bold) are as follows. The empty chevrons << >> indicate the position of the interrupting clause.

1   Grown-ups, << >>, **felt let down** by the movie

2   <<who **were** equally **bewitched** by J. K. Rowling's book>>

3   it **followed** the letter of the tale

4   but **missed** the spirit,

5   **mistaking** special effects for magic.

The only example of coordination is between clauses (3) and (4).

The other clause complexes are joined by a different kind of clause linking known as subordination, where an independent clause is linked to a dependent clause – a dependent clause is one that cannot stand on its own as a sentence.

The clauses *who were equally bewitched by J. K. Rowling's book* and *mistaking special effects for magic* are both dependent and are linked to independent clauses. As such, both are examples of subordination.

ACTIVITY 4   (allow about 10 minutes)

Identify the three clauses in the second-to-last sentence and the two clauses in the last sentence (reproduced below) of Text 4. There is another interrupting clause in this text (the author marks it with dashes).

As a first step, locate all the clause boundaries. Can you identify the independent clause in each of these sentences? Once you have done that, identify the dependent clauses and, hence, further examples of subordination.

> Wanting to give the movie the benefit of the doubt, I avoided reading 'Harry Potter and the Chamber of Secrets' before I saw Columbus's follow-up. This time the twists and turns of Harry's adventures at Hogwarts – where he encounters even greater perils – could take me by surprise.

COMMENT

You should have found the clauses indicated in bold below as the independent clause in each sentence. And so the relationship between these clauses and the others in their respective sentences is one of subordination. There is also an example of an interrupting clause (whose position is indicated by the empty << >>), which is interrupting the independent clause.

> Wanting to give the movie the benefit of the doubt,
> **I avoided reading 'Harry Potter and the Chamber of Secrets'**
> before I saw Columbus's follow-up.
> **This time the twists and turns of Harry's adventures at Hogwarts**
> << >> **could take me by surprise**.
> <<where he encounters even greater perils>>

Subordination involves the linking of a potentially independent clause with one or more dependent clauses. Dependent clauses cannot stand alone and act to supply supportive, background or modifying information for other clauses, or act to elaborate or extend those **main clauses** in some way. So the dependent clause *Wanting to give the movie the benefit of the doubt* gives a reason why the author saw the film before reading the book. The interrupting dependent clause *where he encounters even greater perils* elaborates on Harry's school *Hogwarts*.

The term 'main clause' is used to indicate an independent clause to which other dependent clauses are subordinated. But see further discussion of the term on pages 175–6.

3.3 Circumstantial dependent clauses

ACTIVITY **5** (allow about 10 minutes)

Consider these examples of clause complexes involving subordination, which have been taken from Texts 1, 2, 3 and 4. Clause boundaries have been inserted.

Identify the dependent and independent clause in each example.

What differences are there between the dependent clauses across the six examples? Are you able to reverse the order of the clauses in each example? What happens to the conjunctions in (1) to (4) when you do this?

1   When we got there ‖ we went to 'Toys 'r' Us'

2   If you're the only one looking in the house ‖ he follows you

3   We left Keswick on the night train ‖ because it was the cheapest alternative

4   After collecting our luggage, ‖ we took a taxi to our relatives

5   <it>missed the spirit, ‖ mistaking special effects for magic

6   Wanting to give the movie the benefit of the doubt, ‖ I avoided reading 'Harry Potter and the Chamber of Secrets'

COMMENT

The bold indicates the independent clause in each example.

1   When we got there ‖ **we went to 'Toys 'r' Us'**

2   If you're the only one looking in the house ‖ **he follows you**

3   **We left Keswick on the night train** ‖ because it was the cheapest alternative

4   After collecting our luggage, ‖ **we took a taxi to our relatives**

5   <it>missed the spirit, ‖ mistaking special effects for magic
6   Wanting to give the movie the benefit of the doubt, ‖ I avoided reading 'Harry Potter and the Chamber of Secrets'

The non-bold parts are examples of subordination through what can be termed **circumstantial dependent clauses**: those which supply circumstantial or background information (similar to circumstances within a clause) – they tell: when, where, why, to what extent, for what purpose, in what manner, under what condition. They may also act to indicate that the main clause is in some way anomalous or contrary to expectation.

Circumstantial dependent clauses can begin with a subordinating conjunction such as *when, if, because, after*. The order of the main and the dependent clauses in such structures can be readily reversed. In the case of these subordinated structures, the conjunction 'binds' with the dependent clause. When we reordered the clauses, the conjunctions *when, if, because* and *after* remained with, i.e. were 'bound to', their original clause. This is in contrast to the clauses linked by coordinating conjunctions, where the conjunctions do not move with the clause.

There are also circumstantial dependent clauses without these 'binding' conjunctions. However, circumstantial dependent clauses of this kind are much less common.

3.4 Finite and non-finite clauses

Another useful distinction we can make here is between **finite** and **non-finite clauses**. In Unit 5, we introduced the notion of a finite verb phrase. To distinguish between finite and non-finite clauses we look to see if the verb phrase is marked for tense and modality. Finite verbs are marked for tense and modality, whereas non-finite verbs are not. Tense and modality can be tested by the presence of a temporal or a modal finite (auxiliaries) in the verb phrase. A verb phrase which has the simple present or the simple past is also finite. For example *He completed all his assignments* has tense marked by the '-ed'.

Extending this to clauses, we can say that a clause with a finite verb phrase is a finite clause and a clause with a non-finite verb phrase is a non-finite clause.

ACTIVITY 6 (allow about five minutes)

Go back to the examples in Activity 5 (p. 168) and indicate which of the dependent clauses are finite and which are non-finite.

COMMENT

The first three circumstantial dependent clauses (1), (2) and (3) are finite and the last three are non-finite. You will see from these examples that you can have non-finite clauses with a conjunction (*After collecting our luggage*) and non-finite clauses without conjunctions (*mistaking special effects for magic, Wanting to give the movie the benefit of the doubt*).

Further examples of non-finite circumstantial clauses are outlined in the table below. The dependent clauses in (8) and (11) are non-finite clauses involving the use of the '-ing' form of the verb. But, as you can see, they can also involve the '-ed' form as in (9) or the infinitive form of the verb as in (7).

7	To finish on top,	‖ they had to win every game.
	non-finite dependent clause	independent clause
8	Being a generous soul	‖ he bought everyone drinks.
	non-finite dependent clause	independent clause
9	Asked what he thought of his friend,	‖ he just went quiet.
	non-finite dependent clause	independent clause
10	In order to finish on time	‖ she took some short cuts.
	non-finite dependent clause	independent clause
11	By getting the application in early	‖ we gave ourselves a good chance.
	non-finite dependent clause	independent clause

Note that the non-finite dependent clause in (9) also contains an embedded *finite* clause: *what he thought of his friend.* Embedding will be discussed further in Section 6 of this Unit.

Because they are not realising tense or modality, non-finite circumstantial clauses are necessarily dependent clauses. We can also say that all independent clauses are finite.

Another point to make here, and one which we shall take up later when discussing embedding, is that we are more likely to see non-finite clauses in written language than in spoken language.

4 ELABORATING THROUGH RELATIVISERS

Let's now consider the two examples of subordination from Text 4 (the Harry Potter review) which involve the use of what your reference grammar terms a **relativiser** (see p. 282). A relativiser is either a relative pronoun (*which, who, whom, whose, that*) or a relative adverb (*where, when, why*).

1   Grown-ups, **who** were equally bewitched by J. K. Rowling's book, felt let down by the movie.
2   This time the twists and turns of Harry's adventures at Hogwarts – **where** he encounters even greater perils – could take me by surprise.

These kinds of clause are **relative clauses** and act to elaborate the main clause by adding details. The function of the elaborating clause is to specify the meaning of the main clause in some way – by clarifying it, giving more detail, restating it in different terms or by providing an example.

ACTIVITY 7 (allow about 10 minutes)

Now read the section on relative clauses in your reference grammar, pp. 279–80. At this point we focus on non-restrictive (non-defining) clauses, whose presence in a written text is often marked by a preceding comma. We shall deal with restrictive (which we shall call embedded clauses) towards the end of this unit.

COMMENT

Relative clauses may be classed by their function as either restrictive or non-restrictive.

Elaboration is the primary function of **non-restrictive relative clauses**. These are typically clauses beginning with the relative pronoun 'which' (often following a comma). For example:

He was mowing his front lawn, ‖ **which** had grown rapidly over the last few weeks.

We say that *which had grown rapidly over the last few weeks* is a clause because it has its own process with an associated set of participants and circumstances:

process = *had grown*
participant = *which* (the subject of the clause and standing in for *his front lawn*)
circumstances = *rapidly*; *over the last few weeks*.

Here we see that the which-clause acts to elaborate the main clause (*He was mowing his front lawn*) by providing additional information about the lawn.

Elaborating relative clauses can also begin with 'where' or 'when':

> He entered his old classroom, where he had suffered so many humiliations as a young boy.

Here the where-clause elaborates by providing additional details about one element of the main clause, about the *classroom*. We say this is a separate clause because it contains its own process – *had suffered* – and associated participants and circumstances:

> process = *had suffered*

> participants = *he; so many humiliations*

> circumstances = *as a young boy; where* (standing in for *in the classroom*).

Here in another example:

> Margot comes from a different era, **when** you had to show respect to your elders.

In this example, the when-clause gives specifying information about the *era*:

> process = *had to show*

> participants = *you; respect*

> circumstance = *to your elders; when* (standing in for *in that era*).

Elaborating (non-restrictive) relative clauses often begin with 'who' and these typically 'interrupt' the main clause. We call them interrupting clauses. Consider the following example:

> Frank Lloyd Wright, **who designed the Guggenheim**, is considered one of America's finest architects.

Here the main clause is *Frank Lloyd Wright is considered one of America's finest architects*. The elaborating clause *who designed the Guggenheim* has been placed in such a way that it interrupts that main clause. Once again, the function of the elaborating clause is to provide specification by giving additional details of one element of the main clause. It just happens that the clause is elaborating on an element which does not come at the end of the main clause.

Other types of clause, including non-finite clauses such as *looking up* in the example below, are able to interrupt the main clause in this way.

> The ball was moved inside and Zola, **looking up**, noticed an overlap by Babayaro down the left.

You have seen examples of interrupting clauses earlier in the unit. On p. 166 *who were equally bewitched by J. K. Rowling's book* is an elaborating relative clause that interrupts the main clause *Grown-ups felt let down by the movie*. On p. 167 *where he encounters even great perils* is an elaborating relative clause that interrupts the main clause *This time the twists and turns of Harry's adventures at Hogwarts could take me by surprise.*

To identify the boundaries of interrupting clauses we use double chevrons << >>. So the two examples above with clause boundaries written in would appear as follows.

1   Frank Lloyd Wright, <<**who designed the Guggenheim**>>, is considered one of America's finest architects.

2   The ball was moved inside ‖ and Zola, <<**looking up**>>, noticed an overlap by Babayaro down the left.

Alternatively these clause complexes can be written out with one clause per line as follows. (This style was used on pp. 166–7 for the interrupting clauses in the Harry Potter article.)

Clause complex (1):

(a)   Frank Lloyd Wright, << >>, is considered one of America's finest architects.

(b)   <<who designed the Guggenheim>>

Clause complex (2):

(a)   The ball was moved inside

(b)   and Zola, << >>, noticed an overlap by Babayaro down the left.

(c)   << looking up>>

⑤ REPORTING AND QUOTING

5.1 Reporting what others say – 'indirect speech'

There is one final type of clause complex which needs to be accounted for. This is to do with the resources we have in language for **quoting** what people said, either directly as in *She said 'I am leaving'* or indirectly as in *She said she was leaving*. We also have many ways of reporting what others think, once again as the direct kind of quote: *Alfred thought 'We will succeed'*. And if someone were **reporting** what Alfred thought they would say: *Alfred thought we would succeed*.

A C T I V I T Y **8** (allow about five minutes)

Identify the parts of Text 5 where someone is being quoted and where someone is reporting what someone said. When are quotation marks being used?

Text 5

A cry for help and a desperate struggle to reach safety failed tragically for scallop diver Paul Buckland yesterday.

Pulled aboard his boat after being savaged by a white pointer shark, the 23-year-old died in his deckhand's arms from his 'horrific' injuries.

Mr Buckland, a member of a well-known Port Lincoln family, was diving for scallops 1.8km offshore about 13km west of Smoky Bay on the West Coast when the shark struck about 12.30pm.

Family friend and experienced diver Norm Craig, who had been comforting the Buckland family, said last night: 'It's too early to say anything at the moment, it's all too raw right now.'

Chief Inspector Malcolm Schluter, officer in charge of the West Coast local service area, said Mr Buckland had been in the water for about five minutes when the shark struck.

'He surfaced and called out to his mate something about a shark,' he said. 'His mate was able to drag him aboard and then realised he suffered horrific injuries ... he died within a minute or two of being brought on the boat.'

It is understood that Mr Buckland's left leg was bitten off and he had severe torso wounds.

South Australian Ambulance spokesman Lee Francis said the shark had grabbed Mr Buckland as he was being pulled out of the water. The deckhand called for an ambulance at 12.41pm and sped to the Smoky Bay boat ramp.

(*The Advertiser*, South Australia 2002)

COMMENT

You may have found the following examples.

1 Family friend and experienced diver Norm Craig said last night: 'It's too early to say anything at the moment, it's all too raw right now.'

2 Chief Inspector Malcolm Schluter, officer in charge of the West Coast local service area, said Mr Buckland had been in the water for about five minutes when the shark struck.

3 'He surfaced and called out to his mate something about a shark,' he said. 'His mate was able to drag him aboard and then realised he suffered horrific injuries ... he died within a minute or two of being brought on the boat.'

4 South Australian Ambulance spokesman Lee Francis said the shark had grabbed Mr Buckland as he was being pulled out of the water.

This kind of quoting and reporting occurs when clauses organised around verbal processes (like *to say, to announce, to declare*) or mental processes (like *to believe, to understand, to think, to decide, to feel*) act to frame a subordinate clause.

You can see that there is a difference between (1) and (2) above. In (1), we get to read the exact words that the family friend, Norm Craig, spoke some time after the shark attack. In contrast in (2) we get the reported words of Chief Inspector Malcolm Schluter. His exact words might have been 'Poor bloke, he'd only been in the water for five minutes or so when it attacked'. These words get reconstrued into the 'indirect' *Mr Buckland had been in the water for about five minutes when the shark struck.*

So (1) and (3) are quoting and (2) and (4) are reporting.

Consider this example from the text:

It is understood that Mr Buckland's left leg was bitten off.

This is another example of reporting, although less obvious than the above. Less obvious because it may be that no one has said 'His leg was bitten off' as no one was certain that this did actually happen.

Both reporting and quoting represent further ways in which we can link clauses into clause complexes. As we shall see, reporting involves subordination and quoting involves coordination. We look at both these kinds of clause linking a little more technically now, beginning with two slightly shortened versions of the examples above. Consider the following examples.

1 Malcolm Schluter said Mr Buckland had been in the water for about five minutes

Malcolm Schluter said	‖ Mr Buckland had been in the water for about five minutes
main 'projecting' clause	dependent 'projected' clause

2 It is understood that Mr Buckland's left leg was bitten off

It is understood	‖ that Mr Buckland's left leg was bitten off
main 'projecting' clause	dependent 'projected' clause

Here we have what would traditionally be termed 'indirect speech', with the main clause 'indirectly' reporting what is said or thought. We call this main clause the **projecting clause** and the clause that it projects, the **projected clause**. Note that the structural element 'that' can be omitted as in (1). Where it does appear, it can signal that **projection** is taking place.

We have used the term 'main clause' here, where in some previous discussions of clause complexes we have used the term 'independent clause'. We do this because the projecting clause is clearly not capable of acting independently of the dependent clause that it frames or projects – *Malcolm Schluter said*, for example, is not so obviously capable of operating on its own.

Structures involving such indirect speech are seen as involving subordination – they involve a main projecting clause and a subordinate (dependent) projected clause.

The only kinds of process that can project in this way are mental (thinking, feeling, sensing) and verbal (saying) processes. Looking at the corpus reports (your reference grammar, Section 10.5.2), we see a number of interesting findings in regard to projection. We see, for example, that the verbs 'think', 'say', 'know' and 'see' are the four used most to project. Incidentally, they are also four of the top six most frequently used verbs in English (Biber et al., 1999, Section 5.2.2.1, p. 373). However, the way they are used differs across registers.

ACTIVITY 9 (allow about 10 minutes)

Now look at the table of corpus data in your reference grammar, Section 10.5.2.

Compare how often 'think' is used in conversation as against the written registers (see the rest of Section 10.5.2). What do you think explains the difference in frequency across these registers? What explanation does your reference grammar give for the low frequency of mental verbs like 'know' and 'think' in academic prose?

COMMENT

One explanation is that in academic registers there are more indirect ways of saying what you think, as in 'It is obvious that' which is in some sense equivalent to 'I think it is obvious that'. Another part of the explanation lies in the use of more nominalised forms of mental and communication verbs in academia. So instead of 'She thinks that', 'He believes that', 'They claim that', we find nominalised versions such as 'Her view that', 'His belief that' or 'Their claim that'.

Nominalised forms are abstract nouns formed from verbs or adjectives. See your reference grammar glossary on nominalisation.

5.2 Quoting what others say – 'direct speech'

In contrast to indirect speech, direct speech structures involve coordination. For example, using two shortened versions from Text 5:

1 Norm Craig said last night: 'It's too early to say anything at the moment.'

Norm Craig said last night: ‖ 'It's too early to say anything at the moment.'

  main projecting clause   independent projected clause

2 'He surfaced and called out to his mate something about a shark,' he said

He surfaced and called out to his mate something about a shark   ‖ he said

        independent projected clause   main projecting clause

Both the directly quoted clause and the projecting clause are treated as grammatically equal as both are, to some degree, independent.

Further examples of quoting are as follows. Examples (3) and (4) are from newspapers and (5) is from a narrative.

3 'The situation is a catastrophe. This applies to southern and northern Bohemia ... Prague is comparatively well off, but only in a relative sense,' said Foreign Minister Cyril Svoboda.

4 'He was a warrior of the sea and he died a warrior's death,' David said. 'He would do anything, he knew all the dangers as we all do.'

5 'I'm afraid you ain't fond of Miss Polly,' he grinned.

   'As if ever anybody could be fond of her!' scorned Nancy.

(Porter, 1987)

In (5) Porter has used the processes *grinned* and *scorned* as substitutes for the verbal processes 'said with a grin' and 'said scornfully'. This is a common stylistic choice in fiction where authors try to add variety to colour their texts. Often these choices are omitted in conversation.

⑥ EMBEDDING

Embedded phrases

A common form of embedding occurs at the rank of phrase when one phrase is put inside another phrase. Consider the following clause which we have seen earlier.

Even though every room in the school had an air conditioner...

The prepositional phrase *in the school* is acting as a qualifier inside the phrase *every room* [[*in the school*]]. Here, *in the school* is embedded in the phrase *every room in the school*. You met examples of this kind of embedding when looking at noun phrases in Unit 4.

Embedded clauses

Up to this point, most of the clause combinations considered have involved the linking together of clauses in a chain. Although some clauses were capable of operating independently and others were dependent, they nevertheless operated at the same level or rank of grammatical analysis. Thus, when we consider the possible levels at which we can identify grammatical constituents – words, phrases, clauses/clause complexes – we can say that all the clauses operated at the level of clause/clause complex, i.e. the highest or broadest level of analysis.

However, it is possible for clauses to operate at the lower grammatical rank of phrase. Consider the following example.

The first book [[she wrote]] was her best.

If we ask the question 'What was her best?', we get the answer *The first book she wrote,* which is therefore a participant realised as a noun phrase, with the clause *she wrote* **embedded** within it. Another way of saying this is to say that the clause *she wrote* has been downranked. This means that we no longer see this as a clause in its own right (i.e. independent), but as part of the noun phrase *The first book she wrote.* This downranking can occur when a clause is inserted (embedded) into a participant or a circumstance, typically to play a role in a noun phrase.

One of the most obvious situations where clauses operate at the lower level of phrase is when they act as the postmodifier of the head word of a noun phrase. For example:

1   People who are sixty-five must retire before the end of the year.

This example has two processes – *are* and *must retire* – and therefore might be said to contain two clauses. Well, this is true, but only in part, because one of the clauses is operating not at the rank of the clause but at the rank of phrase. Consider the role of *who are sixty-five*. Its function is to identify those people who must retire – those that have reached the age of sixty-five. In other words, not everyone has to retire, only those who are sixty-five. The role of this clause therefore is to identify which participant performs the process of retiring. The same role of identification could have been performed by, for example, a prepositional phrase ('at sixty-five' as in 'People at sixty-five').

But now consider the following clause complex.

> 2 Peter and Joan, who are sixty-five, must retire before the end of the year.

It is clear in (2) that the people who must retire before the end of the year are Peter and Joan. The clause *who are sixty-five* is interrupting the main clause and its function is to provide some additional information about Peter and Joan, not to identify them. It is not an embedded clause; it is an interrupting clause. If you read aloud both clause complexes (1) and (2), you will see that there is a difference in the intonation patterns across the two. Example (1) will be read with a single 'tone-group', whereas (2) has two separate tone-groups. This reflects the punctuation, with (2) having commas before and after the interrupting clause.

Intonation is the topic of Unit 7, where tone-groups are discussed in detail. A tone-group is the phonetic device that delivers one information unit, i.e. one block in the message that the speaker is communicating. A tone-group usually corresponds to a clause.

We could represent this diagrammatically as follows.

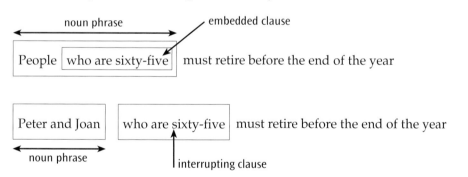

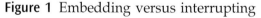

Figure 1 Embedding versus interrupting

We have already considered the role of these embedded clauses in postmodifying the head of a noun phrase – in Unit 4 we saw how they perform the role of qualifier in noun phrases (a function they share with prepositional phrases and adverbs). We can say that embedded clauses frequently occur as one part of a noun phrase – typically located after the head noun (in a postmodification position) – and operate to specify the head noun in some way. When embedded clauses function in this way they can be referred to as restrictive relative clauses. You have also been introduced to the use of double square brackets [[ ]] to indicate embedded clauses.

ACTIVITY **10** (allow about five minutes)

Both the following examples have embedded clauses. There is one embedded clause in (1) and two in (2). Using [[ ]], locate all three.

1 More than half of the health sector personnel surveyed for the new study had experienced at least one incident of physical or psychological violence in the previous year.

2 Some of the 200,000-plus residents who were evacuated from their homes were allowed to return to several areas of the city that escaped the worst of the flooding.

(Hanna, 2002)

COMMENT

Example (1) has two processes, *surveyed* and *had experienced*, so there are two clauses. However, one of the clauses *surveyed for the new study* is identifying the personnel who were surveyed and is therefore part of the noun phrase *More than half of the health sector personnel surveyed for the new study*. In other words it is embedded.

Example (2) has three processes, *were evacuated, were allowed to return* and *escaped*, indicating three clauses. If we ask the question 'Who were allowed to return?' we would get the answer *Some of the 200,000-plus residents who were evacuated from their homes*. In this participant/noun phrase the clause *who were evacuated from their homes* functions to identify which residents were allowed to return – those who had been evacuated. It is therefore an embedded clause.

Turning to the third process, *escaped*, we can apply the same procedure, only this time we ask the question 'Where were they allowed to return to?' and the answer would be *several areas of the city that escaped the worst of the flooding*. This therefore forms a circumstance in the main clause. We can see that the clause *that escaped the worst of the flooding* is now defining which area of the city the writer is talking about – the area that escaped the worst of the flooding. It is therefore an embedded clause.

So analysed, the above clauses would look as follows.

1 More than half of the health sector personnel [[surveyed for the new study]] had experienced at least one incident of physical or psychological violence in the previous year.

2 Some of the 200,000-plus residents [[who were evacuated from their homes]] were allowed to return to several areas of the city [[that escaped the worst of the flooding]].

There is one final form of embedded clause. Here the clause fills all of the noun phrase slot rather than merely being part of a larger noun phrase structure. When this happens, the clause functions as a participant in its own right in the clause structure. Here are some examples.

The best part	is	[[when they start arguing.]]
We	watched	[[the ship sailing away.]]
They	remembered	[[which way to go.]]
participant	process	embedded clause as participant

[[What I really hate]]	is	[[him being so smug.]]
embedded clause as participant	process	embedded clause as participant

Embedding, by repackaging information contained in one clause into another, increases the lexical content of the clause. This typically occurs in written texts where information can be built up around the noun through postmodification with embedded clauses.

Take the example from the activity above (lexical items are in bold):

Some of the **200,000**-plus **residents** [[who were **evacuated** from their **homes**]] were **allowed** to **return** to several **areas** of the **city** [[that **escaped** the **worst** of the **flooding**]].

In this clause we have 11 lexical items. If we take out the embedded clauses, we would have the simpler clause:

Some of the **200,000**-plus **residents** were **allowed** to **return** to several **areas** of the **city**.

Now there are only six lexical items in the clause and so it contains much less lexical information than the original clause.

In spoken language, on the other hand, we see far fewer embeddings as spoken language typically relies on getting the meanings out in shorter clauses. The shorter clauses are complex in the intricacy in the relations between the clauses, but quite simple lexically.

These patterns are reflected in the corpus findings in your reference grammar (sections 9.8.1 and 9.8.2) where the use of relativisers is discussed. Relativisers are the relative pronouns (*which, who, whose, whom, that*) and adverbs (*where, when, why*) that can be used to form non-restrictive and restrictive (embedded) clauses. With embedded clauses, 'that' and 'which' are the most common, but their distribution varies across registers. The use of 'that' is the least common.

⑦ COMPLEXITY IN SPOKEN AND WRITTEN TEXTS

Drawing on the understanding we have developed about the way clauses can combine into clause complexes and on your understanding of noun phrases from Unit 4, we now focus briefly on one of the key differences between spoken and written language: their different kinds of complexity. Spoken language is marked by a complexity in clause relations, written language by the complexity of its noun phrases.

ACTIVITY 11 (allow about 20 minutes)

Read the following two texts. The first is a transcript taken from a video *Sticks and Stones* which was used as part of a racial-harassment awareness training programme.

Identify the clause boundaries in each of the bold sections of the two texts. Use [[ ]] to identify the two embedded clauses in the bold section of Text 7.

What would you say are the major differences between these two texts? In what ways is Text 7 more complex than Text 6? In answering this question, comment on coordination, subordination and embedding.

Text 6

If it had been more openly name-calling, it would've been easier to handle because I could've said well it was. I thought it was normal teasing but they found that I was dragged down so much by it, that it was even better for them to carry on. ... Well, I'd just put up with anything, just to try and be liked. **I think if I'd been more confident and sure of myself, it would never have happened or I would have just ignored it, but because I wasn't really sure about myself at that time, I took everything and I thought they were, they were telling the truth.** It was the worst thing that's ever happened to me because it made me feel so low and like I wasn't worth knowing.

(CTE, 1990)

Text 7

The phenomenon known as 'road rage' emerged and attracted much attention in the news media in the 1990s. This article reports the findings from a study on representations and

understandings of road rage in Australia. **Over 600 news items published between 1995 and 2000 in the two major Sydney newspapers (the** *Sydney Morning Herald* **and the** *Daily Telegraph***) were analysed using discourse analysis**. After a discussion of the ways in which road rage was first introduced to readers, my analysis centres on the major themes emerging in later years of reporting. I conclude that the newspapers' representations of road rage, like those engendering other moral panics, sought to position the phenomenon as a negative outcome of contemporary urban society. Unlike most other moral panics, however, the villains identified as 'road ragers' are not members of minority subgroups or subcultures. Rather, every road user is portrayed as potentially capable of road rage, due to their exposure to the stresses of everyday life.

(Upton, 2001, pp. 23–5)

COMMENT

To highlight the differences between the two texts, we now consider the clause complexes from the emboldened sections in each text.

Example (a) from Text 6

1   I think
2   if I'd been more confident and sure of myself,
3   it would never have happened
4   or I would have just ignored it,
5   but because I wasn't really sure about myself at that time,
6   I took everything
7   and I thought
8   they were, they were telling the truth.

Example (b) from Text 7

1   The phenomenon [[known as 'road rage']] emerged
2   and attracted much attention in the news media in the 1990s.
3   This article reports the findings from a study on representations and understandings of road rage in Australia.
4   Over 600 news items [[published between 1995 and 2000 in the two major Sydney newspapers (the *Sydney Morning Herald* and the *Daily Telegraph*)]] were analysed using discourse analysis.

First focus on the noun phrases in each example. There is a major difference between the very brief noun phrases in (a) (*I, it, everything, it, the truth*) compared with (b) (*The phenomenon known as 'road rage', much attention in the news media in the 1990s, the findings from a study on representations and understandings of road rage in Australia*). Also the embedded clauses in (b) are adding lexical information to the head noun in (1) and (4). There are no embeddings in (a). This means that the lexical density, which is a measure of the number of lexical items per clause, is considerably higher in (b) than in (a). Also the nature of the noun phrases is different, with those in (a) focusing on people and those in (b) on abstract items (*the phenomenon..., the findings..., items...*). In summary, we can say that (b) is far more lexically complex than (a).

If we now turn to the relationships between the clauses within these clause complexes, we see a different kind of complexity. In (a) we see, for instance, a series of eight simple clauses linked by coordination and subordination to form a rather intricate clause complex. If you delve into this intricacy, you will see that it is quite difficult working out how clause (6) relates to clause (5), which in turn relates to the previous clauses.

This not the case with the clause complexes in (b) which are very straightforward. The first clause complex consists of only two clauses linked by coordination, with the second and third clause complexes each consisting of just one clause. In other words, there is a kind of simplicity in the clause relationships, which is in contrast to (a).

So we have different kinds of complexity and simplicity operating within these two texts. In Text 6 we see that, while it is lexically simple as seen in the brief noun phrases, its complexity lies in the intricate way the clauses are linked to each other. In Text 7, however, we see that the noun phrases are much longer with more embeddings, which contributes to their lexical complexity. The way they are linked to each other is quite simple.

The texts in the above activity reflect the general pattern we find with spoken and written language: spoken language is lexically simple but grammatically complex. Written language, in contrast, is lexically complex but grammatically simple.

⟨8⟩ COURSE READER AND CD-ROMS

In much of Book 1, you have been looking at how grammatical form relates to grammatical function. Jim Martin's article in the course reader, which you read earlier, takes you through different grammatical traditions.

ACTIVITY 12 (allow about two hours)

Now read for a second time Section 4.3 and, in addition, Sections 4.4 and 4.5 of Jim Martin's article (Chapter 4) 'Grammatical Structure: What Do We Mean?', in the course reader, *Applying English Grammar*.

(1)   Why might it be useful to use different function labels for different languages?

(2)   How does Halliday's complementary structure perspective and system perspective highlight some differences and similarities between English and Tagalog?

(3)   In what sense is Halliday's systemic functional approach a tiered approach?

COURSE CD-ROMS (allow about four hours)

Now work through the tasks for this unit on the Concordancer and Corpus CD-ROM using the *Corpus Tasks* booklet (allow about two hours).

When you have done this, work through the activities for this unit on the Activities CD-ROM (allow about two hours).

Conclusion

We focused initially on what constitutes a clause and on the possible groupings that can combine together as a clause. From there we moved on to look at how clauses can combine together to form clause complexes. We considered in some detail the various ways of describing the relationships that emerge when clauses combine, whether they involve coordination, subordination or embeddings. We finished with a discussion on the differences between spoken and written language, which brought together an understanding of clausal relationships and the composition of noun phrases.

Learning outcomes

After completing this unit, you should have developed a knowledge and understanding of:

◆   the composition of the clause and of clause complexes

◆   the ways that clauses can combine to form clause complexes and the nature of the relationships between the clauses

◆ embedded clauses and their role as a clause constituent
◆ differences in clause relationships within written and spoken texts.

In the light of your increased understanding, you should be able to:

◆ describe different patterns of clauses in spoken and written texts.

Key terms introduced and revisited

circumstance	non-restrictive relative clause [non-defining clause]
circumstantial dependent clause	participant
clause	process
clause complex	projected clause
coordination	projecting clause
dependent clause [subordinate clause]	projection
embedded clause	qualifier
embedding	quoting [direct speech]
finite clause	rank scale
independent clause	relative clause
interrupting clause [included clause]	relativiser
main clause	reporting [indirect speech]
nominalisation	restrictive relative clause [defining clause]
non-clausal unit	subordination
non-finite clause	

Near equivalents are given in [ ].

Unit 7

Intonation: turning pandas into killers

Prepared for the course team by Martin Rhys

CONTENTS

Materials required

While studying this unit, you will need:

> your reference grammar (Sections 6 and 7)
>
> the Activities CD-ROM (throughout the unit).

Since this unit is about intonation, you need to listen to audio files and watch video clips as well as carrying out activities. The audio files and video clips are on the Activities CD-ROM. You should listen to each file as you read its transcription in this unit. The audio files are numbered 7.1–7.73 and 7A1–7A8. The video clips are individually named.

Knowledge assumed

From Foundation Grammar:

> adverbial
>
> stance adverb.

From Unit 1:

> differences between spoken and written English
>
> dysfluency
>
> systemic functional grammar.

From Unit 2:

> function and lexical words.

From Unit 3:

> grammatical units
>
> interrogative and declarative clauses
>
> participant
>
> circumstance.

From Unit 4:

> head word of a noun phrase
>
> postmodifier
>
> premodifier.

From Unit 5:

> independent and dependent clauses
>
> projecting and projected clauses
>
> subordination.

Introduction

We have been looking at differences between speech and writing in English. But we have not explored an important aspect of English speech which makes it very different from writing – how meanings in English can be made through sound. In this unit we focus on how **intonation** is bound up with the making of meaning in the spoken mode.

You may be wondering what a unit on intonation is doing in a course about grammar. If this is not your first foray into the field of linguistics, you will be well aware that courses concerned with grammar do not normally concern themselves with the way a language sounds. You might like to spend a few minutes pondering why this should be the case: think about issues of accessibility and transcription.

This unit, along with some follow-up work later in the course, will begin to address the lack of attention given to intonation in studies of English grammar. It will by no means offer comprehensive coverage of the subject, but it will bring to your attention a range of the functions – grammatical, informational and attitudinal – which intonation fulfils in spoken (and, less directly, in written) language.

Since the focus of this course is on English grammar, there will be little space to prepare you for any particularly intricate level of auditory analysis. Some of the activities may involve quite difficult tasks, particularly where the intonation of naturally occurring conversation is concerned.

In this unit, like the others in this book, we shall be dealing with differences between spoken and written English. However, our focus is, as you would expect, on features of speech, specifically intonation. To that end, we provide a general introduction to the systems of English intonation, paying particular attention to their informational and grammatical functions within spoken language. While this can be understood only through analysis of the language that we hear (hence the frequent use of the Activities CD-ROM), we also look at the various means – particularly punctuation – by which writers have tried to capture intonation on the written page.

The title of this unit is derived from the following story.

The panda story

A panda walked into a restaurant and asked the head waiter for a table for one. He was shown to his table, a waiter took his order and brought him his meal. When he had finished his dessert, the panda pulled out a gun and shot the waiter. He then stood up and made to leave the restaurant. A shocked head waiter called out to stop him and asked the panda what he thought he was doing. The panda sneered over his shoulder and growled, 'I'm a panda. Look it up.' He slammed the door behind him.

The puzzled head waiter went immediately to find a dictionary and looked up the entry for *panda*. He read the definition: 'large, bear-like creature indigenous to Asia with black and white markings. Eats shoots and leaves.'

The first question is: Do you find this story amusing?

Assuming you do, the second question is: Why? What makes this story funny?

The problem with questions like these, of course, is that, even if you found the story funny when you first read it, analysis of why you found it funny will very soon result in making it not funny any more. Unfortunately, that is a risk we have to take. This is, after all, a course about grammar – not jokes. Unfortunately.

So what makes it funny? The comic absurdity of the whole situation of a panda eating a meal in a restaurant and then shooting the waiter cumulates in the proffered explanation in the punch line of the final sentence – *Eats shoots and leaves*. More precisely, the comedy centres on the potential ambiguity in the final sentence.

If we were to read that sentence in the context of a dictionary definition of a panda, there is little doubt that we would immediately grasp the dictionary's intended meaning and probably not give a thought to possible alternatives. The possible alternative which the story requires us to comically conceptualise in order to find the story funny is itself created by the circumstances of the story. It provides the scenario of a panda eating a meal, killing a waiter with a gun and then leaving. The context creates the ambiguity.

If you showed this story to prescriptive grammarians of the sort mentioned in Unit 1, they would, no doubt, argue with some indignation that no ambiguity actually exists, since the more absurd meaning outlined at the end of the preceding paragraph would require a comma between *eats* and *shoots*. In reality, though, writers are notoriously inconsistent and even capricious with their use of commas. And if the story were told instead of written, as most stories of this type are – well, commas do not appear in speech.

Or do they? Obviously we do not punctuate what we say in the same way that we punctuate our writing. As Biber et al. (1999) point out, 'Whereas the sentence has been treated ... as the fundamental structural unit of grammar, such a unit does not realistically exist in conversational language.' But this is not to say that speech does not have its own ways of organising meaning along the lines that punctuation does for written language.

Activities CD-ROM (allow about five minutes)

Now watch the video clip 'Punctuated conversation' on the Activities CD-ROM.

Take a look at Danish comedian Victor Borge's clever attempt at inserting commas and stops into his speech to hear what punctuated conversation might sound like.

Look again at the final sentence of the panda story.

(1) If you wanted to make it unambiguously clear (and at the same time completely spoil the story) that the panda had shot the waiter and then left, how would you say those four words?

(2) If you wanted to make it unambiguously clear that the panda was a consumer of leaves and shoots, how would you change the way you said those words?

Consider the challenge: you have a sequence of four words and you have to convey two quite different meanings by changing the way you utter them. And you can do this quite easily. In fact, stories like the above rely on the fact that you can do it.

So how do you do it?

Information unit and tone-groups

Meeting the above challenge lies initially in the way you organise your message into 'units of information' which are conveyed as 'tone-groups'. An **information unit** signals the way in which the speaker organises the message, distributing it into blocks. This process is realised phonologically by the utterance being organised or divided into tone-groups. A **tone-group** is a unit of the language's phonology in much the same way as a clause or phrase is a unit of the language's grammar. Units of information and tone-groups are usually coextensive.

If you wanted to convey meaning (2) in the panda story – the dictionary definition – you would probably deliver your message as one information unit conveyed by one tone-group (tone-group boundaries are marked by //):

7.1 // eats shoots and leaves //

If, on the other hand, you wanted to convey clearly meaning (1), you would probably opt for three information units conveyed by three tone-groups with a slight pause between each one:

7.2 // eats // shoots // and leaves //

A reminder – the audio version of this example (and all following examples) is on the Activities CD-ROM. It is accessed from the Unit 7 page.

This is fairly typical of the way in which we use tone-groups to signal items in a list, for example:

7.3   // I came // I saw // I conquered //

7.4   // we beat Germany // Argentina // Brazil // and Italy //

7.5   // I heard it knocking // I heard it scratching // I heard it come in //

7.6   // anyway // anyhow // anywhere //

ACTIVITIES CD-ROM   (allow about three minutes)

Now do Activity 1 'Intonation and meaning' on the Activities CD-ROM.

 TONALITY

1.1 Breaking up information

Each time we speak, one of the set of options we have is how we distribute or break up the information in our message. We select how many units of information we wish to use in order to convey as clearly as we can our message to the listener.

The way in which we divide an utterance into tone-groups describes its **tonality**. Tonality is one of the subsystems of the overarching system of English intonation. Other subsystems will be dealt with shortly.

When we refer to tone-groups and information units, we are, in effect, dealing with the same unit. They are, in other words, coextensive – they begin and end at the same point. The difference between them is that they belong to different stages of the speech process. The information unit belongs to the informational level of speech, where the speaker makes the decision regarding how best to organise the information in the message for the benefit of the listener. The tone-group, on the other hand, is what the speaker articulates and the listener hears. It belongs to the phonological level of the speech process. The information in the message is conveyed by the tone-groups when it is converted into the physical sounds of speech. On one level, then, the message is organised into information units. On another, the utterance is divided into tone-groups. The latter is the phonological expression of the former. The tone-group, in technical terms, is the phonological realisation of the information unit. For example, we could say the following sentence in a number of ways.

I remember she sent me a postcard.

We can organise it into one or two information units:

7.7 // I remember she sent me a postcard //

7.8 // I remember // she sent me a postcard //

(7.7) comes as a single information unit – the speaker remembers that the person being talked about sent her/him a postcard. This information is packaged in a single tone-group.

In (7.8) the speaker decides to package the information as two units – first, that he/she remembers, and second, what it is that he/she remembers – hence two tone-groups.

A tone-group, then, is a unit of the language's phonology, in much the same way as a clause and a phrase are units of the language's grammar. We shall return to explore the relationship between tone-groups and grammatical units a little later in the unit, but first we need to look briefly at how a tone-group is structured.

1.2 Tone-group structure

Grammatical units generally have a structure. A noun phrase, for instance, has an obligatory element which is the head word and can be preceded by premodifiers and followed by postmodifiers (see Unit 4). In a similar way, the tone-group also has a structure. It has an obligatory element which can be preceded and followed by optional elements.

Tonic syllable

A tone-group must have a single **tonic syllable**, which is the most *prominent* syllable within the tone-group and, to put it another way, the syllable which the hearer notices most. The tonic syllable is thus an obligatory constituent of any tone-group. Indeed, the tone-group may consist of the tonic syllable (underlined) on its own:

7.9 // No //

7.10 // Yes //

Or it may consist of a word containing the tonic syllable:

7.11 // Hello //

7.12 // Saturday //

Different varieties of English have different patterns of rhythm, in terms of which syllables within a word are accorded prominence. In Singaporean English, for instance, the most prominent syllable in *Saturday* is usually the final one, i.e. // Saturday //. All the examples in this unit – unless specifically mentioned otherwise – are taken from British English. The activities which ask you for some level of analysis (such as the next activity) require the analysis to be made of the given examples – which are spoken in British English.

ACTIVITIES CD-ROM (allow about three minutes)

Now do Activity 2 'Tonic syllable (1)' on the Activities CD-ROM.

Pretonic

As well as the tonic syllable, the tone-group may contain a rather longer **pretonic** element (in bold) which precedes the tonic syllable:

7.13 // **it was twenty years ago to**day //

7.14 // **Sergeant Pepper taught his band to** play //

7.15 // **they've been going in and out of** style //

ACTIVITIES **CD-ROM** (allow about four minutes)

Now do Activity 3 'Pretonic' on the Activities CD-ROM.

Posttonic

The tone-group may also contain a **posttonic** element (in colour) which follows the tonic syllable:

7.16 // <u>won</u>derful to see you //

7.17 // <u>thrilled</u> to be here //

7.18 // <u>love</u> to take you home with us //

ACTIVITIES **CD-ROM** (allow about four minutes)

Now do Activity 4 'Posttonic' on the Activities CD-ROM.

Pretonic and posttonic

Both these elements – pretonic and posttonic – may be present within a tone-group on either side of the tonic syllable:

7.19 // **it took me** <u>years</u> to write it //

7.20 // **meeting a man from the** <u>mo</u>tor trade //

7.21 // **when I was so much** <u>youn</u>ger than today //

Tone-group structure summary

The structure of the tone-group, then, can be represented as follows (the brackets around pretonic and posttonic indicate their optionality, whereas the tonic syllable is an obligatory component):

     (pretonic)   tonic syllable (posttonic)

2 TONICITY: DIFFERENT TONIC SYLLABLES

The allocation of a tonic syllable to each tone-group describes the tone-group's **tonicity**. Looking back to (7.8), if tonality divided this utterance into two tone-groups, then tonicity would allocate a tonic syllable to each of them from a number of potential choices, for example:

7.22   // I remember // she sent me a postcard //

7.23   // I remember // she sent me a postcard //

7.24   // I remember // she sent me a postcard //

7.25   // I remember // she sent me a postcard //

7.26   // I remember // she sent me a postcard //

You will notice that the second tone-group in each case has a different tonic syllable placement, and that the different placements generate slightly different meanings or implications for elsewhere in the text. For instance, if you heard someone say (7.23), you would assume that the item *postcard* had probably already been mentioned, for example, as in (... indicates a pause):

7.27   // Last year Alice was in Italy // I didn't get a present // didn't get a postcard ... // No wait // I remember // she sent me a postcard //

If, on the other hand, you heard (7.24), then the implications for the context would be slightly different. The item *postcard* would probably again have been mentioned previously, but there is now the hint of some sort of contrast, for example, as in:

7.28   // I can't recall whether she sent a postcard to anyone else in the office // but // I remember // she sent me a postcard //

The contrast is between tonic *me* and the *anyone else in the office* from a previous tone-group. It is fairly typical, though not necessarily always the case, that when the tonic syllable co-occurs with a function word such as the pronoun *me* in (7.24), then there will be some sort of contrast implied with another section of the text. We see this in the remaining two examples. Example 7.25 has the tonic syllable allocated to a function word, an indefinite article, and the contrast which is implied here could be between one postcard and many, for example, as in:

7.29   A: // She must be very fond of you // considering the number of postcards you got // from Italy //

   B: // You do exaggerate // I remember // she sent me a postcard //

And in (7.26), the contrast could be between the sender of the postcard and some other person(s):

7.30 // Last <u>sum</u>mer // I got postcards from <u>A</u>lice // from <u>A</u>lan // from <u>Ka</u>tie // in fact from everyone except <u>De</u>lyth // no <u>wait</u> // I re<u>mem</u>ber // <u>she</u> sent me a postcard // as <u>well</u> //

The contrast in (7.30) is an additional one (Delyth as well as <u>A</u>lice, <u>A</u>lan, <u>Ka</u>tie and the others) and not an oppositional one (Delyth as opposed to <u>A</u>lice, <u>A</u>lan, <u>Ka</u>tie and the others) as in (7.28) and (7.29). These types of contrast are discussed in greater detail in Unit 16.

Now let us see whether you can recognise the tonic syllable within a tone-group, as well as any implications which particular tonic placements may have for the remainder of the text.

ACTIVITIES CD-ROM (allow about 30 minutes)

Now do Activity 5 'Tonic syllable (2)' on the Activities CD-ROM.

ACTIVITY 1 (allow about 20 minutes)

In the CD-ROM activity you identified the tonic syllables in the opening section of Abraham Lincoln's *Gettysburg Address*. The text below displays each tone-group on a separate line and the tonic syllables are underlined.

(1) Where is the tonic syllable in the majority of the tone-groups? (Consider the type of word and its position in the tone-group.)

(2) In what percentage of the tone-groups does the tonic syllable appear in the majority position you identified in (1)?

(3) When the tonic syllable appears in a position other than the position you identified in (1), what are the implications for the remainder of the text in each instance?

(A) // Fourscore and seven years a<u>go</u> //

(B) // our fathers brought forth on this <u>con</u>tinent //

(C) // a new <u>na</u>tion //

(D) // conceived in <u>li</u>berty //

(E) // and dedicated to the propo<u>si</u>tion //

(F) // that all men are created <u>e</u>qual //

(G) // Now we are engaged in a great civil <u>war</u> //

(H) // testing whether that <u>na</u>tion //

(I) // or <u>a</u>ny nation //

(J) // so con<u>cei</u>ved //

(K) // and so de<u>di</u>cated //

(L) // can long en<u>dure</u> //

(M) // We are met on a great <u>batt</u>lefield of that war //

(N) // We have come to <u>dedi</u>cate //

(O) // a <u>por</u>tion of that field //

(P) // as a final <u>res</u>ting-place //

(Q) // for those who here gave their <u>lives</u> //

(R) // that that nation might <u>live</u> //

(S) // It is altogether fitting and <u>pro</u>per //

(T) // that we should <u>do</u> this //

(U) // But in a larger <u>sense</u> //

(V) // we <u>can</u>not dedicate //

(W) // we <u>can</u>not consecrate //

(X) // we <u>can</u>not hallow this ground //

COMMENT

(1) In 18 of the 24 tone-groups (A–X), the tonic syllable appears in the final lexical item.

(2) The fraction 18/24 represents 75% of the time in this small sample. It is claimed that this happens around 80% of the time in conversational English. This is one reason why such tonic placement is known as 'neutral' or 'unmarked' tonicity.

Unmarked (neutral) is the choice that is most typical, compared with **marked** which is a pattern that is not the most typical pattern and therefore has some special meaning or function.

(3) Where tonicity is not neutral – where it is marked – there is usually some textual implication.

(I) // or <u>any</u> nation //

Neutral tonicity would have allocated the tonic syllable to *nation*. Moving it forward to *<u>any</u>* implies that *nation* is retrievable – it has already been mentioned in (C) and (H).

There is also the implication of a contrast – *testing whether any nation, not just this one, can long endure.*

(M) // We are met on a great <u>batt</u>lefield of that war //

Neutral tonicity would have made *war* the tonic syllable. Moving it forward to *battlefield* implies that *war* is retrievable – it has already been mentioned in (G).

(O) // a po̲rtion of that field //

Neutral tonicity would have made *field* the tonic syllable. Moving it forward to *portion* implies that *field* is retrievable – it has already been mentioned as part of *battlefield* in (M).

In (V)–(X) the tonic syllable is c̲a̲nnot and a lexical item (*dedicate, consecrate, hallowed*) follows the tonic item. The moving forward of the tonic syllable signals the lexical item as retrievable. But only *dedicate* has already been explicitly mentioned. However, the sense of the other two lexical words is implicit in the earlier *dedicate a portion of that field as a final resting-place*. An item does not have to be explicitly mentioned in order to be retrievable, as long as the sense of it is present elsewhere in the text.

There is also the implication of a contrast in each – 'what we came to do' but in fact 'cannot do'.

These tone-groups exemplify that implying a tie-up with information elsewhere in the text is a 'cohesive' function of tonicity. The allocation of the tonic syllable can hold the text together by signalling its relationship to information elsewhere in the text. **Cohesion** is the pattern of relations between structures and lexical items which combine together to form a text or discourse. The term 'cohesion' is only touched on here and will be dealt with fully in Unit 15, along with the cohesive function of intonation.

It will not have escaped your notice that, while we dealt with (7.23)–(7.25) above, we did not say a great deal about (7.22). By now you will have realised that (7.22) is an example of unmarked tonicity and, as such, tends not to carry implications for information elsewhere in the text. Tonicity is unmarked in (7.22) because the tonic syllable falls within the final lexical item in the tone-group, which in this case is *postcard*. But there are two syllables in *postcard*. What if the tonic syllable is *card* instead of *post*? All will be revealed in the next section.

2.1 Tonicity and stress

Theoretically, the tonic syllable should be able to be allocated to any syllable within the tone-group. In practice, however, it goes, in the vast majority of cases, to a syllable which is already rhythmically prominent or **stressed**. If a word is composed of more than one syllable, then one of those syllables will be stressed, i.e. will be rhythmically more prominent than the others. For instance, in British English, the stressed syllable (in bold) of the following polysyllabic words is normally:

7.31 **pho**tograph **syl**lable infor**ma**tion pho**to**graphy syl**la**bic infor**ma**tive

Now see if you can recognise stressed syllables by doing the following activity.

◆CTIVITIES **CD-ROM** (allow about three minutes)

Now do Activity 6 'Stressed syllable recognition' on the Activities CD-ROM.

The tonic syllable is usually allocated to a syllable which is already stressed. Hence in (7.22) the tonic syllable is _postcard_ and not _postcard_. This is not to say that _postcard_ is not a possibility. Listen to the following exchange which involves a misunderstanding.

7.32 A: // there's nothing <u>wrong</u> with the postmark //

      B: // I didn't say there <u>was</u> // I said I thought it was a weird post<u>card</u> //

Speaker B switches the tonic syllable to a normally unstressed syllable because the objective is to contrast that syllable with the one which A misheard. Likewise with:

7.33 A: // did you say as<u>tro</u>nomy //

      B: // <u>no</u> // I said <u>gas</u>tronomy //

A similar allocation of tonic to a normally unstressed syllable may occur in a context of language or pronunciation teaching:

7.34 Learner: // and we were <u>sing</u>in //

      Teacher: // and we were sing<u>ing</u> //

The mechanism at work in this unusual allocation of the tonic syllable is not dissimilar to other instances of marked tonicity already dealt with in Activity 1. In all the above cases, a contrast is invoked, that contrast being between the word which contains the tonic syllable and some other word which is retrievable from elsewhere in the text. This suggests that tonic allocation of this type should be characterised as marked, despite the fact that it falls within the final lexical item within the tone-group. In the interest of accuracy, then, we need to expand our definition of **neutral tonicity**, i.e. unmarked tonicity, to one where the tonic syllable falls on the stressed syllable of the final lexical item within the tone-group.

❸ TONE

Tone describes the **pitch** direction of the voice – up, down, both or neither.

We mentioned above that the tonic syllable is the most prominent syllable within a tone-group. How does it achieve this prominence?

Much has been written on this subject (see Wells (1986) and Tench (1996)). Most, if not all of it, lies well beyond the scope of this course. Factors such as loudness and rhythm play a significant part, but it is the choice of **pitch direction** which, in the main, makes the tonic syllable stand out within the tone-group. The next activity will help you to become more aware of the **pitch contours** of speech before we look in detail at the different pitch directions in the system of tone.

ACTIVITIES **CD-ROM**   (allow about 10 minutes)

Now do Activity 7 'Pitch movement' on the Activities CD-ROM.

3.1 Pitch direction

The choice of pitch direction which occurs at the tonic syllable is the third system of intonation: the subsystem of tone.

There are five tones in English.

ACTIVITIES **CD-ROM**   (allow about 15 minutes)

Now do Activities 8–12 'Falling tone', 'Rising tone', 'Level tone', 'Rise-fall tone' and 'Fall-rise tone' on the Activities CD-ROM.

The usual convention of underlining the tonic syllable is contravened in the activities. The non-conventional use of bold enables clearer presentation of the graphics.

No background and feedback to these activities are given within the activities. Each tone is discussed below.

Fall

You have just listened to the following examples in the previous CD-ROM activities.

7.35   // <u>No</u> //

7.36   // He<u>llo</u> //

7.37   // How <u>are</u> you //

7.38   // I <u>knew</u> it was you //

You have heard in these examples that falls are not all the same. In each example, the pitch direction, i.e. the tone, is falling, but the **range** (pitch range) of the fall varies. It is important to understand that we are not talking here about absolute tone, as in music. The range we refer to here is the pitch range of an individual's normal speaking voice. It is, of course, possible to go outside that normal range, but such a choice would constitute either a cohesive function or a signal of speaker attitude, topics to be picked up in Unit 15. It is impossible to specify precisely what sort of attitude, since this depends on so many other features, as noted in Section 4.2 below.

The whole of the fall may take place on the tonic syllable, as in (7.35) and (7.36), or it may begin on the tonic syllable and continue over the posttonic, as in (7.37) and (7.38).

Rise

As the name suggests, this tone is the mirror image of the fall, and is illustrated in (7.39–7.42) (the examples in the above CD-ROM activity).

7.39   // <u>Yes</u> //

7.40   // <u>Really</u> //

7.41   // Was it <u>raining</u> earlier //

7.42   // Is <u>that</u> what you expect me to do //

Level

There is no upward or downward pitch movement in the level tone.

7.43   // <u>Well</u> //

7.44   // <u>Consequently</u> //

7.45   // If it's <u>trouble</u> you want //

7.46   // For the <u>second</u> time of asking //

You have just listened to these examples in the previous CD-ROM activity.

The remaining two tones of English differ from the preceding three in that they are not unidirectional. They comprise combinations of tones already discussed.

Rise-fall

The pitch begins to rise from its onset on the tonic syllable, then generally falls to a point lower than where it began. The examples below illustrate this.

7.47   // <u>Well</u> //

7.48   // Hel<u>lo</u> //

7.49   // Is <u>that</u> what you call it //

7.50   // I should <u>think</u> so //

You have just listened to these examples in the previous CD-ROM activity.

In (7.47) and (7.48), the whole of the rise-fall takes place within a single syllable. In (7.49) and (7.50), on the other hand, the rise component of the tone is realised by the difference in pitch between the tonic syllable and the one which follows it.

Fall-rise

The fall-rise is the mirror image of the rise-fall.

7.51   // <u>Well</u> //

7.52   // <u>Actually</u> //

7.53   // A <u>river</u> runs through it //

7.54   // I don't <u>think</u> so //

You have just listened to these examples in the previous CD-ROM activity.

In (7.51) the whole of the fall-rise (which may include a short rise prior to the initial fall) takes place within the tonic syllable. In the remaining examples, the fall-rise begins on the tonic syllable and continues over the posttonic.

3.2   Recap: intonation systems

We have three different but interdependent systems – tonality, tonicity and tone – which together make up the intonation of English.

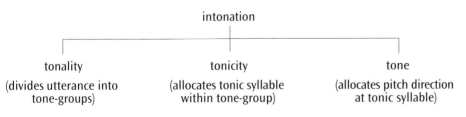

intonation

tonality	tonicity	tone
(divides utterance into tone-groups)	(allocates tonic syllable within tone-group)	(allocates pitch direction at tonic syllable)

④ TONE AND MEANING

The association of tone and meaning has received much attention in studies of English intonation over the last 80 years or so. Such is the diversity of the roles played by tone, however, that it has been difficult to pin it down to any particular function, as is acknowledged by O'Connor and Arnold (1961):

> It has often been pointed out, and rightly, that no tone group is used exclusively with this or that sentence type – question, statement and the like – and also that no sentence type always requires the use of one and only one tone group ... the fact is that intonation is too complex and too flexible to be confined within such narrow rules.
>
> (O'Connor and Arnold, 1961, p. 32)

4.1 Complete and incomplete information

One function generally attributed to tone by most commentators is its function of signalling whether information has been completed or whether there is more to come. How do we know when speakers have finished what they have to say? How do we know when they have not? Of course, there are other cues we follow as well as tone: syntactic (a speaker would be unlikely to finish in the middle of a noun phrase) and **paralinguistic** (a speaker unwilling to make eye contact generally wants to keep the conversational turn). But intonation, particularly the choice of tone, also plays an important part.

> Paralinguistic features are features which accompany language, but are not part of the language system itself, such as volume, gesture and facial expression.

Generally speaking, the rising tone signals incompleteness. We shall take an earlier example and listen to alternative versions of it, one with a rising final tone, the other with a falling final tone:

7.55 // I heard it <u>knock</u>ing // I heard it <u>scratch</u>ing // I heard it come <u>in</u> //

7.56 // I heard it <u>knock</u>ing // I heard it <u>scratch</u>ing // I heard it come <u>in</u> //

With the rising tone on *in* in (7.55), we are left waiting to hear what else the speaker heard 'it' doing. It would be most odd if the speaker simply finished the story like that. When *in* takes the falling tone in (7.56), however, we are satisfied that this particular section of the narrative is complete. That is not to say that the speaker cannot continue, of course, but we understand that the list of what 'it' did has come to an end.

The level tone can fulfil the same function as the rising tone in this respect, as illustrated in (7.57).

7.57 // I heard it <u>knock</u>ing // I heard it <u>scratch</u>ing // I heard it come <u>in</u> //

We could extend the notion of incompleteness across, as well as within, conversational turns. The rising tone can signal that there is something to come by requiring a response from the listener. For instance, an interrogative form is a question, whether accompanied by a falling or rising tone, and, as such, usually demands an answer by virtue of the syntax:

7.58   // Are you going <u>home</u> //

7.59   // Are you going <u>home</u> //

A declarative form with a falling tone tends to be a statement, while a declarative form with a rising tone tends to be an alternative method of forming a question:

7.60   // You're going <u>home</u> //

7.61   // You're going <u>home</u> //

The rising tone in (7.61) again signals incompleteness – but this time incompleteness of the exchange rather than of what the speaker is saying – by requiring an answer to a declarative form which has been turned into a question. In written language, the sentence would be followed by a question mark:

You're going home?

Bearing in mind O'Connor and Arnold's (1961) salutary warning quoted above, it would be foolhardy to claim as an invariable rule the association between rising tone and incompleteness, and falling tone and completed information. The following examples of fall followed by rise give no impression of being incomplete.

7.62   // There's another <u>riot</u> // in <u>Man</u>chester //

7.63   // They're quite far to the <u>right</u> // po<u>lit</u>ically//

7.64   // It was <u>snowing</u> // this time last <u>year</u> //

The final rising tone in the second tone-group of (7.62)–(7.64) does not signal that there is more to come, but rather that the information in that particular information unit is of secondary importance. In Halliday's (1994) terms, it is 'minor' information as opposed to the 'major' information of the first tone-group in each example, which has a falling tone. This particular function of the rising tone is discoursal in nature, signalling the status of information, and is connected with its status as either 'given' or 'new' information which is dealt with more fully in Unit 15. Other discoursal functions of tone in English will also be picked up at a later stage in the course.

The bidirectional tones – the fall-rise and the rise-fall – can fulfil similar functions of signalling whether information is complete or not. In some dialects of British English (e.g. the West Midlands of England), the fall-rise is used more frequently than the rise to indicate that there is more information to come, while in other dialects (e.g. Belfast in Northern Ireland) the rise-fall is used more frequently than the fall to show that information is complete. In many dialects of English, these bidirectional tones fulfil other discoursal functions such as the signalling of a contrast (see Activity 1). The regional variation inherent in a speaker's tone selection is one factor which makes a consistent statement of association between tone and meaning difficult to achieve.

4.2   Tone and attitude

'It's not what she said, it's the way that she said it.'

'Don't use that tone of voice with me.'

These two oft-heard statements demonstrate the clear link in people's minds between the attitude of the speaker and the intonation of what is being said. In cases like these, the words used are not that important – *It's not what she said*. However, other features of speech which accompany the words are crucial in conveying the attitude of the speaker and in creating the all-important effect on the hearer. For speakers of English, those features are summed up in the phrase *tone of voice*.

Phonologists have followed a similar route to linguistics in trying to link intonation and attitude. Ignoring their own warning about the complexity and flexibility of intonation, O'Connor and Arnold (1961) dedicated much energy to providing 'a description of the attitudes conveyed by the different tone-groups in association with the various sentence types'. So a combination of a particular fall with a statement becomes 'phlegmatic, detached, reserved, dispassionate, dull, possibly grim or surly'. A high fall (a fall which begins from a high pitch) with a general question expresses 'mild surprise but acceptance of the speaker's premises.'

But can such attitudes be specified so accurately using just intonation as a cue? Or, when we talk about tone of voice, are we taking other features of face-to-face interaction into account?

Following O'Connor and Arnold (1961), several commentators have tried to link choice of tone to the speaker's attitude, but, as we shall see below, the paralinguistic parameters available to the speaker with which to convey attitude in face-to-face interaction often take precedence over the choice of tone. Not only do these parameters – facial expression, gesture, eye-contact, proximity – occur alongside choice of tone, they will, more often than not, be found to be more significant in determining the listener's perception of the speaker's attitude – as the following video clips demonstrate.

ACTIVITY 2 (allow about 40 minutes)

On the video clips you will hear the same sequence of words spoken eight times with the same tonic syllable but with two different tone configurations. The first four are spoken with a falling tone on the tonic syllable and the second four with a rising tone. The width of the pitch contour has been kept constant, i.e. each fall and each rise begins at the same pitch height and ends at the same pitch height. In other words, the same intonation contour is maintained for each group of four examples. However, the accompanying paralinguistic features differ in each video.

In each of the video clips the following tone-group is spoken:

// You're going <u>home</u> //

For each of the eight video clips:

(1)　Describe the speaker's attitude.

(2)　Make a note of the features that signal the speaker's attitude.

These eight video clips 'You're going home (1–8)' are accessed from the Unit 7 page on the Activities CD-ROM.

COMMENT

Paralinguistic features are variations in the message which are not part of the conventional sound-shape of words, such as a creaky or breathy voice and intonation.

If intonation was a concise guide to the conveying of attitude, then clips (1)–(4) should be within one particular attitude category while clips (5)–(8) should be within a quite different one. Instead there are four different attitudes conveyed in clips (1)–(4), and very similar attitudes to these are conveyed in clips (5)–(8) despite the change in tone selection.

(1) (falling tone) Sad attitude conveyed by head tilting to one side in sympathy and eyebrows raised diagonally towards centre.

(2) (falling tone) Happy attitude conveyed by eyebrows raised in high arch, eyes smiling, extensive display of teeth in smile, mouth turned slightly upward at edges forming slight bulge in cheeks and forward positive movement of head.

(3) (falling tone) Threatening aggressive attitude conveyed by more emphatic segmental pronunciation particularly of word initial consonant (e.g. **g**oing), raised hand and pointing finger, eyelids raised to display whites of eyes and taut facial area around mouth.

(4) (falling tone) Puzzled attitude conveyed by head tilted to one side, eyes narrowed and eyebrows dropped.

(5)–(8) convey very similar attitudes to (1)–(4), i.e. (5) is sad, (6) is happy, (7) is threatening and (8) is puzzled. The tone in (5)–(8) has changed to a rising tone but the other paralinguistic features noted above remain largely the same.

It seems that a change of tone makes minimal difference to the conveying of attitude, whereas the paralinguistic features such as facial expression and hand/head gestures are very influential.

In later units we shall deal with each intonation subsystem as and when it becomes relevant to the topic under discussion. Tonicity and tone are picked up in more detail later, particularly in relation to discourse functions. For the remainder of this unit, the main focus is the role of tonality.

◈ SPOKEN AND WRITTEN LANGUAGE

As a student of language, you will no doubt have thought and read about the relative advantages of spoken and written language. Written language, for instance, can give the writer time and the opportunity to reshape and redraft their text. The resulting product has the advantage of relative permanence over the more ephemeral spoken form. This permanence allows readers the luxury of absorbing written material at their own pace. They can read a sentence, a paragraph or a page over and over again for the pure pleasure of it or until they understand what the writer is trying to communicate. The text can be read in a different country, continent or century from the one in which the writer was writing. As we saw in Unit 1, none of these benefits accrue to spoken language.

But one huge advantage which spoken language has over written is rooted in the range of features available to us in the immediacy of face-to-face interaction, including the versatility of the human voice. As listeners, we may not be able to read over again a difficult sentence, but a furrowed brow or a puzzled look will usually prompt the speaker to reiterate the point and rephrase it in a more accessible manner until he/she is satisfied that the listener has signalled understanding.

Our intonation systems give the speaker the opportunity of distributing the information in a way which will facilitate comprehension for the listener, as well as emphasising certain syllables and choosing certain pitch directions in order to make a cohesive text. Further tone selections, along with a range of paralinguistic features, show (or disguise) the way the speaker is feeling – as you saw in the video clips in the last activity.

5.1 Intonation and fiction

How does written language deal with the unspoken interactions in face-to-face communication? For certain registers, such as academic writing and news reports, the overt or explicit conveying of attitude is not usually a requisite; indeed, it is often seen as something to be avoided. However, in the world of fiction it is a different matter, as demonstrated in the next activity.

ACTIVITY 3 (allow about 40 minutes)

In the text below the novelist Jonathan Franzen in *The Corrections* describes a conversation in a Lithuanian airport between two young American women. The cameo is made all the more effective when the topic of the conversation is seen against the context of a military coup, cancelled flights, tanks on the runway and general chaos.

If you are not familiar with contemporary American English usage, it may be worth pointing out that the word *like* when following a noun or pronoun + *be* is a recent alternative usage for *said*; hence *my dad's like* is equivalent to *my dad said* and *I'm like* is equivalent to *I said* in British English. The word *hello* as used in the conversation would usually be an expression of incredulity at the interlocutor's lack of awareness of the situation or lack of comprehension of what is being said. When used in this way, it almost invariably takes its own tone-group and an exaggerated fall-rise tone.

7A1   // hello //

Read the text below, which is a short extract from the conversation.

> Cheryl said to Tiffany: 'So my dad's like, you've got to sublet if you're going to Europe, and I'm like, I promised Anna she could stay there weekends when there's home games so she can sleep with Jason, right? I can't take a promise *back* – right? But my dad's getting like all bottom-line, and I'm like, hello, it's *my* condominium, right? You bought it for *me*, right? I didn't know I was going to have some stranger, you know, who, like, *fries* things on the stove, and sleeps in my bed?'
> Tiffany said: 'That is so-gross.'
> Cheryl said: 'And uses my pillows?'
>
> (Franzen, 2001, pp. 525–6)

Make notes in response to the following questions.

(1) Look at the different types of punctuation mark used in the text. Describe the ways in which they represent the intonation features of each girl's speech.

(2)   By which device does the author make sure we recognise some of the tonic syllables? What are the implications for the rest of the text when the tonic syllable falls on a function word, for example *my* in 'it's *my* condominium, right?' and *me* in 'You bought it for *me*, right?'?

(3)   What is the intonational effect of hyphenating *so* and *gross*?

(4)   Look again at the punctuation. Which punctuation mark ends all Cheryl's sentences? What does this imply about Cheryl's favoured use of tone?

COMMENT

(1)   Tonality is generally signalled quite faithfully by commas, which, for instance, separate the reporting structure (e.g. *I'm like*) from the direct speech (e.g. *I promised ... right?*).

The absence of commas in Cheryl's response to her dad (*I promised ... Jason*) suggests the possibility of a single tone-group as the whole reply is machine-gunned into one information unit, which in turn implies that it is well rehearsed, having been narrated several times previously.

The request for confirmation *right* is always isolated (usually by a comma) at the end of a sentence in its own tone-group. The use of a dash instead of a comma in one instance suggests a rather more emphatic deployment of tone – something like a high rise which travels outside the normal voice range.

The proliferation of commas in Cheryl's:

> But my dad's getting like all bottom-line, and I'm like, hello, it's *my* condominium, right? You bought it for *me*, right? I didn't know I was going to have some stranger, you know, who, like, *fries* things on the stove, and sleeps in my bed?

may or may not suggest separate tone-groups. We should certainly expect tone-groups for the insert *you know*, but the next insert *like* may simply be part of a stuttering pretonic which conveys her outrage at the idea of sharing her space with someone who '*fries* things'. Intonationally, it might look like this:

7A2   // I didn't know I was going to have some <u>stranger</u> // you <u>know</u> // who ... like ... <u>fries</u> things on the stove //

(2)   The instances where the author wants us to be in no doubt about the location of the tonic syllable are the words in italics. Of the four italicised words (*back, my, me, fries*) two are marked tonics since they are attributed to the grammatical items (function words) *my* and *me*. Placing the tonic syllable on a grammatical item

generally (though not always) sets up some sort of contrastive expectation whereby some other item is implied in the discourse which is retrievable for the listener by contrast with the tonic item. Hence

7A3   // it's <u>my</u> condominium // <u>right</u> //

implies 'not yours', i.e. that it does not belong to her father, who is already present in the text via Cheryl's narrative.

Likewise,

7A4   // You bought it for <u>me</u> // <u>right</u> //

implies 'You didn't buy it for yourself'.

(3)   The hyphenating of *so-gross* constitutes a rather less obvious, but proportionately far cleverer, marker of tonic placement. The 'intensifier' (an **intensifier** is an adverb or adverbial that amplifies meaning) *so* is combined with the adjective *gross* to make a new member of the lexeme *gross*, carrying a meaning something like 'an intensified degree of grossness'. Intonationally, if the words were separate we should expect the tonic syllable to fall on *gross*:

7A5   // That is so <u>gross</u> //

The hyphenation, however, shifts the tonic placement forward to the intensifier *so*, the most prominent syllable within the new item:

7A6   // That is <u>so</u>-gross //

(4)   Each of Cheryl's sentences ends with a question mark. Often this is because they end with the demand for confirmation: *right*. Her last two sentences, however, are declarative (see Unit 3), yet they are still punctuated by question marks. This signals strongly Cheryl's proclivity for the rising tone. Although an overgeneralisation, the rising tone is associated with the question form (see Section 4.1). A declarative format accompanied by a falling tone is usually going to be a statement:

7A7   //it's <u>that</u> way //

When accompanied by a rising tone, however, the same declarative form can become a question:

7A8   //it's <u>that</u> way //

Cheryl's repetitive use of the rising tone as a norm signals an intonational trend which has become recognisable in several dialects of English over recent years, noticeably in the USA and Australia but also the UK, particularly among younger people. It signals Cheryl's tendency to require confirmation from the listener of everything she says.

5.2 Spoken and written intonation

Following on from the last activity, we look further at the ways in which intonation operates in spoken and written language. Let us look again at an example from Section 1 to see how the systems of tonality, tonicity and, to a lesser extent, tone may be conveyed on the page.

7.7   // I remember // she sent me a postcard //

These two tone-groups might be transcribed as any of the following.

1   I remember. She sent *me* a postcard.

2   I remember: she sent *me* a postcard.

3   I remember; she sent *me* a postcard.

4   I remember, she sent *me* a postcard.

5   I remember ... she sent *me* a postcard.

6   I remember – she sent *me* a postcard.

The various alternative punctuation marks between *remember* and *she* unambiguously signal a tone-group boundary, while the italic makes it clear that *me* is the tonic syllable in the second tone-group. We might also italicise the second syllable of 're*mem*ber' – or, indeed, the whole word – if we wanted to show the speaker's choice of a particular tone for contrast or emphasis. There is, in turn, the strong implication from the italic – without actually specifying the pitch direction – that the tone selection on *me* is quite a dramatic one such as a high fall or a rise-fall. Selections of tonic syllable and tone along these lines would, of course, have implications for what else is going on in the text, but the cohesive function of intonation will be left for later units.

The fact that tonality can be conveyed in written language by punctuation signals the close correspondence between phonological tone-groups and grammatical units. In (1)–(2) above, the punctuation marks signal each tone-group as an independent clause. However, we do not want to give the impression that tone-groups and clauses are always so neatly coextensive as the above examples suggest. Far from it.

We defined tonality as the system that allows the speaker to organise their message into units of information. One of the primary motives which guides tonality choices must be consideration for the listener. The speaker wants to ensure that the message is arranged and delivered in such a way that will make the message easy for the listener to understand and absorb. This entails the efficient distribution of the message into units of information.

ACTIVITIES CD-ROM (allow about 50 minutes)

Now do Activity 13 'A news report' on the Activities CD-ROM.

⑥ TONALITY AND CONVERSATION

The news item in the activity concerned us with the relatively straightforward process of deciding how best to organise information units for the listener within a piece of written language which had already been composed. Most news broadcasts share this characteristic of scripted speech – language which has been written in order to be spoken – along with other registers such as lectures, political speeches, plays and film scripts.

Normal conversation is an example of unscripted speech and places altogether different demands on the speaker. Whereas the writer has the luxury of perfecting the process (e.g. drafting, seeking advice, research, reflecting, redrafting) until sufficiently satisfied with the final product, for the scriptless or spontaneous speaker the process and the product are more or less one and the same. Hence the 'processing constraints' are revealed most obviously in the product by the dysfluency features – such as hesitations, repetitions and 'false starts'. (A speaker may stop in the middle of saying something and try to make a **repair**. When a repair is at the beginning of an utterance it is called a **false start**.)

ACTIVITY 4 (allow about 10 minutes)

Now read sections 13.2.5 and 13.3.1 in your reference grammar. Make notes on the types of dysfluency – for use in the next activity.

COMMENT

A **lexical bundle** is a sequence of words which is in frequent use. A **syntactic blend** is a sentence or clause that finishes in a way that is grammatically inconsistent with the way it began. The term **reduced form** includes reduction processes such as elision, contraction and ellipses. A speaker may resort to **local repetition** to relieve planning pressure and incomplete utterances occur for many reasons.

The processing constraints of spontaneous conversation can also take their toll on intonation patterns. The following activity illustrates this point.

ACTIVITY 5 (allow about 25 minutes)

The text below is from a conversation in a television programme on the relative values of mainstream and alternative medicine. The main speakers are a general practitioner (GP), an alternative-medicine practitioner (Debra) and the chair (Chair). The extract starts some way into the programme and any inhibiting effects of the cameras seem to have evaporated. The transcription has no punctuation other than pause markers (...).

(1)   Read the text and observe that it is not easy to understand.

GP and I think as Debra has expressed some of this tonight ... she really doesn't see that in fact ... or perhaps she does see ... but ... I mean ... it didn't come over from what she said ... that she thinks ... or her image ... of a ... going to a GP with a headache was that she'd get two paracetamol ... surely it would ... might be equally useful for the general practitioner to find out what was about ... her headache was about by taking a decent history ... erm ... I ... I find this very worrying ... er ... er ... Debra who seems a delightful person has already fallen ... got into the other camp so to speak ... rather than um

CHAIR Do you ... do you ... do you feel that about ... about ... about real ... about normal medicine ... do you feel that way about it?

DEBRA I was slightly exaggerating ... I was slightly exaggerating

CHAIR [Attempted intervention]

DEBRA I mean ... I ... but I do think that ... that ... that allopathic medicine doesn't have the tools to necessarily find out what the cause of headaches are

GP I think an awful lot of

DEBRA I mean because it doesn't have the questions ... because it doesn't have the concepts

GP Well I think a lot of tools are there ... perhaps they haven't ... you happen to have had the bad luck that no-one's used them on you ... but I ... I think ... perhaps...

DEBRA   Well

GP a lot of it ... the tools are that in fact the patient will very often tell you what is wrong with them ... if you give them half a chance ...

('Alternative Medicine', 1988)

(2)   Watch and listen to the video clip 'Medicine discussion'.

The video clip is accessed from the Unit 7 page on the Activities CD-ROM.

(3)   Follow the tone-groups and tonic syllables given in the following text as you watch and listen to the video again.

GP // and I think as Debra has expressed some of this to<u>night</u> // ... she really doesn't <u>see</u> that // in <u>fact</u> // ... or perhaps she <u>does</u> see // ... but ... I mean ... it didn't come over from what she <u>said</u> // ... that she <u>thinks</u> // ... or her <u>image</u> ... // of a ... going to a GP with a <u>head</u>ache // was that she'd get two para<u>ce</u>tamol ... // <u>surely</u> it would ... // might be equally <u>useful</u> // for the general practitioner to find out what was a<u>bout</u> // ... her headache was a<u>bout</u> // by taking a decent <u>his</u>tory ... // erm ... I ... I find this very <u>worry</u>ing // ... er ... er ... Debra who seems a de<u>light</u>ful // <u>per</u>son // <u>has</u> // al<u>rea</u>dy fallen // ... got into the other <u>camp</u> so to speak // ... rather than um

CHAIR // Do you ... do you ... do you feel that about ... about ... about real ... about normal <u>medi</u>cine // ... do you feel that way a<u>bout</u> it? //

DEBRA // I was slightly e<u>xagg</u>erating // ... I was slightly e<u>xagg</u>erating //

CHAIR [Attempted intervention])

DEBRA // I mean ... I ... but I do <u>think</u> // that ... that ... that allopathic medicine doesn't have the <u>tools</u> // to necessarily find <u>out</u> // what the cause of headaches <u>are</u> //

GP // I think an awful lot of

DEBRA // I mean because it doesn't have the <u>ques</u>tions // ... because it doesn't have the <u>con</u>cepts //

GP // Well I think a lot of tools <u>are</u> there // ... perhaps they haven't ... you happen to have had the bad <u>luck</u> // that no-one's used them on <u>you</u> // ... but I ... I think ... perhaps...

DEBRA // Well

GP a <u>lot</u> of it // ... the <u>tools</u> are // that in fact the patient will <u>very</u> often // tell you what is <u>wrong</u> with them // ... if you give them half a <u>chance</u>... //

(4)   Make a list of the dysfluency features in the first 'turn' (the GP's) of the conversation and explain why they occur.

(5)   Look at the tone-groups which have been selected from the text
and placed in groups A and B below. Write notes on the different
ways in which dysfluency features have an effect on the tonality
within each group.

Group A

// and I think [as] Debra has expressed some of this to<u>night</u> //

// but ... I mean ... it didn't come over from what she <u>said</u> //

// Do you ... do you ... do you feel that about ... about ... about real
... about <u>nor</u>mal medicine //

// that ... that ... that allopathic medicine doesn't have the <u>tools</u> //

// ...perhaps they haven't ... you happen to have had the bad <u>luck</u> //

Group B

// <u>sure</u>ly it would ... // might be equally <u>useful</u> //

// for the general practitioner to find out what was a<u>bout</u> // ... her
headache was a<u>bout</u> //

// al<u>rea</u>dy fallen // ... got into the other <u>camp</u> so to speak //

C O M M E N T

(1)   Speakers and listeners have no time to revise or reconsider the
grammatical structures being produced during spontaneous
speech. As a result, conversational grammar typically lacks much
of the elaborate structure of the written sentence.

(2)   The video illustrates some of the many types of dysfluency.
Dysfluency describes the ways in which unplanned speech departs
from smooth-flowing grammatically well-formed utterances. It
results in the use of hesitators (*erm, um*), pauses and repetitions
which reflect the difficulty of mental planning at speed. These
types of dysfluency are discussed in Unit 1.

(3)   As you follow the video clip again you will probably notice some
other types of dysfluency. You have read about dysfluency in your
reference grammar in an earlier activity. The reading introduced
two more types of dysfluency that are illustrated by the
conversation:

A syntactic blend is a sentence or clause that finishes in a way that
is grammatically inconsistent with the way it began.

A false start is an unplanned repeat and is called more precisely
a 'retrace-and-repair sequence'.

(4) Each new structure (where a grammatical inconsistency occurs) begins a new line in the layout below.

1 and I think as

2 Debra has expressed some of this tonight

3 ...she really doesn't see that

4 in fact

5 ...or perhaps she does see ... but...

6 I mean

7 ...it didn't come over from what she said

8 ...that she thinks

9 ...or her image ... of a

10 ...going to a GP with a headache was that she'd get two paracetamol

11 ...surely it would

12 ...might be equally useful for the general practitioner to find out what was about

13 ...her headache was about by taking a decent history

14 ...erm ... I ... I find this very worrying

15 ...er ... er

16 ...Debra who seems a delightful person has already fallen

17 ...got into the other camp so to speak

18 ...rather than um

Most of the dysfluency features arise from the dual triggers of processing constraints and the competitive nature of the conversation. The GP's opening turn, for instance, is crammed with false starts and syntactic blends where she changes her mind part way through one structure and begins another.

The GP is also constrained by politeness. She is attacking Debra's point of view and tries to compensate for this by praising the rival's personality: *Debra who seems a delightful person* (16). In the same vein, she changes the potentially insulting *fallen* (which we have to assume was going to lead to 'into the trap') for the more cumbersome but less insulting *got into the other camp* (17). Her awareness of the clumsiness of this phrase is supported by her adding *so to speak*.

The GP's hesitations are indicated by the ellipses (...) and the filled pauses by *er ... er* (15), *in fact ...* (4) and *... I mean ...* (6). These fillers serve the dual purpose of giving the speaker time to think of how to continue and also of how to avoid a silence which another speaker could fill by taking over the turn. Debra uses fillers (*I mean*) and repetition for the same reason a little later (*I was slightly exaggerating ... I was slightly exaggerating ... that ... that ... that*). She uses repetition quite frequently, but understandably so, since she is under pressure from the GP to give up her turn. Eventually, the GP talks across Debra to take the turn forcibly.

(5) In Group A the dysfluency features are assimilated into the tone-group. Look, for instance, at the Chair's contribution:

> // do you ... do you ... do you feel that about ... about ... about real ... about <u>nor</u>mal medicine //

Without the dysfluency features of repetition (*do you ... do you ... about ... about ... about*) and a lexical switch (from the word *real* to the word *normal*), this would read:

> // do you feel that about <u>nor</u>mal medicine //

The dysfluency features more than double the number of words used, but the information is still delivered within a single tone-group. The dysfluency, in this case, does not affect the tonality.

In Group B the syntactic switch in each structure has the effect of aborting one tone-group and forcing the speaker to begin another, for example:

> // <u>sure</u>ly it would ... // might be equally <u>use</u>ful //

In the above structure the switch is between modals (from the word *would* to the word *might*).

In:

> // for the general practitioner to find out what was a<u>bout</u> // ... her headache was a<u>bout</u> //

the switch is a structural change to the clause with the insertion of a subject *her headache*.

In:

> // al<u>rea</u>dy fallen // ... got into the other <u>camp</u> so to speak //

the switch is a change of verb phrase. The GP was going to say 'fallen into the trap' when she realised it would be rude and so changes to the less idiomatic and more clumsy *got into the other camp* to avoid giving offence. She acknowledges the change and clumsiness with the comment *so to speak*.

It is noticeable that in Group B the tonic syllable has already occurred when the syntactic switch takes place, which is not the case in Group A.

⑦ TONALITY AND GRAMMAR

We now return to a selection of those cases where tonality has a clear grammatical function, often reflected in the punctuation of the written version. Look again at (7.7) and (7.8) (repeated below) to see how distinctive choices from within the system of tonality can signal different relationships between clauses. (Given that we are primarily concerned with the function of tonality here, we shall exclude, for the time being, placement of the tonic syllable.)

7.7   // I remember she sent me a postcard //

The single tone-group in (7.7) makes it clear that this is a sequence of two clauses where the second is subordinate to the first. In traditional grammar, the second clause *she sent me a postcard* would be termed a 'that-complement clause', where the missing *that* is a complementiser. You can find out more about that-clauses and their function as complements in sections 8.15.1 and 10.2 of your reference grammar. Recall also a slightly different analysis from Unit 6 which comes from (Hallidayan) systemic functional grammar. In this analysis, *I remember* is a projecting clause and *she sent me a postcard* is a dependent (i.e. subordinate) projected clause.

7.8   // I remember // she sent me a postcard //

We now have two tone-groups, where tonality has signalled a change in the grammatical relationship between the two clauses. We have a sequence of two independent clauses: the relationship of projecting and projected that we saw in (7.7) has been destroyed, since there is no longer any projection. Notice now that *remember* is used with just one participant – *I*. We saw in (1)–(6) in Section 5.2 how this relationship could be expressed in written form by punctuation. A similar analysis could be operated to distinguish between the following:

7.65   // I don't think I know //

7.66   // I don't think // I know //

The uncertainty of (7.65) (an independent clause followed by a dependent clause) is replaced by the absolute confidence of (7.66) (two independent clauses).

Phrases as well as clauses can be delimited by tonality:

7.67   // After that talking to // the police will be a breeze //

7.68   // After that // talking to the police will be a breeze //

The tone-group boundary following *talking to* in (7.67) indicates that the first tone-group comprises the prepositional phrase *After that talking to,* as illustrated below.

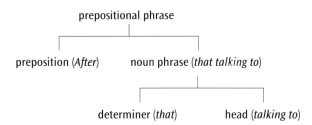

In (7.68), however, the shift of the tone-group boundary means that the initial prepositional phrase becomes *After that*:

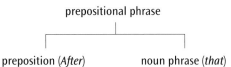

In both (7.67) and (7.68), the clause begins with a circumstance as opposed to the more normal pattern of beginning with a participant. When this happens, the initial circumstance almost invariably takes its own tone-group, as in the following examples.

7.69   // That way // you can have your cake and eat it //

7.70   // Wednesdays and Fridays // we go to the gym //

The sequencing of clausal elements is dealt with further in Book 3 under the topic of 'theme'.

◆**CTIVITIES CD-ROM** (allow about 45 minutes)

Now do Activities 14–22, on various aspects of tonality and grammar, on the Activities CD-ROM. These activities illustrate how intonation can distinguish between different grammatical structures so that the same sequence of words can convey different meanings or fulfil different grammatical functions according to the accompanying intonation. The activities revisit topics from Units 1–6.

⑧ A DIVERSION: TONALITY AND UNCONVENTIONAL PUNCTUATION

This section examines some examples where the informational function of tonality has influenced the punctuation of a written text in a way which would be considered a contravention of traditional notions of correctness.

Example 1

In (7.69) and (7.70) we have observed instances within clause structures where a marked 'theme' (such as a circumstance beginning the clause) is allocated its own tone-group, whereas an unmarked theme (such as the subject beginning the clause) does not. Here are two further examples.

7.71 // Next year // the chairman resigns his post //

7.72 // The chairman resigns his post next year //

This information structure would be echoed in written language by the use or absence of a comma:

> Next year, the chairman resigns his post.

> The chairman resigns his post next year.

However, where a subject element becomes elongated and lexically more dense, the tendency in speech is to award it its own tone-group in the interests of optimising information distribution to aid listener comprehension, for example:

7.73 // The chairman of the UK's latest dotcom disaster company //
      resigns his post next year //

The growing trend – which we emphasise would be marked as incorrect punctuation by your tutor – seems to be to reflect the function of tonality of optimising information distribution to aid the listener, by the use of a comma, in writing:

> The chairman of the UK's latest dotcom disaster company, resigns his post next year.

The initial element of a clause is called its **theme**. The theme is informationally the most important part of a clause, hence its positioning. The general pattern of clausal elements in English is to begin with the subject of the verb. When this happens, the theme is said to be 'neutral' or 'unmarked'. Where a theme and the subject are not the same, the theme is 'marked'. A fuller treatment of theme will be found in Section 4 of Unit 9 in Book 2, Sections 3 to 5 of Unit 14 in Book 3, and Section 2.2 of Unit 17 in Book 4.

Example 2

The punctuation conventions change halfway through the following Australian advertisement for a car (sentences are numbered).

> (1) Building such a car isn't all that difficult, actually; the Europeans, in particular, have been doing it for years. (2) The clever part, of course, is doing it for a sensible price.

(3) The new Ford Fairlane Ghia. (4) At around $48,000, it's world class in every area. (5) Except price.

The first two sentences follow traditional written conventions: full-stops and semicolon denote the boundaries of independent clauses. A comma and semicolon and the pair of commas isolate parenthetic information such as the stance adverbials (*actually, of course*). Sentence (4) follows the same pattern, this time with a comma dividing off a marked theme (*At around $48,000*).

Sentences (3) and (5), on the other hand, use full stops in a way more akin to information distribution than to an indication clause and sentence structure. Sentence (3) comprises a noun phrase and sentence (5) a short prepositional phrase. We would probably expect a conventional written version to combine the last three sentences into one:

> At around $48,000, the new Ford Fairlane Ghia is world class in every area, except price.

However, written convention in this instance (and in many others like it) is sacrificed in order to reflect the way the advertisement would sound in spoken form. The subject (*The new Ford Fairlane Gia*) is 'fronted' (moved to initial position) and given its own information unit, unsurprisingly so since the whole purpose of the advertisement is to highlight and sell it. The main selling point is the price, which is also drawn attention to by receiving its own information unit (*At around $48,000*).

> Moving a clause element to initial position is **fronting**.

But this could have been achieved by conventional punctuation within the confines of the single sentence:

> The new Ford Fairlane Ghia, at around $48,000, is world class in every area, except price.

However, the allocation of a sentence each to the subject noun phrase (sentence (3)) and to the prepositional phrase (sentence (5)) not only ensures them a tone-group of their own. The full stop demands a greater pause than the comma would have done, thus ensuring greater 'foregrounding' of the significant elements (the particular car and its price). The punctuation highlights the tonality.

> **Foregrounding** elements gives them pronounced, but uncustomary, prominence.

Example 3

In January 2003, the UK Government's Secretary of State for Education, Charles Clarke, published a strategy for funding within higher education.

The devolved Welsh Assembly Government has responsibility for education policy within Wales, though the question of higher-education funding is a murky area. Consequently, the Welsh Assembly

Government felt it appropriate to publish a cabinet statement in response to that made by Charles Clarke. The first sentence of that statement read as follows:

> Charles Clarke today published his strategy for higher education, in England.

In conventional terms, the comma should not have appeared, since the prepositional phrase *in England* acts as a postmodifier for (higher) education. Were the statement to be spoken, *in England* would normally appear in the same information unit as *strategy for higher education*:

> // his strategy for higher education in England //

However, the presence of the comma demands a separate information unit for *in England*:

> // his strategy for higher education // in England //

Such a reading suits the purposes of the Welsh Assembly Government who would wish to draw attention the fact that Clarke's statement, albeit generally operable within England and Wales, is nevertheless liable to adaptation within Wales, and should therefore be seen at this stage to apply in its fullness only to England. Giving *in England* its own information unit by means of the comma highlights this fact.

Conclusion

Intonation in English is made up of the subsystems of tonality, tonicity and tone.

Tonality describes how a spoken text is divided by the speaker into tone-groups, which reflects how the information in the message is distributed into information units.

Tone describes the selection of pitch contour at the most prominent point within the tone-group. That most prominent point is known as the tonic syllable. There are five tones in English: fall, rise, level, rise-fall and fall-rise.

The location of the tonic syllable comprises the tonicity.

Learning outcomes

After completing this unit, you should have developed an understanding of:

◆   intonation

◆   subsystems of intonation

◆   the structure of a tone-group

◆ the role played by intonation in the information structure of scripted and unscripted speech

◆ the role played by intonation in distinguishing between grammatical categories

◆ how intonation can be conveyed in written language

◆ how intonation can influence punctuation.

In the light of your increased understanding, you should be able to:

◆ recognise that stretches of speech are divided into tone-groups

◆ recognise that each tone-group has a tonic syllable

◆ recognise that each tone-group carries a pitch pattern

◆ interpret how a change in intonation can signal a change in grammatical structure

◆ describe the ways in which written language is able to convey patterns of intonation.

Key terms introduced and revisited

circumstance	pitch
cohesion	pitch contour
dysfluency	pitch direction
false start	postmodifier
foregrounding	posttonic
fronting	premodifier
head	pretonic
incomplete utterance	range [pitch range]
information unit	reduced form
intensifier [amplifier]	repair
intonation	stressed syllable
lexical bundle	syntactic blend
local repetition	theme
marked tonicity	tonality
neutral tonicity [unmarked tonicity]	tone
noun phrase	tone-group
paralinguistics	tonic syllable
participant	tonicity

Near equivalents are given in [ ].

Review of Book 1

In this book you have been introduced to a number of concepts about what grammar is and how it can be analysed. You will have seen that this course takes a descriptive rather than a prescriptive approach to language, investigating how and why people speak and write in varying ways, without seeking to impose external rules for language behaviour. Within this descriptive tradition, we have also drawn on two particular theoretical models of grammar: traditional/structural (specifically, the framework set out in your Longman reference grammar) and functional (specifically, Hallidayan systemic-functional grammar), which provide complementary perspectives on the texts we look at. The practical skills of structural grammar which you have been acquiring – classifying words as determiners, pronouns and so on, identifying noun and prepositional phrases, dividing texts into clauses, etc. – will provide a valuable foundation for the mainly functional types of analysis which will be covered in the next two books. Functional concepts such as process types, participants and commands have been briefly outlined, and will be revisited in greater depth later.

While acquiring this descriptive framework, you have also begun to explore some of the broad differences between the modes of speech and writing, as revealed by lexicogrammatical features including use of question tags, lexical density, noun and verb phrase structure, complexity of clause linkage and use of intonation. (The next two books will continue to explore differences between registers, but with an increasingly narrow focus.) In this exploration, the role of corpus evidence and concordancing software will have become apparent. Reference to large collections of naturally occurring texts selected according to specified criteria enables us to draw more reliable conclusions about language use than reliance on the intuitions of native speakers. Computers permit much faster and more accurate collection of statistical data on our corpora – such as frequency counts – than could be achieved by hand, and the software's clear presentation of concordance lines can often reveal collocational patterns in data which would not have been accessible through intuition alone. You have been learning a range of analytical techniques from the field of corpus linguistics, and while these have so far mainly been applied to the exploration of structural features (due to the lack of functionally tagged corpora at the present time) you will later learn how to extend your searches to provide data for some types of functional analysis.

By relating the research findings and practical skills covered in this book to your own experience of speaking and writing English, and of hearing and reading English texts around you, we hope you will have come to a greater understanding of – and deeper interest in – English grammar. You may also find ways to apply your new insights in developing your own writing skills, and this application will be extended in the next two books.

Applications (extension study)

If you have time in your study schedule, you may now find it interesting to look at a professional application of some of the grammatical and corpus-based skills and findings introduced so far. Work through Chapter 1 of *Applications: Putting grammar into professional practice* on lexicography, 'Putting grammar into the dictionary', by Gill Francis and Barbara Mayor.

This study is **optional** and will not be compulsorily assessed.

Key terms from Book 1

To help remember and revise important terminology, you might find it useful to pick a few words from the following list and try to write a brief definition of them. Contrast each term with other related terms where relevant, e.g. **finite clause** vs. **non-finite clause**, and think of a couple of examples to illustrate the concept, e.g. *didn't he?, isn't it?* as instances of question tags. If you are unsure about any of your definitions or examples, use the index to Book 1 and/or the index to your reference grammar to look up fuller discussions of these terms. The course *Glossary* also provides useful short definitions and examples.

active voice	adjective	**adjective phrase**	**adverb phrase [adverbial group]**
agent	antecedent	**article**	aspect
attributive adjective	**auxiliary verb**	backchannel	**circumstance**
circumstance adverbial	**circumstantial dependent clause**	**classifier**	**clause**
clause complex	closed class	cohesion	**collocate**
collocation	**command**	concord	concordance line
concordancing program [concordancer]	constituent	**context**	coordination
coordinator	co-text	**corpus/corpora**	corpus-based grammar
declarative	deictic word	**demonstrative**	**dependent clause [subordinate clause]**
describer [epithet]	**descriptive grammar**	**determiner**	dialect
dialogue	discourse marker	dysfluency	**ellipsis**

embedded clause	embedding	false start	**finite**
finite clause	foregrounding	fronting	**function word**
functional grammar	head [central element]	head [preface]	hesitator
imperative	incomplete utterance	**independent clause**	information unit
insert	intensifier [amplifier]	**interrogative clause**	**interrupting clause [included clause]**
intonation	key word in context [KWIC]	**lemma [lexeme]**	**lexical bundle**
lexical density	**lexical verb**	lexical word	lexicogrammar
lexicogrammatical pattern	**lexis**	local repetition	main clause
marked tonicity	**material process [action process, activity verb]**	**mental process [mental verb]**	**modal finite [modal auxiliary, modal verb]**
modality	**mode**	monologue	**morpheme**
morphology	neutral tonicity [unmarked tonicity]	node/key word	nominal
nominalisation	non-clausal unit	**non-finite clause**	**non-restrictive relative clause [non-defining clause]**
noun	**noun phrase [nominal group, noun group]**	**numerative**	open class
orthographic word	paralinguistics	**participant**	**passive voice**
pedagogic grammar	**phrasal verb**	**phrase [group]**	pitch
pitch contour	pitch direction	**possessive**	postmodification
postmodifier	posttonic	predicator	**premodifier**
pre-numerative	**prepositional phrase**	prescriptive grammar	pretonic
process	**projected clause**	**projecting clause**	projection
pronoun	qualifier	**quantifier**	**question**
question tag	**quoting [direct speech]**	range [pitch range]	rank
rank system [rank scale]	**realised by**	reduced form	**register/subregister**
relational process	**relative clause**	relativiser	repair

reporting [indirect speech]	**restrictive relative clause [defining clause]**	sociocultural context	**speech act [speech function, speech-act function]**
stance adverbial	'standard' English	**statement**	stressed syllable
string	**structural grammar [traditional grammar]**	subcorpus	**subject [grammatical subject]**
subordination	**subordinator**	syntactic blend	tail [tag]
temporal finite [primary auxiliary]	**text**	**theme**	token
tonality	tone	tone-group	tonic syllable
tonicity	transcript	type	**type-token ratio**
utterance	**verb phrase [verbal group, verb group]**	**verb phrase complex**	**verbal process [saying process, communication verb]**
wildcard	word	**word class [part of speech, grammatical class]**	

Near equivalents are given in [ ]. Emboldened terms are particularly important to learn at this stage in the course.

References

The Advertiser (2002) 'Shark attack', *The Advertiser* (South Australia), 1 May 2002, Adelaide, South Australia.

'Alternative Medicine' (1988) Transcript of an extract from *After Dark Series 2*, Channel 4/ITN Archive.

Alexander, S. and Beer, M. (1998) *Stephanie Alexander & Maggie Beer's Tuscan Cookbook*, Australia, Viking/Penguin Books.

Ansen, D. 'Mild About "Harry"' in *Newsweek* (Pacific edn), vol. 140, no. 21, 18 Nov 2002.

Biber, D., Conrad, S. and Leech, G. (2002a) *Longman Student Grammar of Spoken and Written English*, London, Pearson.

Biber, D., Conrad, S. and Leech, G. (2002b) *Longman Student Grammar of Spoken and Written English Workbook*, London, Pearson.

Biber, D., Conrad, S., Johansson, S. and Leech, G. (1999) *Longman Grammar of Spoken and Written English*, London, Longman.

Brazil, D. (1995) *A Grammar of Speech*, Oxford, Oxford University Press.

Coates, J. (1993) *Women, Men and Language*, London, Longman.

Coulthard, M. and Sinclair, J. (1975) *Towards an Analysis of Discourse*. Oxford, Oxford University Press.

CTE (1990) *Sticks and Stones* (*Replay, Reinforce, Remember*) [video], London, CTE.

Derewianka, B. (1990) *Exploring How Texts Work*, Sydney, PETA.

Eggins, S. E. and Slade, D. (1997) *Analysing Casual Conversation*, London, Cassell.

Franzen, J. (2002) *The Corrections*, London, Fourth Estate.

Halliday, M. A. K. (1985) *Spoken and Written Language*, Deakin University, Geelong, Australia.

Halliday, M. Matthiessen, C. (ed) (2004) *An Introduction to Functional Grammar*, 3rd edn, London, Arnold.

Hanna, M. (2002) 'Prague cleans up as threat continues', CNN.com [online]. Available at http://www.cnn.com/2002/world/europe/08/16/czech.floods/index.html [Accessed 13 February 2004.]

Hewings, A. and Hewings, M. (2004) *Grammar and Context*, London, Routledge.

Hunston, S. (2002) *Corpora in Applied Linguistics*, Cambridge, Cambridge University Press.

Irving, J. (1981) *The Hotel New Hampshire*, London, Jonathan Cape.

Keller, H. (1980) *The Art of the Impressionists*, London, Phaidon Press.

Lupton. D. (2001) 'Constructing "road rage" as news', *Australian Journal of Communication*, vol. 28(2), 2001.

McCarthy, M. (1998) *Spoken Language and Applied Linguistics*, Cambridge, Cambridge University Press.

The National Institute for the Prevention of Workplace Violence (2000) 'Road rage causes fatal accident' [online]. Available at http://www.workplaceviolence411.com/WVContactUs/wvcontactus.html [Accessed 9 December 2003.]

O'Connor, J. D. and Arnold, G. F. (1961) *Intonation of Colloquial English*, London, Longman.

Parks, T. (1992) *Italian Neighbours*, London, Minerva.

Partridge, L. and Gems, D. (2002) 'A lethal side-effect', *Nature*, vol. 418, 29 August 2002.

Plum, G. (1988) 'Text and contextual conditioning in spoken English: a genre-based approach,' unpublished PhD thesis, University of Sydney, vol. 2, Text 1.6.

Porter, E. H. (1987) *Pollyanna*, London, Angus and Robertson (first published 1913).

Roadragers (2003) 'Road rage' [online]. Available at http://roadragers.com/cgi-bin/query/display.pl?sortdate=20030626090044 [Accessed 21 January 2004.]

Schiermeier, Q. (2002) 'Central Europe braced for tide of pollution in flood aftermath', *Nature*, vol. 418, 29 August 2002.

Sinclair, J. McH. (1990) *Collins Cobuild English Grammar*, London, Collins.

Tench, P. (1996) *The Intonation Systems of English*, London, Cassell.

Upton, D. (2001) 'Constructing road rage as news: an analysis of two Australian newspapers', *Australian Journal of Communication*, vol. 28, no. 3, pp. 23–35.

Webb, A. (1987) *Talk About Sound*, London, Franklin Watts.

Wells, W. H. G. (1986) 'An experimental approach to the interpretation of focus in spoken English' in Johns-Lewis, C. (ed.) *Intonation in Discourse*, London, Croom Helm.

Further reading on Functional Grammar

Bloor, T. and Bloor, M. (2004) *The Functional Analysis of English: a Hallidayan approach*, 2nd edn, London, Hodder Arnold.

Butt, D., Fahey, R., Feez, S., Spinks, S. and Yallop, C. (2000) *Using Functional Grammar: an explorer's guide*, 2nd edn, Sydney, NSW, National Centre for English Language Teaching and Research (NCLTR Macquarie University).

Eggins, S. (2004) *An Introduction to Systemic Functional Linguistics*, 2nd edn, London, Continuum.

Halliday, M. and Matthiessen, C. (eds) (2004) *An Introduction to Functional Grammar*, 3rd edn, London, Arnold.

Humphrey, S. and Droga, L. (2002) *Getting Started with Functional Grammar*, Berry, Australia, Target Texts.

Martin, J. R. and Rose, D. (2003) *Working with Discourse*, London, Continuum.

Thompson, G. (2004), *Introducing Functional Grammar*, 2nd edn, London, Hodder Arnold.

Acknowledgements

Grateful acknowledgement is made to the following sources for permission to reproduce material in this book.

Units 1, 2, 3 and 4

Reprinted with permission from *Nature*, vol. 428, 29 August 2002, p. 921, Gems, D. and Partridge, L. (2002) 'A lethal side-effect'. Copyright © 2002 Macmillan Magazines Limited.

Reprinted with permission from *Nature*, vol. 418, 29 August 2002. Schiermeier, Q. (2002) 'Central Europe braced for tide of pollution in flood aftermath', Copyright © 2002 Macmillan Magazines Limited.

Unit 5

Road Rage Causes Fatal Accident, Copyright © 2004 Associated Press. All Rights Reserved.

Reprinted with permission from *Nature*, vol. 428, 29 August 2002, p. 921, Gems, D. and Partridge, L. (2002) 'A lethal side-effect'. Copyright © 2002 Macmillan Magazines Limited.

Unit 6

'A cry for help', *The Advertiser*, 1 May 2002. The Advertiser, Adelaide, South Australia.

Unit 7

'Alternative medicine' (1988). Extract from 'After Dark Series', Channel 4/ITN Archive.

Video clip

The Best of Victor Borge: Acts I and II. Copyright © Victor Borge Estate, Gurtman and Murtha, New York.

Course team acknowledgements

The course team wishes to thank and acknowledge the assistance of the following in the production of this book.

Michael Hoey (external assessor)

Ron Carter, Susan Feez, Michael Halliday, Geoffrey Leech (general course consultants)

Susan Hunston (adviser)

Mohammad Awwad, Safinaz Shariff, Najib al-Shehabi (Arab OU critical readers)

Judy Anderson, Frank Xiao Junhong, Ahmed Sahlane, Cristina Scarpino (developmental testers)

E303 Associate Lecturers, particularly Marisa Lohr (revisions to course materials)

Index

Page references in bold type refer to the most significant treatment of the subject. Words in italic refer to usage of those words.